WIVES WITHOUT HUSBANDS

GENDER & AMERICAN CULTURE

A complete list of books published in Gender and American Culture is available at www.uncpress.unc.edu.

ANNA R. IGRA

WITHOUT HUSBANDS

MARRIAGE, DESERTION, & WELFARE IN NEW YORK, 1900–1935

The University of North Carolina Press Chapel Hill

Set in Scala types by Keystone Typesetting, Inc.
Manufactured in the United States of America

The paper in this book meets the guidelines for permanence and durability of the Committee on Production Guidelines for Book Longevity of the Council on Library Resources.

Library of Congress Cataloging-in-Publication Data
Igra, Anna R.
Wives without husbands : marriage, desertion, and welfare in New York, 1900–1935 / by Anna R. Igra.
p. cm. — (Gender and American culture)
Includes bibliographical references and index.
ISBN-13: 978-0-8078-3070-3 (cloth: alk. paper)
ISBN-10: 0-8078-3070-4 (cloth: alk. paper)
ISBN-13: 978-0-8078-5779-3 (pbk.: alk. paper)
ISBN-10: 0-8078-5779-3 (pbk.: alk. paper)
1. Poor women—New York (State)—New York. 2. Women heads of households—New York (State)—New York. 3. Jewish women—New York (State)—New York—Social conditions. 4. Jewish women—New York (State)—New York—Economic conditions. 5. Absentee fathers—New York (State)—New York. 6. Desertion and non-support—New York (State)—New York. 7. Public welfare—Government policy—New York (State)—New York. 8. Welfare recipients—New York (State)—New York. 9. National Desertion Bureau, New York—History. 10. National Desertion Bureau, New York—Case studies. I. Title.
HV1447.N5I47 2007
362.83′9—dc22 2006026996

An early version of chapter 3 appeared as "Male Providerhood and the Public Purse: Anti-Desertion Reform in the Progressive Era," in *The Sex of Things: Gender and Consumption in Historical Perspective*, ed. Victoria de Grazia, with Ellen Furlough (Berkeley: University of California Press, 1996). An early version of chapter 5 appeared as "Likely to Become a Public Charge: Deserted Women and the Family Law of the Poor in New York City, 1910–1935," *Journal of Women's History* 11, no. 4 (2000): 58–81; copyright © 2000 by Indiana University Press. Portions of the introduction and epilogue appeared as "Marriage as Welfare," *Women's History Review* 15, no. 4 (September 2006): 601–10; copyright © Taylor & Francis.

11 10 09 08 07 5 4 3 2 1

contents

illustrations

acknowledgments

The generosity of many people nurtured this book. I am grateful for the assistance of librarians and archivists at the New York Public Library, the New York State Library, Rutgers University, Carleton College, Columbia University, the Tamiment Institute, the Rockefeller Archive Center, the Library of the Association of the Bar of the City of New York, the Center for Advanced Jewish Studies, the American Jewish Historical Society, and the American Jewish Archives. Lauren Benditt made some timely trips to the University of Minnesota libraries for me. The staff at the YIVO Institute for Jewish Social Research, particularly Marek Web, Frume Mohrer, Aviva Astrinsky, and Leo Greenbaum, provided crucial support for my research on the National Desertion Bureau. I thank the Jewish Board of Family and Children's Services for permission to use the National Desertion Bureau case files. The staff of the Staten Island Courthouse kindly allowed me to read docket books in their basement. I would also like to acknowledge those who provided funding for my research: the American Historical Association, for a Littleton-Griswold grant; the Rutgers Center for Historical Analysis; the New York University School of Law, especially William Nelson, for a Samuel I. Golieb fellowship; and Carleton College, for a Faculty Development Endowment grant.

I benefited from the insightful comments of numerous colleagues, including Beth Wenger, Anne Meis Knupfer, Jane Sherron De Hart, Alan Kraut, Carole Turbin, Kirk Jeffrey, Carl Weiner, Shurlee Swain, John Gillis, Ellen Ross, Richard L. McCormick, Deidre Moloney, Victoria de Grazia, Belinda Davis, the late Megan McClintock, and especially Joanne Goodwin. The anonymous peer reviewers guided my revisions with their valuable queries and suggestions. Several editors at the University of North Carolina Press devoted effort and talent to bringing this book to publication: Lew Bateman, who acquired the project; Kate Torrey, who chaperoned it during a crucial time; and Chuck Grench, whose commitment reenergized me and the project. Paul Betz polished my prose with his meticulous copyediting. Amanda McMillan, Katy O'Brien, and Paula Wald were ever-dependable navigators, steering the manuscript toward completion.

I thank my family for believing I could write this book and especially my father, Jacob Igra, for help with translations. The unwavering support of Bob Levy and Rachel Lavine sustained me through my sojourn in a chilly climate. Paul Clemens brought his broad knowledge, careful reading, and probing questions to the early stages of the manuscript. I am grateful to Amy Swerdlow for her encouragement, thoughtful criticism, and commitment to feminist scholarship. Norma Basch's enthusiasm in the initial stages of the project fueled my own; I thank her in particular for teaching me that the law is not just for lawyers. Jan Lambertz and Lisa Norling read the entire manuscript, providing smart suggestions, reassurance, and gentle nudging as needed.

Linda Kerber's generosity made all the difference: she read several drafts of the manuscript and kept it moving in the right direction. Suzanne Lebsock's comments on the book at a critical stage improved it immensely; I thank her, too, for her intellectual rigor, steadfast support, and wry good humor. Alice Kessler-Harris is a brilliant inspiration. I could not have completed this book without her keen insight, patient attentiveness, faith in the project, and sound advice at all stages of the manuscript's development. For all that cannot be quantified, I thank my *bashert*, Howard Oransky.

introduction

"Marriage is the foundation of a successful society." So declares the opening statement of the Personal Responsibility and Work Opportunity Act, the founding document of contemporary welfare policy for poor families in the United States.[1] Marriage, most Americans believe, is not a matter of money but rather an affair of the heart. So why would an act to address poverty begin with a credo about marriage? How did marriage become such a central concern of welfare policy?

The assumption that marriage belongs in any program of welfare reform has a long history, stretching back to the early twentieth century. At that time, an optimistic generation of reformers tackled what they identified as the mounting problems of urban industrial life. Rejecting the stoic and pessimistic view that poverty was an inevitable and eternal feature of human existence, these men and women placed their confidence in new social-scientific theories: a well-ordered, harmonious society, they believed, could be engineered through the application of their expertise in a more activist government. Marriage had long provided a metonym for the larger social order, and reforming one often involved remaking the other.

Concerns about marriage and poverty intersected with particular force in the efforts of reform-minded lawyers and social workers to combat husbands' and fathers' desertion of wives and children. This book focuses on antidesertion reform and its effects on a particular population of poor women as they encountered the welfare system in a particular time and place: deserted Jewish women in New York City in the first few decades of the twentieth century. Especially in the pre–New Deal years, the "welfare state" in the United States was a patchwork of primarily local initiatives that mixed state regulation with other agencies, often religious or ethnic organizations. Jewish organizations played a leading role in making desertion a focus of family and welfare reform. Working with their non-Jewish peers, Jewish social workers and lawyers participated in creating an antidesertion system that consisted of special domestic relations courts, laws, and welfare policies. They built a model legal aid agency for Jewish deserted women, the National Desertion Bureau (NDB), headquartered in New York City.

Although official definitions varied, in social welfare parlance the term "desertion" was more about money than the absence of the husband.

"Desertion" occurred when the family became destitute and applied for assistance of some sort. A man living with his family could become a "deserter" by withholding his wages; a man who left his family was not a deserter if he sent money or if his family could manage without him. A woman who agreed to separate from her husband could become a deserted woman at a later date if she became so poor that she required assistance from a public or private welfare agency. It was a woman's marital status combined with her application for aid that earned her the label "deserted woman."[2] While recognizing that desertion was sometimes actually mutual separation, I use the term "deserted woman" to refer to someone who was placed in the "deserted" category by social welfare agencies.

Deserted women occupied a liminal category; neither widowed nor unwed, they were wives without husbands. Studying liminal groups such as deserted women turns common sense into curiosity, assumptions into questions. Those who fall between categories can make visible elements that thread through an entire system of classification. Like other female welfare clients who were sorted according to their past relationships with men, deserted women were incorporated into the heterosexual system of welfare classification. When approached by a destitute woman, the charities wanted to know: are you married? divorced? widowed? deserted? unwed? What Alice Kessler-Harris terms the "gendered imagination" shaped social agencies' assumption that marital status should govern women's access to economic assistance.[3] The desire of welfare reformers to anchor deserted women in the category of "wives" reveals a larger commitment to using marriage to contain women's poverty.

The centrality of marriage in early American welfare policy is often assumed by historians but rarely made fully visible. Feminist historians alert us to the ways in which gender and state development have been mutually constitutive. Their recent work focuses on the construction of women as mothers. They have illuminated the important role women played in the creation of the American welfare state and female reformers' special "maternal" concern with the protection of children and mothers.[4] "Maternalists" valorized motherhood while also making moral distinctions between worthy widows and "fallen" unwed mothers. Scholars of "maternalism" often note the preference of social welfare reformers for the male breadwinner/female dependent family form. Yet men have frequently dropped out of the historical picture, as maternalist programs are depicted as concerned with relations among women and between women and children.

Focusing on deserted women enables us to give sustained attention to welfare policy's expectation of male breadwinning and uncovers the paternalist underpinning of maternalist programs. Casting themselves as protectors of women, antidesertion reformers—most of them men—sought to lift deserted families out of poverty by regulating male breadwinning. Although antidesertion reformers did sometimes employ maternalist rhetoric, they were more concerned with men as fathers and husbands than with women as mothers. Many of the most active antidesertion reformers were men who conceived of themselves as disciplinary fathers and chivalrous defenders of women and the public good. By characterizing working-class deserters as "cowardly" and "shiftless" husbands, male reformers highlighted their own fiscal responsibility and solicitude for women. Yet, as is so often the case in relations of rescue, working-class women paid a price for the protection offered by male legal and social welfare professionals.[5] Ultimately, the antidesertion system disciplined women at least as much as the men who were its ostensible targets.

In their antidesertion campaign, middle-class professional men struggled with working-class men over the meaning of manhood. The turn of the century was a critical moment in the redefinition of manhood.[6] Changes in the workplace were undermining the nineteenth-century ideal of the sturdy producer, while a burgeoning consumer culture was encouraging a reorientation of masculine identity away from labor and toward consumption. Workingmen, argues the historian Lawrence Glickman, gave up their long resistance to the wage system and instead staked their manly dignity on the ability to command earnings adequate to sustain an "American standard of living" for their families.[7] As workingmen moved to underscore their status as breadwinners, the locus of their identity increasingly shifted from the workplace to the household.[8] Ideals, however, often generate resistance even as they appear to become enshrined. Men—and not only working-class men—betrayed ambivalence toward breadwinning. Recognizing the attractions of alternative modes of masculinity, antidesertion reformers worried that the lure of consumer pleasures might weaken, rather than strengthen, working-class men's commitment to breadwinning.

As numerous historians have observed, the family wage system, with its ideal of male breadwinning, was never fully realized in working-class families. Most men simply did not earn enough. But there was another problem with the ideal: it assumed that men would share their earnings with their wives and children. Feminist scholars have documented the conflicts within working-class families over the division of a man's pay.[9] Given their intimate knowledge of such conflicts, antidesertion reformers' optimism about male breadwinning as the solution to women's and children's poverty is perplexing. Marriage was a particularly unstable footing for social policy, yet it seemed unfair to reformers that the public should be required to compensate for inadequate providers.

In tracing the efforts of antidesertion reformers to resurrect marriages and protect the public purse, I describe a legal system that scholars of family law might find surprising.[10] Until recently, the history of family law tended to follow a narrative of modern family history as the progressive development of the private, affective nuclear family whose members are increasingly recognized as rights-bearing individuals by the state, rather than as members of a patriarchal corporate unit. This narrative posits a transition from status to contract, from patriarchal to companionate marriage, as both ideal and practice. Conventional historical wisdom, built on the work of Lawrence Stone and others, teaches that by the twentieth century the concept of marriage as a private matter of romantic love had replaced the view of marriage as a matter of money and power.[11] Feminist historians have cast doubt on this optimistic tale of family modernization, observing that aspects of coverture (the erasure of women's legal identities in marriage) lingered well into the twentieth century.[12]

Middle-class people are thought to have embraced the warm and loving ideal of companionate marriage especially eagerly, yet many middle-class social welfare professionals evaluated poor people's marriages in terms of cold cash. The laws that antidesertion reformers used to prosecute nonsupporting husbands envisioned the family in economic, rather than affective, terms. The statutes governing desertion cases heard in the domestic relations courts belonged to what Jacobus tenBroek labels "the family law of the poor."[13] They applied only to people who were, or were likely to become, charges upon the public. The resources of all family members—whether male or female, parent or child—were treated as a single pool; individual property rights were irrelevant. Aided by charity investigators, judges attempted to rearrange the allocation of family funds. In the New York City domestic relations courts, magistrates dispensed with many of the procedural rules governing criminal cases but retained the power to levy criminal penalties, including incarceration.[14] The complainant in desertion cases was the government, and nonsupport was a criminal act perpetrated against the public.

Antidesertion reformers made both distinctions and connections between appropriate "public" and "private" resources and responsibilities.

The public/private dichotomy was an idiom they used to articulate their social ideals. We should be wary of taking this idiom as a representation of social reality, as demarcating concrete spaces or discrete spheres.[15] But discursive idioms are not inconsequential in their effects. The terms "public" and "private" and their relationship to each other have been redefined over time, shaping not only how people view the world but also how they change it.[16] Attempting to return women and children from the rolls of "public charges" to dependence on particular men, antidesertion reformers translated issues of class and gender into the idiom of public and private. "Public" money, they believed, should not be used to meet "private" working-class duties—such as supporting "other men's" wives and children.[17] Intentionally or not, antidesertion reformers participated in drawing the boundary between familial duty and public responsibility so as to limit social obligations to the poor. At the same time, they connected men's performance of familial duties to their status as masculine citizens.

Reformers' reception of immigrants exposed their evolving definition of citizenship. As they responded to the arrival of millions of immigrants from eastern and southern Europe, social workers and legal professionals reworked the relationships of men and women to the state. The National Desertion Bureau's attempt to assimilate eastern European Jews into conventional gendered families appears to fit neatly into the story of programs to "Americanize" immigrants. However, the antidesertion system was more than an instrument of social control, of professionals using their power and expertise to adapt working-class people to middle-class norms. While defining desertion as an immigrant import into previously respectable communities, reformers also borrowed reform techniques that immigrants brought with them across the Atlantic. Moreover, when American Jewish agencies mounted a campaign against desertion in the immigrant community, they both instructed Jewish men on the responsibilities of citizenship and took up an issue that had already been the subject of periodic agitation in eastern Europe. Paradoxically, by engaging with New York's welfare and legal systems, Jewish agencies may have been most effective in Americanizing themselves.

The challenges involved in studying the antidesertion system are many: to understand not just its design but also its implementation; to figure out not just what the law said but also how it affected the lives of ordinary people in their local courts; to find not only the architects of welfare policy but also their clients. The records of the NDB, long hidden in the subbasement of the YIVO Institute for Jewish Social Research's former home on 86th Street in New York City, provide just such a multifaceted view into the antidesertion system. In rows of rusting file cabinets, I found thousands of historical treasures: the case files of the most prominent privately funded antidesertion agency of the early twentieth century. (As if in anticipation of the grit that would accumulate on my face and arms on each trip to the subbasement to retrieve a folder, there was even an ancient bar of soap in one of the case files.) The files ran anywhere from twenty-five to 200 pages and covered periods of time ranging from a few months to several decades. The bulk of the documents were in English, with most of the rest in Yiddish, along with a smattering of other European languages. Based on the YIVO archivists' estimate that there were 17,000 case files in the cabinets (more were rumored to be in an inaccessible storage facility), I calculated that 300 would be a reasonably representative group. Each file bore a number, preceded by one of four letters, and using randomly selected digits, I gathered the stratified sample of case files that forms the basis of this book.[18]

The NDB case files are exceptionally rich sources. They provide a key to the workings of the antidesertion system in the lives of Jewish deserted women as recorded primarily in social workers' and lawyers' notes. Although such sources contain the biases of agency workers, the case files are not univocal. The correspondence of husbands and wives to one another, as well as to the agency, the reports of neighbors and children, and occasional disagreements among welfare workers help the reader to discern multiple points of view. By itself, each NDB case is idiosyncratic, and any attempt to compile a complete narrative of a particular case is frustrated by breaks in chronology. Even where forms produced by agencies and courts give the appearance of standardization, they often contain blanks or are overwritten with notes that do not correspond to the forms' demands. Only if one puts together pieces culled from a large number of files can one discern patterns and bring the overall system into view.

Read together, the 300 NDB cases permit a view of the entire antidesertion system, beyond the NDB itself. As it located and prosecuted nonsupporting men, the bureau served as a link between social service agencies, the district attorney's office, and the courts, taking referrals from all of them, as well as complaints from deserted women themselves. Although NDB administrative records are not available, the professionals who worked for the bureau were vocal participants in the movement for legal reform, and I draw extensively on their public statements as well as on their advice to clients. Other sources contextualize the more than

5,000 documents from the case files, placing the story of the NDB in the larger history of marriage and social welfare reform.

In the first chapter of the book, I explore the dynamics that led the Jewish community to prioritize the issue of desertion. Between approximately 1880 and 1920, about two million eastern European Jews established their families in the United States, intending to stay. Although their gender norms had already been changing in eastern Europe, immigration accelerated Jews' encounter with a breadwinning ethic enshrined in English common law and, increasingly, in American popular thought. In chapter 2, I show how Jewish lawyers and social agencies worked with their non-Jewish counterparts to hammer out a welfare policy for deserted women and to design a legal structure to regulate male breadwinning. Chapter 3 examines the characterization of desertion as a problem of male self-indulgence. Social reformers sought to orient immigrant men's spending toward supporting respectable families. Yet both working-class and middle-class men expressed ambivalence about the way such respectability might curtail their freedom. Deserted women themselves are the subject of chapter 4. Often reluctant participants in the search for their husbands, deserted women struggled to combine many other strategies in order to manage their lives as "husbandless wives." I explore women's reasons for using the antidesertion system and measure reformers' rhetoric about female dependence against working-class Jewish women's behavior and expectations. In chapter 5, I follow these women into the legal system, a system that relied to a large extent on the unpaid labor of the very women it was supposed to help. I analyze the basis of the laws regarding nonsupport and evaluate their effectiveness in the 300 NDB cases. The final chapter examines women's interactions with the welfare system as it implemented the new antidesertion policy. In the 1930s, Depression relief programs incorporated the changes wrought by the antidesertion movement.

Although with the New Deal the government overtook Jewish and other ethnic charities as the major agent of the welfare system, the legacy of the Progressive Era commitment to marriage-as-welfare lingers in our own time. It turns out that the Jewish community of early twentieth-century New York City is an unusually fruitful, if unconventional, place to begin unraveling the way marriage became a central and lasting concern of American social welfare policy.

They Need Not Become a Burden to the State

> *In this country it is not possible for a healthy man to throw all work and worry about making a living onto his wife while he goes idle . . . , as one sees in every town and city in Russia. The court will compel such a man to do his duty to his wife and children just as his wife desires.*
>
> *The Americans, who are the most civilized people in the world, treat their women with the greatest respect and tenderness. The Talmudic sages teach us also to appreciate and respect our women to the highest degree, but the circumstances of our dark lives in the European diaspora made many men impractical people and idlers, accustomed to living from the toil and care of their wives. In this free land that kind of behavior won't do. Here the man must work and the woman stay at home, run the house, and raise the children.*
>
> *—Educational Alliance, 1903*

At the turn of the twentieth century, a Jewish immigrant could learn what it would mean to become an American by reading the Yiddish pamphlet *Sholom Aleykhem tsu Immigranten* (Welcome, Immigrants), published by the Educational Alliance. Between the opening explanation of the rights of Americans under the Constitution and the closing patriotic songs (the national anthem and "Columbia, the Gem of the Ocean"), the tract instructed new arrivals about the differences between the Old World and the New. The Educational Alliance, a Jewish settlement house in New York City, considered it essential for eastern European immigrants to know that a proper Jewish American husband supported his domesticated wife.[1]

Nonsupport, the Educational Alliance implied, was a throwback to a less civilized place and time. The pamphlet framed immigration as a movement from darkness to light and urged eastern European Jews to adopt "enlightened" American middle-class gender ways. Doing so would not necessitate abandoning Jewish tradition, it claimed, but would instead allow for the fulfillment of ancient prescriptions. A family deserter therefore betrayed both American expectations and those of his own people.

Emphasizing breadwinning as a core component of American manhood was by no means unique to the Educational Alliance or the Jewish community. Nor was the equation of middle-class gender norms with "civilization."[2] Indeed, Jewish family reformers were able to galvanize the campaign against desertion in New York precisely because other Progressives shared such values. They built on a long-standing middle-class ideal of men as providers that was increasingly shared by working-class men. Before coming to the United States, Jewish men had already encountered the image of the male breadwinner as a sign of modernity. Jewish charity workers, like their Catholic counterparts, participated in solidifying this masculine ideal through their work with immigrants.[3]

Among ethnic groups absorbing an influx of new immigrants, Jews were unusual in the attention they gave to desertion. The Catholics who did address desertion as a public issue tended to belong to the Society of St. Vincent de Paul, an all-male organization particularly concerned with male behavior. The major Catholic charities dealt with deserted families on an individual basis, but they did not define desertion as a distinct social problem requiring major policy initiatives. In contrast, Jews campaigned against desertion in their community and at the same time pressed for it to receive priority on the agenda of American Progressive reform.

The greater Jewish emphasis reflected the way desertion as a communal concern developed abroad and crossed the Atlantic with immigrants. Perhaps more significantly, the composition of the immigrant population presented the established American Jewish community with both opportunities and potential problems. Unlike many immigrant groups, Jewish arrivals comprised entire families of men, women, and children. Clearly, the Educational Alliance viewed this as an opportunity to reconstruct gender. But the possibility also existed that immigrant men would remain unreconstructed. Anxious American Jews envisioned the many Jewish women and children who would be left destitute and potentially dependent on charity. A large and visible dependent Jewish population, they believed, would threaten both future immigration and the acceptance of Jews by their host country.

REMAKING JEWISH GENDER

Two million eastern European Jews entered the United States in the decades between approximately 1880 and the First World War. The majority came from the Russian Empire, where most had been confined to the twenty-five western provinces that constituted the Pale of Settlement. Leaving behind increasing economic hardship and antisemitism, they came to stay. They were met by an American Jewish community itself made up of relatively recent immigrants. Between 1830 and 1870, approximately 150,000 Jews came to the United States from central Europe seeking political emancipation and economic opportunity.[4] Their story had been one of remarkable upward mobility, and by the time the eastern Europeans arrived, they had built a substantial middle class. The eastern European newcomers, in their vast numbers, heightened the visibility of Jews in America just as the community was facing resurgent antisemitism and nativism. Motivated by a sense of kinship as well as trepidation about the effect of the immigrants on American public opinion, more established Jews sought to protect, aid, and uplift the new arrivals.[5] The National Desertion Bureau (NDB), an agency that aimed to regulate the behavior of working-class Jewish husbands, reflected the interaction between the philanthropic and Americanizing impulses of the established community and the legacy that the newcomers brought with them from eastern Europe.

The post-1880 Jewish immigration was a family affair. Compared to other immigrant groups, eastern European Jews had a more even sex ratio and a higher proportion of children. Over half traversed the ocean in complete family groups, while others sent someone ahead—typically a husband or a daughter—who brought the rest over within two or three years.[6] There were very few "birds of passage"—men who, like many Italian immigrants, came without their families and planned to return home after working and saving in the United States. Jews came to stay—and most of them stayed in New York City, where by 1915 they constituted one-fourth of the population.[7] Relatives and *landsleit* (immigrants from the same place) eased the transition to their new home, and charities instructed immigrants on how to adjust to American ways of work and family.

Immigration neither "uprooted" immigrant Jews from a stable, traditional society nor completely "transplanted" their eastern European way of life.[8] Jews in eastern Europe were already experiencing rapid change before coming to the United States. In the last decades of the nineteenth century, they faced worsening economic conditions, aggravated by occupational and residential restrictions, and dislocations caused by the beginnings of industrialization in the Russian Empire. Those who emigrated were primarily skilled urban artisans facing rapid downward mobility, not rural peasants. In the United States, they adapted to available opportunities by parlaying their manufacturing experience into jobs in the garment industry and other consumer goods industries.

Culturally as well as economically, immigration represented neither an abandonment of tradition in favor of modernity nor the wholesale relocation of an age-old way of life. Even before eastern European Jews had crossed the ocean, many had begun to reassess their lives as Jews, as men and women, and as family members. New literary and intellectual currents encouraged the development of secular perspectives, instead of or in combination with traditional Judaism. The Russian government interfered with the rabbinate and fomented distrust of communal leaders charged with implementing oppressive government policies, contributing to the fragmentation and decline in rabbinic authority. Changing economic conditions only aggravated the challenges to Jewish mores and ways of life, including marriage and family life, that loosened the control that rabbis, communal leaders, and parents exercised over the young. These developments contributed to the sense of instability that was captured in a domestic metaphor: the "crisis in the family" that became a topic of debate in eastern European Jewish communities in the era of mass migration.[9]

Jews in nineteenth-century Russia had both emotional and material incentives to form families. They married for love, affection, and companionship, even when parental control over the match precluded free choice of a partner.[10] In Jewish culture, a woman fulfilled her highest calling by marrying and caring for her children and her husband; a spinster's life was difficult and considered pitiful. Men were obligated to marry under rabbinic law. Though a man could excel in other arenas—for example, by becoming an accomplished scholar—marriage also provided many advantages. First, there was the dowry provided by his wife's parents for his use during the marriage (it was to be returned to the wife in the event of a divorce). Whether it was a sum of money or a stake in a business, the dowry contributed to the couple's ability to maintain themselves and their children. A husband might also receive *kest*—a number of years when his wife's parents supported him in their home while he continued his Talmudic education or learned a trade. While the move to the wife's family home could generate some tension and a longing for his own parents, a young man could profit materially from a match.[11]

Only rarely, however, did a Jewish husband enjoy the luxury of remaining a Talmudic scholar supported by his wife and her family. Most men scrambled to make a living. Jewish artisans were employed seasonally, often steadily for only ten or twelve weeks a year, and making ends meet was a constant struggle for all but a small elite. Therefore it usually took more than one person to maintain a family. When a man married, he gained an economic partner in his wife, who would make a critical contribution to their family's survival. Although legally men were responsible for supporting their wives and children, in fact couples typically formed what Susan Glenn has aptly designated a "breadwinning partnership."[12]

Jewish women took on the essential tasks of housekeeping and caring for children. They developed the arts of bartering and bargaining in order to stretch the family's income. In addition, women engaged in a range of gainful activities. The most common occupation for married women was petty commerce—peddling goods in the marketplace, from house to house, and even on the road, traveling from town to town. Women's contributions to the family economy also included production for the market, typically in the sweatshop style of domestic manufacturing of goods then sold by middlemen. In the 1870s, the Singer sewing machine became a fixture in many Jewish homes in the Pale, transforming them into small garment shops in which women worked alongside their husbands and children. Women made clothing and bedding, baked bread, and cultivated small gardens of "Jewish fruits"—carrots, beets, onions, and cucumbers. Often they sold a portion of what they produced. Other occupations for women included shopkeeping, taking in washing, midwifery, matchmaking, hand sewing, rolling and baking *matzah* for Passover, and working at the *mikvah* (ritual bath).[13] Knowing how crucial the woman's contribution to family support would be, young men and their parents typically sought a prospective wife with commercial talent, especially one who spoke the local language in addition to Yiddish.[14]

While shared responsibility for family support among Russian Jewish families was customary, it was not uncontroversial. In the nineteenth century, an intellectual elite influenced by the Haskalah developed a critique of Jewish gender arrangements. The Haskalah was the Jewish "enlightenment" initiated by eighteenth-century western European Jewish intellectuals who sought to reconcile Judaism with modernity. "Enlightened" eastern Europeans caricatured traditional Jewish marriage as a loveless, commercial venture imposed on very young people by insensitive and calculating parents.[15] They represented themselves as protectors of exploited Jewish womanhood, advocating the expansion of female education and the withdrawal of wives from the income-producing portion of their "double day."

Maskilim—the Haskalah's self-conscious modernizers of eastern European Jewry—urged husbands to support their wives. Some maskilim viewed wives' participation in the economy as degrading, associating women's marketplace activity with crass deportment and even promiscuity.[16] Other maskilim turned their harshest criticism on men, accusing them of overburdening their wives with both domestic and income-earning work.[17] The Yiddish novelist Shomer (the future father-in-law of NDB chief counsel Charles Zunser) contrasted his productive mother Hadassah to his unenlightened father. Hadassah was known for her "knowledge of arithmetic and four languages," while his Talmud scholar father was "one of the study hall regulars with their hands in their pockets who despise all work and fail at every trade."[18] To his female readers, Shomer offered a critique of such gender arrangements and an alternative vision of loving marriages in which women could depend on their enlightened husbands. The pamphlet *Sholom Aleykhem tsu Immigranten,* which characterized Russian Jewish men as "idlers, accustomed to living from the toil and care of their wives," echoed maskilic criticism of Jewish husbands.

Some of the ideals of the Haskalah coincided with changes occurring in the Jewish community in the second half of the nineteenth century. Their idealization of marriage for love instead of money, with a partner freely chosen, was echoed in the Yiddish popular literature of the second half of the nineteenth century and in the vision of young Jews embracing new political and social currents. When presented with the opportunity, Jewish women increased their education—though not necessarily with the sole aim of becoming refined wives and mothers. As new industries offered work to young people, the marriage age rose and couples became more capable of setting up independent households without an extended stay with the wife's parents. However, the maskilim's attack on the participation of women in the marketplace had little pragmatic effect. Particularly after 1881, as Russian Jews faced more severe economic restrictions and increased antisemitism, women's economic role remained essential to the mass of impoverished families.[19] The male breadwinner ideal would take hold among immigrants to the United States, but in eastern Europe it had only limited resonance.

Although eastern European Jewish marriages involved an economic partnership, they were not necessarily characterized by a harmonious unity of interest. Indeed, the divorce rate signaled the existence of marital dissatisfaction: among Jews it was higher than among any other European group. (Only Americans had a higher divorce rate.) Jewish law, the primary arbiter of family relations in nineteenth-century Russia, allowed divorce on broad grounds, including mutual incompatibility. Under Jewish law, only the husband could initiate a divorce, but it was normally complete only after the wife accepted the *ghet* (divorce certificate) before two witnesses. However, some men managed to evade the latter requirement, leaving their wives technically married but without husbands.

These women were *agunot*—like women whose husbands died without two witnesses, disappeared, or married non-Jews—"chained women" unable to remarry. The high divorce rate and the plight of the *agunah* contributed to the "crisis" in the Jewish family that concerned maskilim and also many in the Orthodox rabbinate who were otherwise their foes.[20]

The deserted *agunah* made her voice heard in the pages of the Jewish press, where personal announcements appeared describing the missing husband and the circumstances surrounding his disappearance. In the late 1860s, deserted women's pleas for assistance in locating their husbands appeared in *Ha-magid*, a Hebrew-language weekly published in a small town on the border between Prussia and the Russian Empire.[21] *Agunot* appealed regularly in the 1890s to readers of *Hamelits*, another Hebrew-language paper, in which a typical notice read: "It has been two years since my husband left me and my child in deprivation and great poverty because, six weeks after our marriage, he deceptively took [our] money, saying he was going for a few days to the town of Bialystok." A description of the man accompanied the notice: "tall, with black hair, a short black beard" and "a long nose, with one crooked and short leg."[22] Under Jewish law, unless the missing husband was found and agreed to provide a *ghet*, this wife of six weeks could not remarry. However, for several decades after the Russian Great Reform of 1864, which made secular courts more accessible, some women also appealed to authorities beyond the community to get around the aspects of Jewish law that "chained" women to their absent husbands.

In the first decade of the twentieth century, the Yiddish press brought tales of desertion to a wide readership. *Der Fraynd*, a popular daily newspaper, carried stories similar to those that had appeared in the smaller-circulation Hebrew papers. It stoked readers' appetite for scandal, for example, by its extensive coverage of a man who married and then deserted thirty women. At the same time, it spread suspicion and disapproval of irresponsible husbands who abandoned their familial duties. As Sarah Abreyva Stein speculates in her study of *Der Fraynd*, deserted women may have viewed advertising in the widely circulated popular paper as more effective than appealing to the more geographically circumscribed and attenuated authority of the rabbinate.[23]

The public consternation over the plight of the *agunah*, the Enlightenment critique of Jewish family life, and the relatively high divorce rate, all indicate that marital strife and public attention to it had already begun before the period of emigration. The erosion of rabbinic authority in the nineteenth century had weakened community control over the formation and breakup of marriages. Jewish immigrants brought this legacy with them to the United States, where they were met by an established American Jewish community that took pride in upholding bourgeois norms of respectable family life.

A BLOT ON THE FAIR NAME OF ISRAEL

Anxiety about family instability struck a chord with the older American Jewish community that greeted the influx of eastern European immigrants. Even middle-class Jews were not entirely comfortable in America, wary of the judgments that Gentiles might make of the entire community if any Jew violated dominant American standards of conduct or even was simply too conspicuous. They were highly self-conscious about their reputation among non-Jews and hoped to combat negative stereotypes through unimpeachable behavior. As Naomi Cohen observes, " 'Mah yomru hagoyim?' ('What will the gentiles say?') became well-nigh an obsession."[24] In particular, American Jews sought to prove their acceptability based on their pure and respectable family life—defined as the gender arrangements of the American upper middle class. In language that echoed the themes of American middle-class domestic discourse, middle-class Jews praised refined wives and mothers—those with "a sweet temper and good manners" who could say of their husbands, "he earns abundantly because he is a happy man."[25] Harmonious homes, domestic wives, and reliable male providers were a credit to the Jewish community. Of course, Jews did not uniformly embody these ideals. Especially in the first generation, German Jewish women worked alongside men in family businesses, contributing to the upward mobility that would later allow the adoption of middle-class lifestyles. Some Jewish men did not hold to their husbandly duties; instead, they joined those who abandoned their families in the hope of making a fortune in the West.[26] Nevertheless, middle-class Jews considered their standard of family life to be one of the strongest proofs of their worthiness as Americans.[27]

American Jews also prided themselves on their philanthropic efforts both for needy members of the community and for non–Jewish Americans. Charitable work allowed the donors to fulfill the traditional obligation of *tzedakah*—which translates as "justice"—to the poor. Some among the small, very wealthy German Jewish elite also adopted a Carnegie-like attitude toward the poor. The German-born Jewish American banker and philanthropist Jacob Schiff, for example, saw his wealth as entailing the obligation of stewardship, since the "surplus wealth we have gained, to some extent, at least, belongs to our fellow beings; we are only the temporary custodians of our fortunes."[28] However, there was a difference: it was especially urgent that wealthy Jews appear generous rather than grasping, lest they conjure up antisemitic stereotypes associating Jews with usury and greed.

Like contributors to Catholic charities, Jewish philanthropists took a "proprietary" approach to their community's poor and to immigrant absorption. Both Catholics and Jews sought to protect their needy coreligionists from the judgment and proselytizing that could accompany Protestant aid. When more established Catholic groups, such as the Irish and Germans, assisted immigrants from southern and eastern Europe, they established their own sober respectability and sense of responsibility.[29] By "taking care of their own," Jewish charities similarly demonstrated the independence of the community. Jews prided themselves on maintaining the so-called Peter Stuyvesant Pledge—the promise made by Sephardic immigrants to the governor of New Amsterdam in 1654 that Jews would take care of their own and never become a burden on the non-Jewish public. Jewish charity workers claimed to hold to that pledge until the 1930s, and historians have echoed their words.[30] However, the influx of millions of eastern European immigrants challenged the ability of the Jewish community to remain self-sufficient.

Eastern European Jews themselves strove to create a self-sufficient community and avoid dependence on the charities. They formed thousands of *landsmanshaftn*, mutual aid societies comprised of immigrants from the same hometown. Primarily male in membership, *landsmanshaftn* provided a range of health, unemployment, and burial benefits, as well as small payments to widows. They signified a commitment to breadwinning among Jewish immigrant men, who rarely earned enough to support a family. As a writer for the *Tageblat* wrote, a sick member of a *landsmanshaft* "suffers no degradation . . . because he asks no charity. He is given what he is entitled to. It is mutual aid."[31] The *landsmanshaft* preserved men's self-respect, along with that of the eastern European Jewish immigrant community, by protecting their dignity from the condescension of the charities.

By the time of the mass immigration, those charities were taking the initial steps that would transform them from an array of often fraternal and sororal benevolent societies to amalgamated "scientific" charity organizations. Beginning in the 1870s, some American Jewish leaders joined their Protestant counterparts in criticizing "inefficiency" in the administration of charity. Critics such as Meyer S. Isaacs, editor of the *Jewish Messenger*, sought to address what they viewed as indiscriminate giving by groups and individuals, as well as overlapping and competing organizational fund-raising campaigns. In 1874, five New York Jewish philanthropic groups merged to form the United Hebrew Charities (UHC), which in 1926 became the Jewish Social Service Association.[32] In 1900 the National Conference of Jewish Charities (NCJC) was formed to connect agencies across the country.[33]

The UHC and its counterparts in the NCJC marked a shift in American Jewish leadership, from rabbis and editors to wealthy businessmen. The UHC was funded from 1891 to 1914 by the Baron de Hirsch Fund, set up by the Munich-born Baron Maurice de Hirsch, whose railroad enterprises in Europe reaped a fortune. In the United States, the fund was administered by the new, largely German-born elite, including the bankers Jacob Schiff and Jesse Seligman and the first director of the UHC, the dry goods manufacturer Henry Rice.[34] The first president of the NCJC was Max Senior, also a businessman. It was often such donors who insisted on "scientific charity" measures. Henry Rice, who was also a member of the Charity Organization Society, the major non-Jewish "scientific charity" in New York, insisted that "sentiment should be subordinated to strict investigation."[35] Although professionals and eastern European Jews did increasingly join the ranks of charity administrators and workers, the power of the purse strings remained with the wealthy donors. Employees of the charities had a sometimes testy relationship with the wealthy benefactors who paid their salaries. The social worker Morris Waldman, for example, publicly accused Jacob Schiff of "benevolent despotism" and felt his career had been hampered as retribution for the remark.[36]

The new leadership was not only wealthy; it was also overwhelmingly male. Jewish women had their own tradition of participating in philanthropic work as volunteers in sewing societies, ladies' auxiliaries, and other benevolent groups. The federated charities created in the 1870s absorbed many women's organizations, as Jewish men asserted their claim to represent and control the philanthropic face of the community. Reacting against the American association of benevolence with femininity, Jewish men promoted masculine administration as more rational and efficient than the groups they incorporated. Frequently relegated to subsidiary roles, women continued to deal with clients and to raise funds for charities in which they had little decision-making power.[37]

Women became distinctly junior partners in the new amalgamated charities.[38] Even the handful of women who gained high positions had to struggle to be heard. Minnie Low, the superintendent of the Bureau of Personal Service of the Associated Jewish Charities of Chicago, attained the office of president of the NCJC in 1914. Yet all five other officers of the organization and the entire twelve-member executive committee were male. On seeing a draft of the program for an upcoming conference, Low complained to David Bressler, president of the National Association of Jewish Social Workers, about the token representation of women: "While you very graciously accord women the opportunity of being Session Chairmen, you have not accorded a place to any woman—north, east, south or west—on the program proper." When Bressler attempted to mollify Low by pointing out that every New York member of the executive committee planned to vote for the proposed state suffrage amendment, Low replied: "You know, women not only like to vote, but they like to talk once in a while. . . . In fact, if you want to retain the interest of the rank and file, you must give women a chance to be heard. . . . It is merely a question of justice, because surely you could have found one fair dame in the width and breadth of this land, who could bring something valuable to the Conference."[39]

Needless to say, women fared better in their own organizations. The National Council of Jewish Women (NCJW), founded in 1893, gathered together clubs and benevolent societies from across the country. It launched a social reform program that included the promotion of Jewish education as well as many typical Progressive causes, such as the prevention of juvenile delinquency. Populated primarily by middle-class Jews, the NCJW joined the aid effort for eastern European immigrants. Like their male counterparts, they did so out of feelings of kinship and responsibility for the new arrivals. They also sought to protect the community's image. As Rebekah Kohut, first president of the New York section of the NCJW, observed, "Because the Jew is criticized and attacked as a tribe, he is obliged to defend himself as a tribe, whether he likes it or not."[40] The members of the NCJW took immigrant women, especially young women, to be their special responsibility, focusing on preventing the recruitment of girls into prostitution. Older immigrant women were treated as mothers, rather than as wives, in most of the NCJW programs for them, such as parenting classes and health education. Desertion, in contrast to prostitution, was apparently of relatively marginal concern to the NCJW.[41]

The male-led charities made desertion a central issue. Like the NCJW, they saw the threat to Jewish women, and by extension to the community, as coming from disreputable Jewish men. Desertion among working-class immigrants threatened the reputation of Jewish family life, and the poverty of abandoned families challenged the resources of the charities. By making men responsible for their dependents, charity workers would demonstrate their own responsibility for the independence and respectability of the community.

The American Jewish establishment's sensitivity to non-Jewish opinion and eastern European Jews' concern over the plight of the *agunah* converged in a series of programs aimed at combating desertion. The NCJC's committee on desertion issued its first report in 1900. Two years later, the UHC created in New York a Department of Desertion that worked in cooperation with the Educational Alliance's Legal Aid Bureau, which had been handling desertion cases since it was established. In 1905, the NCJC created the Committee for the Protection of Deserted Women and Children, funded by the UHC and directed by Charles Zunser, a young attorney. The National Desertion Bureau was created in 1911 by the NCJC and eventually came under the umbrella of the New York Federation of Jewish Philanthropies. It was funded through the New York Foundation by the multimillionaire Heinsheimer brothers and by contributions from Jewish charities around the country.[42] Zunser served as the NDB's chief counsel from 1922 to 1948.

The NDB, a Jewish legal aid agency with a name notably not signaling ethnicity, reflected the anxiety about respectability that colored Jewish charity work. Among the first resolutions on desertion proposed by the NCJC was one recommending that Jewish social agencies "elevate the general tone of our poorer coreligionists."[43] The involvement of Jews in antidesertion reform, like their participation in the campaign against prostitution, stemmed in part from fears of antisemitism.[44] Desertion was, uptown Jews believed, a "blot on the fair name of Israel."[45] Fearing that they would be identified with the problems of working-class Jewish communities, middle-class Jews sought to defend the reputation of the Jewish community as a whole. A similar dynamic operated among Catholics who worried that social problems identified with immigrants would reinforce stereotypes about their group. Responding defensively to commonplace views of Irish immigrant drunkenness, primarily male Catholic organizations encouraged temperance among immigrant men. Jewish reformers worried that impoverished eastern European Jews would fuel the campaign for exclusionary immigration quotas by becoming public charges. "The subject of how to avoid wife desertion is most important," argued one participant in an NCJC discussion on desertion, because "in order to stop anti-immigration laws we should feel morally responsible to our government to keep all Jewish poor off our streets, to take such care of our Jewish women and children that they need not become a burden to the State."[46]

The fears of antisemitism were not unreasonable. Although antisemitism was less pronounced in the United States than in Europe, it was increasingly institutionalized in the late nineteenth century as schools, clubs, and vacation spots excluded Jews. Furthermore, in the period of mass immigration, nativity became racialized in both scholarly and popular culture. Irish, Jewish, or Italian "racial" traits were seen as causes of immigrants' aberrant social behavior by those native-born whites concerned about the new arrivals' "fitness for self-government." In the American racial hierarchy, European immigrants—"probationary whites," to use Matthew Frye Jacobson's term—were arrayed between African Americans and Anglo-Saxons.[47] Some social workers, seeking to legitimize their profession through association with science, elaborated racial categories into "diagnoses" of their clients' economic and social problems.

The practice of employing racial explanations for social problems was employed with striking forthrightness in a four-part series, titled "Racial Factors in Desertion," that appeared in 1922–23 in the *Family*, a publication of the American Association for Organizing Family Social Work. The author, the social worker Corinne Sherman, identified "racial" reasons for desertion among Italians, Slavs, Irish, and African Americans. In her schema, Italians had a "racial propensity for roving . . . overwhelming passion; and an irresponsible love of pleasure." She contended that Slavic customs were "more primitive than civilized," with the women characterized by "extreme undesirability"; Ruthenians were "especially low grade." The Irish, Sherman believed, were "essentially animalistic and anthropomorphic," had a "natural love of philandering," and bore an "emotional instability natural to their race." And she explained desertion among African Americans by contending that they descended from "easy-going savages" with "no real homes, home-keepers and home makers."[48]

These "racial characteristics" apparently were not intractable: Sherman believed that Americanization, or "assimilation," could stem desertion. She reserved the term "American" for whites whose families had been in the United States for at least three generations. Their "racial characteristics" included "a tendency toward well-considered, purposeful action, especially in comparison with other races, along material lines." Viewing the "American" cases as more "individual," Sherman did not employ "illustrative cases," as she had in other parts of the series. Indeed, the section on "Americans" stressed deserters' deviation from, rather than expression of, traits identified as "racial." Sherman looked forward to a time when science would provide social workers with the "laws of racial psychology" as tools for case work.[49]

Although comments made in passing reveal that Sherman felt that Jews were not "Americans," she did not include a section on Jewish deserters.[50] Her "data" were the case files of the Charity Organization Society (COS), which did not handle Jewish cases. A superintendent of the COS, Frederick Bauer, did express his opinion on the subject of Jewish desertion, asserting that "the Hebrew whom we have always considered the model father—the man who we were led to believe stood by his family to the last ditch, is the chief offender."[51] The NDB attempted to gain a monopoly on Jewish desertion cases, in effect protecting clients—and the Jewish community at the same time—from this kind of outside judgment. The bureau and its affiliates among Jewish welfare societies became the experts on Jewish desertion and maintained control over statistics on Jewish desertion and their interpretation.

Yet Jewish agencies' posture was often defensive, revealing the fear that Jewishness would be associated with desertion itself. They argued that desertion was not a characteristic "Jewish problem" but rather a temporary aberration, a symptom of the disruptions caused by migration. In 1910, a year before the NDB opened its doors, discussants at the meeting of the NCJC speculated about "the origin of Jewish desertion cases" in the unsettling effects of immigration from "some dark Russian settlement" in a "land of oppression" to a "land of civilization." They imagined that marriages fell apart when men immigrated before their wives. As one participant characterized the problem facing such a husband, "When his wife arrives he is shocked to find that whereas he has become an American and has associated with Americans, his wife is a far different being." The conference participant argued that therefore Jewish desertion cases "differ from desertions ordinarily."[52] As it turned out, the NDB rarely encountered this type of desertion. Instead, most of their clients found their mates on the American side of the ocean after settling into the new landscape.[53] Their marriages—and desertions—were less different from those of their fellow Americans than some Jewish charity workers wished to believe.

Indeed, a second strategy for defusing the fear that desertion would be seen as a particularly Jewish problem was to argue that it occurred among non-Jews as well. For example, after reviewing numerous studies, Morris Waldman asserted that "family desertion is by no means a distinctly Jewish problem. . . . It is not a Jewish question alone, but is just as prevalent among the Gentiles, and from this fact we may take unction to our souls." When his own statistics revealed a greater tendency among Jewish deserters to leave for "other women," he rushed to explain away the impression "that our people are much more immoral." Waldman contended that "the desertion evil . . . does not argue a greater prevalence of moral depravity than exists among other people."[54] Judge Julian Mack, commenting on the report of the Committee on Desertion at the NCJC meeting in 1912, turned the feared slur on the Jewish community into a compliment:

> I like this [antidesertion] work particularly on the part of the Jewish Charities because it shows that we are not afraid to admit our faults. It is not pleasant to say that the Jewish Charities needed a Desertion Bureau, that that is one of our great troubles. It is a blot on the Jewish name, of course, but I think it is a fine thing to be willing to admit it; we admit that we have our faults, but we purpose [*sic*] examining into them and remedying them and as far as possible eradicating them, and I think it is in that spirit that we are setting a fine example.[55]

The board of directors and the staff of the NDB represented a hierarchical alliance of well-to-do American Jews and eastern European immigrants. The bureau's Certificate of Incorporation filed with the State of New York in 1914 bears the signatures and addresses of its first board of directors. They included such prominent figures as Felix Frankfurter and Julius Mayer, and virtually all of them lived "uptown"—shorthand for the middle-class areas of Manhattan north of the Lower East Side's concentration of recent eastern European Jewish immigrants.[56]

However, the bureau's professional staff included a number of Yiddish-speaking eastern European immigrants with ties to the downtown community. Chief Counsel Charles Zunser, for example, was the son of a celebrated Russian Jewish songwriter, poet, and *badchen* (wedding bard), who would have been well known to recent immigrants for his humorous Yiddish writings. Charles's wife, Miriam, daughter of the Yiddish novelist Shomer, was herself an active participant in Yiddish cultural life as a poet and as a playwright for the Yiddish theater.[57] Whether echoing the ideals of the maskilim or those of his adopted country, Charles took pride in his wife's erudition and literary accomplishments, but he did not want her to be the family breadwinner. The dapper Charles turned from writing to a more financially reliable career in the law. His foray into New York City politics as a district organizer for reform mayor John Purroy Mitchel brought in enough money for the Zunsers to cease their annual apartment-hopping and buy a house in a not entirely hospitable non-Jewish suburb.[58] While some bureau staff participated in Yiddish cultural life, others may have shared the political orientation of many downtown workers: Assistant Secretary Samuel Edelstein, for example, described himself as "loyal to the Socialist Party."[59] Charles Zunser's friends included the socialist Rose Pastor Stokes and the Jewish feminist writer Anzia Yezierska. Those who worked for the bureau may have been moving economically and geographically away from the working-class Jewish community, but they maintained ties to the downtown community, even as they received the official backing of the uptown Jewish establishment.

Respectability might well have been of particular concern to the lawyers involved in creating and staffing the NDB. In the early decades of the century, Jewish lawyers found the doors to the most prestigious workplaces, corporate firms, virtually closed to them. Limited to the lowest ranks of the profession, many eked out a meager and irregular living in small solo practices. Members of the Protestant legal elite labeled eastern European Jewish lawyers "shysters" and "ambulance chasers," who could not comprehend American notions of justice and standards of professional conduct. "Without the incalculable advantage of having been brought up in the American family life," warned one prominent Protestant attorney, Jewish lawyers were likely to be unethical.[60]

In the early decades of the century, aspiring Jewish lawyers faced increasingly discriminatory practices and mounting accusations impugning their fitness for the profession. Shut out of corporate jobs and relegated to the least reputable rungs of the profession, Jewish attorneys had few avenues to respectable employment. Even before Jewish lawyers as a group found an alternative route to prestige and social mobility in New Deal government service, some forged careers in public service that demonstrated their commitment to American values. Immigrants and women—both outsiders vis-à-vis the legal power structure—staffed legal aid agencies and found work with the charities. By defending deserted women and regulating breadwinning among Jewish men, Charles Zunser, Fanny Rosen, and other NDB lawyers contributed to establishing their own reputability along with that of the Jewish community as a whole. Their work demonstrated to skeptical American observers that Jewish participation in the legal profession was a public service, not a public menace.[61]

The National Desertion Bureau had a key downtown ally in Abraham Cahan, who joined its board in 1923 and was editor of the influential *Jewish Daily Forward*, a Yiddish-language socialist newspaper with a circulation of 250,000. The *Forward* cooperated fully with the NDB, even as criticisms of "the charities" and of the bureau's parent organization, the UHC, appeared frequently in its pages. Cahan may have perceived the bureau as less distant from the downtown community than the UHC, and

FORWARD — פארווערטס

א גאלעריע פון פערשוואונדענע מענער.

אויב איהר דערקענט זיי, און ווייסט וואו זיי זיינען, לאזט וויסען זייערע פרויען דורך׳ן „פארווערטס“

סעמיועל ראזענבלום.

סעם בלומבערג.

סעמיועל מאסקאוויטש.

לואיס ראזענבלום.

הערי קאודען.

Jewish Daily Forward, *21 April 1912. The* Forward *solicited the community's help in locating deserters with its "Gallery of Missing Men." (The Dorot Jewish Division, The New York Public Library, Astor, Lenox, and Tilden Foundations. Reprinted with the permission of the Forward Association, Inc.)*

he shared the NDB's concern about desertion. Like his predecessors in eastern Europe, Cahan allowed his paper to become a mouthpiece for women who were seeking missing husbands, publishing their letters and developing a column titled "The Gallery of Missing Men" (or "The Gallery of Runaway Husbands"), in which pictures and descriptions of deserters were printed with requests for information about their whereabouts.

Initially, Cahan harbored suspicions of those who wished to meddle in the family lives of his working-class readers. He began his service for deserted women reluctantly, claiming that it did not seem right to "force a man to live with his wife, whether he wanted to or not." Echoing stereotypes of Jewish women as shrews, he asserted that husbands had good reason to leave wives with "poisonous" temperaments. Nevertheless, he took pity on those who appeared to be especially helpless, mothers of small children and elderly or sick deserted women. Thus Cahan came to disregard the readers who claimed that desertion was not an appropriate concern for a socialist newspaper.

"The Gallery of Missing Men" was more than a simple location service. It sent a message to Jewish immigrant men that they should support their wives and children; if they failed to do so, they would be humiliated before the community. Readers understood the power of the "Gallery" to shame Jewish men. One worker who had recently been fired attempted to turn that power against his boss. He brought to Cahan's office a woman whom he introduced as his former boss's deserted wife. After hearing her tragic tale, Cahan agreed to print the manufacturer's picture in the "Gallery." Shortly after it appeared, Cahan was visited by the irate manufacturer—accompanied by the *real* wife—who threatened to sue if the editor did not print an extensive retraction and apology. Realizing that he had been used by the worker as an instrument of revenge, Cahan complied.[62]

After 1911, the *Forward* avoided smearing respectable Jewish breadwinners by relying on the NDB to investigate desertion cases and only printing notices from the bureau in the "Gallery." Readers were told to contact the NDB if they spotted any of the men. The NDB printed similar announcements in the personal columns of English-language newspapers, in trade union papers, and in the foreign-language press (such as the Hungarian-language press). The NDB attempted to make desertion a community-wide concern through the "Gallery." It expanded its network of informants by enlisting the help of labor organizations, fraternal societies, employers and workmates of runaway men, and neighbors of deserted women.

Charity workers hoped that men's desire to protect their reputations and avoid public embarrassment would prevent restless husbands from leaving their families and compel deserters to return home. The head of a Jewish relief agency commended the *Forward* for using the "weapon of publicity" to "create an atmosphere of danger," which he believed would be "the greatest deterrent to desertion." He predicted that on seeing his picture in the paper, a deserter would feel "embarrassed over the situation, and would probably seriously consider a return to his family."[63] Charity workers believed that by shaming individual men before the Jewish reading public, they would protect the reputation of American Jewry as a whole.

The Jewish antidesertion campaign was launched at a propitious moment. During the Progressive Era, energetic reformers were busy laying the foundations of what would become the American welfare state. They used rhetoric about the need to protect women and children to generate support for many of the changes they sought—tenement-house regulation, protective labor laws, workmen's compensation, food and drug safety, and an array of other government interventions. Jewish charity workers joined this tide of reform, finding a receptive audience and making their mark on welfare policy. The NDB's effort to make Jewish men support their families thus represented the confluence of eastern European Jewish immigrant, American Jewish, and more general American reform streams.

The NDB hoped to prevent desertion through its publicity techniques, on the theory that through the "Gallery" men would learn that they would be exposed and pursued if they left their families. But once men left, the NDB aimed most of all to restore marital harmony. As Morris Waldman reported, "Our endeavor has always been to reunite and reconcile, to keep family and home intact." Consistent with its desire to rebuild families and protect marriage, the bureau refused to arrange divorces. "Our very society rests upon the principle of preservation of the family and the home, and this has been a dominant feature in our upbuilding," asserted Waldman.[64] However, given the disinclination of most deserters to acquiesce to antidesertion professionals' desire to arrange marital reconciliations, the bureau relied heavily on the coercive arm of the law to compel men to resume the duty of breadwinning. Paradoxically, Jewish reformers' efforts to limit public responsibility for the Jewish poor led them to call for the expansion of state authority into the community.

chapter 2

The Creation of an Antidesertion System in New York

Family desertion has continued to grow so serious that attempts to diminish it are no longer confined to philanthropists and professional charity workers. The agitation has become general. Public-spirited men in other walks of life have begun to realize the seriousness and extent of this crime and its effect on the Jewish community.

—Morris Waldman, "Family Desertion," 1905

In 1909, the author of a manual for charity workers observed that "fifteen years ago the deserted family was hardly differentiated from any other instance of poverty; it was a family in want, and the mere fact that that want was caused by the desertion of the natural breadwinner did not seem to the philanthropists of the day to have any material bearing on the situation. . . . A deserted family was supposed to occupy the same position as a family which had lost its head by death." By 1909, however, desertion had been "discovered": "The subject is discussed at almost every national or state conference . . . and it is rapidly developing a literature of its own."[1]

American reformers "discovered" numerous social problems in the Progressive Era—poverty, corruption, juvenile delinquency, and so on.[2] In one sense, they found nothing new. Destitution, political scandal, and youth crime had all existed before and had been subject to periodic critique. But at the end of the nineteenth century, they were redefined as problems in need of solutions, often involving government intervention.

The intimate relationships of the poor became targets for reform. Many commentators on family life in the early twentieth century worried that marriage was in peril.[3] The rising divorce rate, women's increased participation in the labor force, and the influx of unattached "homeless" men seemed to confirm their fears. The antidesertion reformer Bernhard Rabbino lamented in 1933 that "America, till about forty years ago, was truly blessed, because it was a land of real homes." Rabbino, a Russian-born rabbi, located the era of decline as the period of mass immigration, when he himself had arrived in the United States. Exhorting his readers to restore the home to its former "pristine position," Rabbino argued that "the only way to put our social structure on a stronger, safer and more durable basis is to go 'back to the home.' "[4] As an aggressive and dramatic publicist for antidesertion reform in the first decade of the century, Rabbino contributed to the movement to stem the supposedly mounting numbers of men who were fleeing their families.[5]

Historians taking a longer view observe that marriage and "the family" seem always to have been in crisis compared to a nostalgically imagined past.[6] Desertion had long been an informal means of divorce. In the eighteenth and nineteenth centuries, men boarded ships harbored in cities such as New York and Philadelphia, bound for other ports and new lives, leaving wives and children behind. They headed west, seeking adventure or fortune or simply escape. Deserted wives responded in several ways. Many simply remarried, despite the absence of a formal divorce. As divorce became more available on a wider range of grounds, some deserted women sought to formalize their unmarried status through state courts and legislatures. If the deserting husband left behind anything—be it property or other assets—it could be seized and used to assist the abandoned family.[7] But around the turn of the century, these measures no longer seemed adequate to social reformers and charity workers.

Jewish charity workers and lawyers such as Rabbino joined their mostly Protestant counterparts in designing the relief policies, laws, and courts that by the mid-1910s comprised an entirely new antidesertion system. No longer would deserted women be treated as widows. The growth of social case work, with its emphasis on individualized "diagnosis" and varied "treatment" of the poor, contributed to the emergence of deserted women as a distinct category of client requiring a specialized approach.[8] Marital status, rather than simply motherhood, became the salient distinction, eventually leading to separate social welfare strategies for deserted women and widows.

FORGING A NEW WELFARE POLICY

There was little discussion among charity workers about specific remedies for desertion until the late 1890s. Before that time, annual reports of social agencies and manuals for charity workers grouped deserted women with widows, both in statistical compilations and in discussions of remedies. The New York Charity Organization Society (COS), for example, kept no separate statistics for deserted women in the 1880s. Although deserted women occasionally appeared in the annual reports' appendix of "illustrative cases," intended both to raise funds and to instruct COS agents, prosecution of deserters was not included as a recommended course of action. Instead, successful resolutions of desertion cases included finding paid work for the woman, sending her children to institutions, or sending both the woman and her children to a (female) relative.[9] The COS treated widows the same way. The United Hebrew Charities (UHC) occasionally raised the issue of desertion in the 1880s, but not until 1897 did it designate deserted wives as a group requiring special attention.[10]

The disaggregation of deserted wives from widows laid the groundwork for increased attention to the prosecution of nonsupporting husbands and fathers. Two trends contributed to the emergence of deserted women as a distinct category in social welfare policy: first, the attempt by charities, overwhelmed by the depressions of the 1890s, to trim their relief rolls and hence their expenditures; and, second, the movement to return institutionalized children to the care of mothers. Antidesertion activists defined their twin goals as restoring family life and saving public and community funds. Beginning in the late 1890s, social welfare workers began advocating treating deserted women differently from widows as a means to accomplish these ends.

Desertion became the subject of debate in the U.S. Congress in 1895, when the Senate Committee on Pensions considered a bill to provide for the deserted wives of Civil War veterans. Some congressmen resisted the proposed extension of government interest into the marriages of veterans, protesting that it offended masculine autonomy: "A provision which would place all the soldiers of the Union Army now receiving pensions under the care or surveillance of anybody . . . would be exceedingly offensive."[11] However, advocates responded by casting the relationship between male citizens and government authority as dependent on men's performance as breadwinners: "The plainest dictates of justice require of the husband the discharge of this duty [to support his wife and children] to the extent of his ability, and it is also the duty of the Government to compel him to discharge this duty to the extent of his ability."[12] After several years of debate, a law was passed in 1899 that allowed a deserted veteran's wife and/or her children to receive half of her husband's pension until his return or death (when she would have to reapply as a widow). Its final, amended language revealed congressmen's concern not only about deserters but also about abandoned wives, specifying that to be eligible a deserted woman had to be "of good character and in necessitous circumstances" and her children "legitimate."[13] Congress periodically found opportunities to endorse the campaign to make husbands support their families, but state jurisdiction over family law and most welfare programs relegated the federal government to a minor role in antidesertion reform until the New Deal.[14]

In New York, COS workers proposed the harshest antidesertion policy: withholding relief from deserted women as a means of impressing on men their breadwinning responsibilities. In 1895, Mary Richmond, then general secretary of the Baltimore Charity Organization Society and later director of the Charity Organization Department of the Russell Sage Foundation in New York City, advised: "In many cases the more heroic treatment of cutting off supplies must be resorted to. . . . When we find that we are dealing with such a man, it becomes necessary to prove that we have more strength of character to resist temptation to help than he has strength of character to resist temptation to work." Richmond warned charity workers not to grow "so sensitive to the charge of hardness" that they allowed the plight of abandoned children to tempt them into generosity.[15]

Fears of "shiftless" husbands contributed to the defeat of an early attempt to pension single mothers. A mothers' allowance bill was introduced into the New York State legislature in 1897, with the goal of returning children from institutional to maternal care. The bill, which applied to the City of New York, instructed the city comptroller to pay to a destitute mother the amount normally expended by an institution for the care of a child in order to keep the child at home. It covered any destitute mother who was compelled by poverty to seek the commitment of her children, whether she was widowed or deserted, whether or not she had an employed husband or wage-earning children. The bill passed both houses of the legislature in 1898, but it was vetoed by the governor under pressure from New York City social agencies opposed to granting public relief to people not living in institutions for the poor.[16]

Those who had opposed the mothers' allowance legislation raised an issue that would shape the policy of social agencies toward deserted women. The bill's opponents labeled it the "shiftless fathers' bill," arguing that giving aid to women with living husbands would encourage desertion by men who could rest assured that the public would support their children.[17] Social agencies chimed in, advocating the policy of withholding relief from deserted women as a "preventative" measure. The arguments surrounding the "shiftless fathers' bill" were echoed in the antidesertion policy debates. C. C. Carstens of the Society for the Prevention of Cruelty to Children (SPCC), for example, warned that "to treat the deserted wife . . . as if she were a widow is giving unbegrudging aid but is also giving a cowardly husband encouragement."[18]

Charity workers feared that if they continued to treat deserted women as widows, men would continue to desert on the assumption that relief would be extended to wives and children. Mary Breed of the Albany Society for the Cooperation of Charities believed that a man was "only led off by the easy-going conviction that his family will get along somehow without him. It would seem to be our business to show him that this conviction is entirely unfounded. This can certainly not be done by giving aid." Breed joined Richmond in arguing that even friends and family of deserters should be urged to withhold help. In cases where it was absolutely necessary to offer assistance, Breed suggested that relief be made "unpalatable" by requiring the woman to give up her children to foster care: "Her very unwillingness to accept it helps us to effect our end, the reestablishment of the home." Commenting on Breed's position, Roy Wallace of the Philadelphia SPCC endorsed a British report that concluded that "deserted women should be relieved only in institutions."[19]

Wallace was particularly anxious that charitable funds not end up supporting men, arguing that "it is socially dangerous to provide for the returned deserter a better home condition than would have prevailed if he had stayed on the job." As C. C. Carstens warned at the New York State Conference of Charities and Correction in 1904, "He may be back tomorrow to enjoy the shelter, food, and fuel that a charitable society or perchance a Lady Bountiful may have provided." The same fear of assisting men drove suspicions that some couples would stage "collusive desertions" if relief were extended to deserted women and children. Carstens worried that "one of the easiest ways of getting relief is by pretending to be a deserted wife, while the husband is away but in actual collusion with the wife or is actually around at certain hours of the day and night." Haunted by such fears of the "man-in-the-house," many charity workers agreed that "it is not practicable . . . to deal with deserted wives on the same plan as we deal with widows."[20] Hence, early policies for deserted women included breaking up families, providing less relief to deserted women than to widows, or denying relief altogether.

The policy of withholding relief from deserted women was not embraced by the Jewish charities, with the exception of the Cincinnati United Jewish Charities. As New York UHC manager Morris Waldman observed at the National Conference of Jewish Charities (NCJC) meeting in 1910, "scientific charity" (termed "scientific selfishness" by another conference participant) had become "taboo . . . a counter reformation in Jewish Charities having apparently set in. The pendulum which ten years ago swung from the heart to the brain in charity work seems now on its return swing." Waldman criticized the Cincinnati agency's refusal to handle desertion cases and its policy of referring women instead to the Humane Society, which used its police powers to track down and arrest deserters. Social workers from around the country attending the NCJC meeting joined Waldman in his condemnation of this method.[21]

Commenting on the Cincinnati policy of not aiding deserted women directly,[22] one Jewish charity worker contrasted Christian charity with the Jewish tradition of justice to the poor: "How could New York refuse to aid a thousand helpless women, who, in taking care of their babies, fulfill their mission. Is it kind to call these women beggars? . . . It is quite true you reduce the number who ask for assistance, but is that a proof they are not in want? . . . We have had 1,800 years of charity giving, let the poor now have justice. . . . You should not close your doors to the family of a deserter. . . . Continue to aid helpless women left to care for their infants."[23] Boris Bogen, the director of the Cincinnati United Jewish Charities, attempted to defend his policy, only to receive the retort of Mrs. Henry (Hannah Greenebaum) Solomon, founder of the National Council of Jewish Women and a conference participant from Chicago, who found "little value" in Bogen's method and believed that charities "should not consider women beggars. . . . They earn all they get, especially those of the [working] class . . . since upon them devolves the burden of carrying the financial question, being the housekeeper, laundress and general burden-bearer."[24]

Offering deserted women less assistance than widows struck many Jewish charity workers as unfair. Lee K. Frankel, manager of the UHC, acknowledged Mary Breed's point that relief for deserted women might increase desertion, but felt that "a deserted woman, with children, who is not at all responsible for the desertion of her husband, is a subject for our sympathy as much as a widow, and should receive the same sort of treatment."[25] Solomon Lowenstein also found it "difficult to see wherein the condition of [a deserted] family differs from that of a widow" and argued that "the cure [for desertion] cannot be sought in the granting or withholding of relief."[26]

In the late nineteenth century, while the COS continued to resist granting outdoor relief for widowed as well as deserted mothers, the UHC was already providing pensions for both groups of women.[27] Although the COS did eventually pension widows, in 1910 its spokespeople at the New York

Conference of Charities and Corrections still balked at providing pensions for deserted women and opposed legislation for publicly financed allowances. The cos suspected that deserted women, and not only their husbands, were undeserving. As Mary Breed argued, "The deserted wife is distinctly below the [moral] standard of the widow deprived of her husband by death. . . . There seem to be, then, few deserted wives to whom we can apply the character test necessary for a pension plan."[28] In contrast, charity workers at the 1910 meeting of the NCJC tended to take the opposite view, in part because they had a history of granting regular relief to deserted women as well as to widows. In 1909, the UHC had sponsored a separate agency to disburse monthly pensions, the Widowed Mothers' Fund Association, with Hannah Einstein at its head. Einstein became an ardent and prominent advocate of public pensions as well.[29]

The distance between the major Protestant and Jewish charities on the issue of providing allowances to deserted women was greater in New York than in other parts of the country. Cincinnati's Boris Bogen shared Mary Breed's perspective, while Charity Organization Societies in states such as Connecticut, Maine, and Missouri granted relief to both deserted and widowed mothers.[30] Over time, the cos in New York changed its perspective: by 1919, its superintendent, Joanna Colcord, reported that social workers had departed from Breed's "stringent" approach. Colcord herself deemed her agency's earlier policy "rigid" and "niggardly."[31]

The New York mothers' pension program established in 1915 bore the marks of charity workers' debates about desertion. Mothers' pension legislation swept the nation like "wildfire," beginning in 1911; by 1920, forty states had instituted programs.[32] The principles that guided the pension movement, if not the implementation of programs, were that children should not be separated from their mothers simply because of poverty, that a good mother's care was superior to institutional care, and that motherhood was a service to the state. Mothers' pension plans varied in the definition of recipients, including any combination of widows, wives of incarcerated or disabled men, deserted women, and unwed mothers. Many states named deserted women as eligible recipients at some point, but there was considerable ambivalence regarding their inclusion. The primary recipient, and the image used to drum up support for pension legislation, was the "worthy widow," the figure least likely to arouse public opposition. By the time the New York legislature enacted a mothers' pension bill in 1915, antidesertion reformers had articulated rationales for disaggregating widows from deserted women and for excluding the latter.

The mothers' pension movement developed alongside the antidesertion campaign. The two movements shared some personnel. William Hard, the editor of the *Delineator* and a prominent proponent of mothers' pensions, urged the passage of antidesertion legislation. Hard, a friend of Jane Addams and a former Chicago settlement house worker himself, used the pages of his magazine to advocate "the increase of women's powers in their homes."[33] The General Federation of Women's Clubs and other female social reformers who took up the cause of children emphasized the need for maternal care and family life for the proper development of young citizens. Antidesertion activists shared these concerns, placing particular emphasis on the expense of orphanage care. Beginning around the turn of the century, social agencies began calculating how much the support of deserted women and children was costing the public. Generally, they estimated that about 10 percent of the dependent population were deserted families and that between 20 and 25 percent of children in institutions had been abandoned.[34] Efforts to remove children from orphanages encouraged both the growth of foster care and the passage of public mothers' pension programs in many states. Jewish agencies did not embrace foster care to the same extent as their Protestant counterparts. A dearth of foster homes for Jewish children and the strength of orphanages slowed the development of placing out in the Jewish community.[35] However, Jewish charity workers emerged as vigorous supporters of publicly funded mothers' pension programs, while non-Jewish private charities were the most vigorous opponents of mothers' pensions.[36]

Debates about mothers' pension legislation echoed earlier discussions about private charity as an incentive to desertion by shiftless men. The New York City commissioner of charities Robert W. Hebberd, an ally of Jewish antidesertion activists and a member of the commission that drafted New York State's pension legislation, warned against making the program a broad one. In a speech supporting the "chivalric" movement for mothers' pensions, he asserted that "there are, doubtless, thousands of men in this country who would be overtempted . . . to desert their families if they could be sure that a 'pension' would be forthcoming as the result of such desertion. . . . It must be evident that society cannot afford to hold out this temptation to the weak or the shiftless heads of families." Hebberd did not want to lend men "any encouragement to waste their means in drink or in any other form of hurtful extravagance." He therefore wished to restrict pensions to "the natural objects of charity," worthy widows, whom he viewed as "a logical charge . . . upon the body politic."[37]

The commission created to make recommendations on mothers' pensions to the New York State legislature included several people who had been immersed in debates about desertion for over a decade, among them William Hard, Robert W. Hebberd, and Hannah Einstein. Their report argued for extending benefits only to widows because "the misfortune that follows upon the decease of the poorer laborer is not caused in any way by those who must suffer. Then, too, adequate relief cannot in any way increase the number of worthy families in distress as can easily be the case with other mothers whose husbands are living. To pension desertion or illegitimacy would, undoubtedly, have the effect of [putting] a premium on these crimes against society."[38] By the time mothers' pension legislation succeeded in New York with the 1915 Child Welfare Act, it had been narrowed to include worthy widows only; it was among the most conservative pieces of legislation of its type in the nation.[39]

By 1915, there had emerged in New York a consensus among social workers that addressed both the fiscal and the familialist concerns of antidesertion reformers. The policy was to return family deserters to their place as providers either by encouraging marital reconciliations or, failing that, by enlisting the coercive power of the law. Aid would be extended to deserted women on the condition that they cooperate in the location and prosecution of their husbands. Both private and public charities in New York adopted this policy, and it was incorporated into mothers' pensions and later into Depression-era agency guidelines. As charity workers turned to legal coercion to accomplish their economic and social goals, they built institutions that offered mechanisms for diverting deserted women away from welfare and toward the legal system instead. They became advocates for legal and court reform, adding legal departments to their own organizations and building domestic relations courts.

THE LEGAL SYSTEM

Antidesertion reformers participated in the Progressive Era "revolt against formalism" in the law. While charity workers were devising a plan for the treatment of deserted clients, Roscoe Pound was developing the rationale for a new sociological jurisprudence that would allow for an expanded role for the law in the regulation of everyday life. Pound argued that judges and attorneys should stop viewing the law as a set of abstract universal principles. Instead, law should be responsive to the contemporary environment—an increasingly urban one undergoing constant change—and judges should consider the social factors shaping particular individuals' behaviors. Antidesertion reformers, engaged less with high theory than with their immediate policy agenda, would have agreed with Pound's assertion that the law should meet "social ends." They brought the concerns of social work to the law, prodding the existing legal system to intervene in cases of desertion and fighting for the creation of a specialized court that exemplified the socialization of the law.[40]

Those instrumental in founding the National Desertion Bureau (NDB), such as UHC manager Lee K. Frankel, and attorneys from the Legal Aid Bureau of the Educational Alliance participated actively in the movement to reshape the legal sanctions for desertion in New York. They also called on the secular legal system to regulate the Jewish practice of granting divorces when requested by men, after finding that deserters were unilaterally divorcing their wives by persuading or paying unscrupulous rabbis to issue *ghets* (divorce certificates). The Educational Alliance succeeded in getting the state legislature to enact a law making it a misdemeanor in New York for anyone to issue a *ghet* unaccompanied by a civil divorce.[41] But the Jewish antidesertion activists' most far-reaching campaigns were aimed at a general strengthening of abandonment laws and at creating new courts.

Joining forces with Protestant charities, the activists first tackled the problem of prosecuting deserters who crossed state lines, a problem that welfare workers and lawyers were debating around the country. In 1900, the NCJC recommended that "charity societies . . . strive to influence legislation in different cities to make abandonment a criminal offense and to insure the rendition of fugitive husbands."[42] In 1903, the New York Conference on Charities and Corrections passed a similar resolution and called on governors to honor requisitions for deserters.[43] Influenced by the 1887 Interstate Extradition Conference resolution that extradition for petty offenses should be discouraged, reformers in New York concluded that if they wanted an effective instrument for prosecuting deserters, they had better make abandonment a felony.[44] The Buffalo Charity Organization Society framed a bill in 1903 and, with support from the UHC, lobbied to have it enacted by the legislature.[45]

Passed by the New York State legislature in 1905, the Child Abandonment Act proved to be ineffective.[46] Disappointed reformers found that government authorities were unwilling to assume the costs of extradition. As Morris Waldman commented, "Unfortunately, the change in the law did not at once change the feeling on the part of the prosecuting attorney and the courts, that family desertion was a largely private affair that did not warrant severe punishment."[47] Fifteen years after the law was passed, Walter Liebman of the NDB was still complaining that "prosecuting attorneys and public authorities generally are not alive to the problem." He continued: "The prosecuting attorneys make these claims: (1) that the

Charles Zunser, chief counsel of the National Desertion Bureau. (YIVO *Institute for Jewish Research*)

process of extradition is too costly to the municipality or to the county; (2) that the wife of the defendant often refuses to prosecute and thus turns the trial into a farce; (3) that very few of the extradited offenders would, in fact, go to jail, and that it is useless, as well as extravagant, to bring back men only to return them to their families." Liebman argued that prosecuting attorneys were unwise, for "a reasonable number of prosecutions in each jurisdiction will act as a deterrent to many men who might otherwise desert."[48]

Governors were reluctant to honor requisitions from other states. Governor S. V. Stewart of Montana admitted, "Since I have been governor of Montana more refusals of requests for requisition have come from other governors in cases of this kind [desertion] than in all other classes of cases, and more resistance has been presented in the matter of honoring requisitions from governors of other states than in all other cases."[49]

Reformers continued to press for greater enforcement of the abandonment act and in 1922 secured an extradition treaty with Canada,[50] but the problem of extradition proved intractable. Over the course of the twentieth century, numerous measures were implemented on the state and federal levels to facilitate the location and extradition of nonsupporting fathers, each one testifying to the failure of the one before it.[51]

Hoping to build on public support for juvenile courts, antidesertion reformers campaigned for domestic relations courts to handle desertion and nonsupport cases. However, according to the *New York Times*, "There is no such demand for [domestic relations courts] as there was for the Children's Court."[52] In the absence of a public outcry for the creation of domestic relations courts, a small group of legal and social welfare professionals worked to build support among New York City magistrates and public charities administrators. Bernhard Rabbino was perhaps the most diligent advocate for the new courts. Beginning in 1905, Rabbino, who was both a rabbi and an attorney for the Legal Aid Bureau of the Educational Alliance, published articles and papers on the subject, distributing them to a wide range of public officials, from local magistrates to President Theodore Roosevelt.[53]

Rabbino and other antidesertion reformers such as Benjamin Tuska, a director of the Educational Alliance, finally got their public platform when the governor appointed state senator Alfred R. Page to investigate conditions in city courts. The Commission to Inquire into Courts of Inferior Criminal Jurisdiction (the Page Commission) began hearings in November 1908 on inefficiencies and corruption in the New York City courts.[54] Recognizing that the investigation provided an opening for his ideas,

Rabbino sent a proposed bill for the establishment of a domestic relations court to Julius Mayer, the counsel for the Page Commission and later a member of the board of the NDB. During the hearings in January 1909, Mayer called Rabbino and Tuska to solicit their views on reforming court procedures in domestic cases.[55]

Mayer pressed numerous representatives of social agencies, judges, policemen, and probation officers to address the idea of a distinct legal arena for desertion cases. Male leaders of Jewish communal organizations, such as attorney Ralph Jacobs and Dr. Henry Fleishman of the Educational Alliance, came ready to support it. The St. Vincent de Paul Society joined Jewish advocates for a domestic relations court. However, when Mayer asked a Catholic clergyman for his view on how to reform the treatment of desertion, the canon recommended Ralph Jacobs as a witness with more knowledge of the issue.[56] Women's organizations, including the NCJW, attended the hearings, primarily to lobby for changes in the handling of young women charged with prostitution in the city courts. Many representatives of these women's groups responded positively to the idea of a special desertion tribunal. However, the gender division of labor in New York Jewish reform was evident at the hearings: the women focused mainly on protecting young female defendants, while the men emphasized finding better ways to discipline nonsupporting husbands.[57]

The hearings marked a turning point in the development of the antidesertion system: the Page Commission recommended that special courts be created to handle cases of desertion and nonsupport. Accordingly, the Inferior Criminal Courts Act of 1910 created domestic relations courts in New York City. The legislation signaled New York State's pioneering role in making desertion the province of socialized courts. Within five years, Chicago, Cincinnati, Boston, and Philadelphia had joined Buffalo and New York City in the effort to use new legal forums to compel men to support their families. Over the next few decades, similar courts would be established in more than twenty other cities and counties across the country.[58]

The role of the Page Commission in spurring the creation of the New York City domestic relations court has largely been forgotten. The commission is best remembered for precipitating reforms in prostitution proceedings, notably its recommendation that any woman convicted of a prostitution-related offense be subjected to a mandatory physical exam.[59] But the Page Commission also recommended the creation of new jurisdictions, a women's night court, a men's night court, and a domestic relations court.

The preoccupation of the commission in designing these jurisdictions seems to have been the separation of men from women and of some women from others based on moral criteria. Sex-segregated night courts were necessary because "the mingling of women with men," the commission's final report argued, "has a demoralizing tendency."[60] Within the women's night court, the commission recommended the segregation of "younger and less hardened" prostitutes from "the older and more hardened," as well as the physical separation of women charged with prostitution from other defendants, for "a young girl or woman charged with petit larceny should not be compelled to come into close association with a prostitute or vagrant." The domestic relations courts were intended in part to separate the "decent woman . . . who is merely poor" from the degraded woman.[61]

The Page Commission's concern for dividing deserted women from the less respectable poor was influenced by the complaints of antidesertion reformers. Bernhard Rabbino described the situation prevailing in the unspecialized magistrates' court: "Huddled together were pickpockets, prostitutes, thieves, forgers, deserted women. . . . How degrading for a decent woman to rub elbows with this rabble, and listen to the annals of vice!"[62] (The *New York Times* responded sarcastically to such arguments offered at the Page hearings: "No doubt many women and a few men are compelled in the pursuit of justice to undergo a certain measure of the kind of torture that results from enforced contact with the unclean and the vicious." Police court cases involving such people "are not nice, but neither are many cases of domestic troubles.")[63]

According to the Page Commission's plan, segregated jurisdictions and holding pens were to be prophylactics against the spread of moral contagion in the courts—although all these groups could be found rubbing elbows in poor neighborhoods. Indeed, the deserted woman and the prostitute might inhabit not only the same social space but even the same body. The separation of deserted women from prostitutes was an uneasy distinction, for antidesertion reformers believed that the former could easily become the latter. As Morris Waldman of the UHC commented: "Who knows how many among the unfortunates who walk brazenly along in the lights of the Great White Ways of our cities, or who skulk shamefacedly in the shadows of our byways, scorned and condemned by the thoughtless of their own sex, and ridiculed or abused by the brutal of the other sex, have been driven to their lives of shame by the cowardly desertion of their husbands."[64]

Proceedings in the domestic relations court, closed to the press and the public, were intended to afford a greater degree of privacy than existed in the other magistrates' courts. The concern for privacy on the part of antidesertion reformers who lobbied for the creation of these arrangements is curious, given their wholehearted support of "publicity" as a means of locating deserters for the purpose of prosecution.[65] It is hard to believe that this protected a deserted woman's privacy, but it did, perhaps, preserve her respectability as a private woman, a wife. Seen in the light of the Page Commission's overall recommendations, the concern of antidesertion reformers for privacy seems to have been a way of distinguishing respectable, private women from nonrespectable "public" women—that is, prostitutes.[66]

Historians note that, ironically, "the state created family privacy in America even as it asserted new authority over family relations."[67] The domestic relations court was dubbed the "Court of Nobody's Business,"[68] but, as Stephanie Coontz observes, "we have made many matters 'everybody's business' in order to win support for making them 'nobody's business.' "[69] Antidesertion reformers attempted to make nonsupport a public concern and to enlist the public in locating deserters, but beyond that they depended on the lack of privacy in working-class homes to accomplish their ends. The judge relied on reports of investigations by agency or court officers that included interviews with neighbors, extended family, workmates, and employers of the husband and wife.

If "privacy" could include the gossip networks of working-class neighborhoods and the scrutiny of social investigators, what then did the term mean to the middle-class professionals who designed the domestic relations court? Barring the press and the public from the legal proceedings did remove nonsupport cases from the spectacle of open police court hearings, affording judges the kind of professional privacy associated with the therapeutic encounters of doctors and psychiatrists with patients. But, while protecting the dignity of presiding judges, domestic relations court procedures and their attendant investigations may have assaulted the dignity of working-class women and men. Occasional comments by both deserted wives and their husbands suggest that they experienced middle-class surveillance and entry into working-class networks as invasions of privacy.[70]

Closed, "private" hearings and the suspension of normal rules of evidence and procedure would, antidesertion reformers hoped, allow the domestic relations court magistrate to act as a healer of broken marriages. The paternalistic protection of deserted women from petty criminals was part of a larger paternalist condescension that pictured judges as fatherly figures knowing better how to manage marital conflict than did disaffected working-class spouses. Opponents of the court doubted that such paternalistic power to orchestrate other people's intimate lives was possible. The *New York Times* agreed with a magistrate who complained that "to manage the affairs of the proposed court properly would require 'a direct descendant of an angel.' Such would be hard to find, because in heaven, where the angels are, 'there is no marrying or giving in marriage.'"[71]

Bernhard Rabbino, who dubbed himself "the Father of the Domestic Relations Court," petitioned for his appointment as its first magistrate, collecting supporting signatures from leaders in Jewish philanthropy and social work, businessmen, and clergy (including both Orthodox and Reform rabbis).[72] Rabbino was not daunted by the requirement of near-divine paternal power. He imagined a tribunal in which the judge would, "like the High Priest of old, act as the angel of peace."[73] Chief City Magistrate Otto Kempner also described the domestic relations court as a paternal forum: "The judge acts more as a friendly and fatherly arbitrator than as a criminal Magistrate. . . . He directs his efforts towards reuniting warring couples by judicious counsel and admonition."[74]

Rabbino was an ardent family preservationist. The subtitle of his collected arguments for the establishment of domestic relations courts, *A Plea for the Preservation of the Home*, and the title of his autobiography, *Back to the Home*, expressed his commitment to rebuilding nostalgically imagined nuclear families. More than any other antidesertion reformer, Rabbino believed that families disintegrated when women were gainfully employed. Calling women wage earners "back to the home" and men back to their families, Rabbino declared with typical grandiosity, "Individuals pass on. The family lives. The burden of my song has been 'Preserve the Home.' It is the foundation-stone of the Republic. Its sanctity spells the well-being of the State. Upon its solidarity rests the power of the Nation."[75] While many antidesertion reformers agreed with Rabbino's conviction that "the preservation of the family as a unit is the first and paramount duty of society,"[76] none concurred with his bottom-line disregard for the expense that might be entailed in creating a new institution. "What of it!" he exclaimed. "The improvement of the morals of the community cannot and should not be measured by dollars and cents."[77]

However, Rabbino's plan for a domestic relations court met with success only when he teamed up with those for whom "dollars and cents" were of primary importance. Robert W. Hebberd, the New York City commissioner of charities, responded to Rabbino's campaign by creating a Domestic Relations Court Committee of prominent New Yorkers, with Rabbino as secretary. The involvement of the commissioner of charities signaled the economic incentives for the creation of domestic relations courts. They were seen by antidesertion reformers as a way to reduce the amount that both local government and private charities expended on poor women and children. As Benjamin Tuska noted, "The communal and legal standpoint is one dictated by self-interest. We must save the community expense."[78] Both paternalistic and fiscal arguments for the creation of domestic relations courts can be found in the writings of antidesertion legal reformers of the period, but the emphasis on nonsupport to the almost complete exclusion of other marital problems was symptomatic of the economic interests involved.

Deserted women who were not already receiving relief, or who were deemed not to be in immediate danger of becoming public charges because they had possessions that charitable agencies believed could be sold or used for support,[79] were excluded from the domestic relations courts. They instead could bring an action for separation and support in the civil courts. For a woman on the borderline of poverty, pursuing such legal action must have presented difficulties, for as one New York judge observed, "This entails considerable expense and delay and women amply justified, are sometimes restrained . . . from proceeding in civil courts even to obtain a separation or partial divorce."[80]

Although antidesertion reformers did not view their efforts as contributing to the inequities of the legal system, they did place the social issue of desertion in the context of the high cost of divorce. Desertion "is known as the poor man's divorce," noted NDB president Walter Liebman. "The rich man resorts to the divorce court. The poor man takes the law into his own hands."[81] Benjamin Tuska believed that

> you create absolutely no essential distinction by calling it separation in one case and desertion in the other. Where the prosperous man has decided to leave his wife, if he does not arrange with her, her lawyers arrange with him. He has the wherewithal to make the arrangements, and her lawyers have an object in fighting. When desertion takes place among the poor, there being usually nothing for the family to live upon but the current joint earnings, the wife cannot afford to engage the compelling power of private law, but is obliged to appeal to the commissioners of charity. . . . There the complainant, as well as the informant, is the community.[82]

The dual system of family law that made one husband's desertion a private separation and another's a public offense persisted in the twentieth century as social welfare workers sought solutions to poverty in the regulation of domestic relations. Public assistance rules and procedures came to rely on the new legal institutions to limit the reach of welfare programs. Private charities' reluctance to assist deserted women was translated into public policy as the framers of pension legislation, fearing the taint of corruption that adhered to state spending in the Progressive Era, attempted to establish themselves as responsible administrators of the public purse.[83] In the process, what appeared to be a concern for the transfer of resources within the family from the wallet to the purse was revealed to be at least as much about the distribution of resources among classes.

The legal machinery for regulating male breadwinning defined men's obligation as the minimum required to prevent social spending on dependent women and children. Social welfare workers feared that if public assistance programs became available to deserted women, then men would shift their spending from household provision to personal consumption. Concerned about subsidizing male "self-indulgence," they looked to the new sociolegal institutions for help in preventing welfare fraud by "shiftless" men.

By the mid-1910s, the elements of the new regulatory system were in place: a fairly uniform welfare policy for deserted women and children; a model sociolegal agency linking the welfare and legal systems; and courts specifically designed to handle cases of nonsupport. The twin objectives of "family preservation" and trimming the charity rolls by containing dependency in the family hinged on restoring deserters to their status as providers.

chapter 3

Ambivalent Breadwinners and the Public Purse

Dear Editor,

This is the voice of thirty-seven miserable men who are buried but not covered over by earth, tied down but not in chains, silent but not mute, whose hearts beat like humans, yet are not like other human beings.

. . . We feel degraded and miserable here. And why are we confined here? For the horrible crime of being poor, not being able to satisfy the mad whims of our wives . . . Even during the worst times of the Russian reaction people didn't suffer as the men suffer here in America because of their wives. For a Jewish wife it's as easy here to condemn her husband to imprisonment as it is for her to try on a pair of gloves. . . .

. . . As soon as the wife tastes an easy and free dollar, as soon as she discovers that the "charities" won't let her starve, she doesn't care that her husband is condemned. She lives a gay life, enjoys herself. . . .

Therefore, it is your duty as editor of the Forward, *the newspaper that is read mainly by the working class, the class that furnishes more than all others the candidates for the workhouse and for grass widowhood, to warn all Jewish women not to take such revenge on their husbands.*

—Thirty-seven inmates of Blackwell's Island Prison workhouse, 1910

Dear Mr. Edelson

I am appealing to you for your servicies in regard to the trouble with my husband. I have always led a miserable life for my husband but always tried to meet the obsticles with a smile. I was always content of denying myself of proper clothing although he could afford it. The last straw came when he left me for the second time destitute. My rent and other bills were long over due and I had the choice of leaving the rooms or being put out. I feal in no way to become a public charge.

—Applicant to the National Desertion Bureau, 1923

Eastern European Jewish immigration to the United States surged during the same period in which the future of American manhood was anxiously discussed by statesmen, trade union leaders, and social workers. The modern workplace—whether corporate office or Taylorized factory—

was taking shape; consumer culture offered compensating comforts for alienated employees. While some—most famously Teddy Roosevelt—urged men to resist the softening effects of modern civilization by adopting a virile, athletic, even martial posture, others embraced the new order for the opportunities it provided for domesticating men. Antidesertion reformers, abandoned wives, and deserters participated in a struggle over the meaning of manhood that centered on the tension between male breadwinning and masculine pleasure. Reformers' sometimes ambivalent commitment to male breadwinning and consumer restraint ultimately shaped public policy for poor women and children.

An urban landscape beckoning with the promise of consumer goods and mass entertainments lay behind the struggles waged by working-class men and women over meager familial resources. In a letter to the editor of the *Jewish Daily Forward*, thirty-seven imprisoned deserters accused their wives of preferring consumer pleasures—clothing ("gloves") and amusements (the "gay life")—to husbands of limited means;[1] appealing to the National Desertion Bureau (NDB) for help, a deserted woman complained that her husband refused to pay for necessary household expenses, "although he could afford it."[2] In their drive to prosecute runaway husbands, antidesertion reformers expressed few doubts about men's ability to pay for upkeep of the home. Desertion, they believed, was willful: men simply refused to take responsibility for breadwinning, instead spending their wages on their own pleasures.

Antidesertion reformers worried about the disintegrative effects of participation in American consumer culture on immigrant families. The historian Andrew Heinze suggests that both immigrants and social reformers understood that acculturation occurred through consumption. According to Heinze, Jewish immigrants from eastern Europe were especially likely to equate freedom with access to American abundance. Many social reformers approved of immigrants' aspirations in the arena of consumption because they viewed the desire for an "American standard of living" as a positive sign of acculturation.[3] But social reformers also worried about the disruptive potential of consumer aspirations and of the equation of American freedom with access to consumer pleasures. "Liberty," they contended, meant the opportunity to provide for a family, not simply the freedom to buy American goods. Although consumption was a route to social integration, antidesertion reformers believed that it also posed the danger of familial and hence social disintegration.

Some men resisted the expectation that they would provide, as the letter of complaint to the *Forward* makes clear. Women's activity as consumers in the United States continued and enhanced the eastern European Jewish female role of "baleboste,"[4] but the American normative expectation of male breadwinning and female dependence generated conflict. The thirty-seven Jewish prisoners may have sharply resented the fact that in the United States the law, the charities, and their wives expected them to be the primary providers. Their bitter condemnation of the "mad whims" of their wives pointed to excessive female desire as the cause of their problems. As Riv-Ellen Prell characterizes popular Jewish representations of gender conflict in the early twentieth century, "The consuming woman and the man who provides for his family became the symbiotic pair that brought one another grief."[5]

The confrontation of Jewish immigrants with modern gender norms was but a heightened case of a wider transformation that had been under way in the United States for decades. Over the course of the nineteenth century, the economic center of the American household had shifted from production to consumption. Although still not complete by the turn of the century, this gradual transformation shaped the gender expectations and behaviors of husbands and wives, as well as the conflicts that afflicted their marriages.[6] Men, who in an earlier time might have derived a sense of identity from their work, increasingly experienced it as the source of a paycheck, rather than as a sign of competent manhood. Organized labor registered this shift by redefining virtue for workingmen as providing their families with a "respectable" standard of living.[7] The consumerist turn made breadwinning more central to normative masculinity, highlighting men's connections to families and households. The complaints of wives, the resistance of husbands, and the ambivalent anxieties of family reformers who feared that the lure of consumer pleasures could erode men's motivation to provide demonstrate that this transition was neither smooth nor comprehensive.

The antidesertion movement sought to regulate male breadwinning.[8] Reformers defined desertion as a problem of economic distribution within the family and linked judgments about a man's use of his wages to notions of respectable manhood and responsible consumption. In debates over the causes of marital dissolution, social reformers pitted working-class men's responsibilities as providers against their desires as consumers.[9] The proliferation of household budget studies in the Progressive Era signaled the assumption that women should and did control household consumption. Antidesertion reformers emphasized men's responsibility to support women as household managers, both by providing the necessary funds and by refraining from personal spending.

Legal and social welfare professionals contended that responsible providerhood among working-class men would also benefit the middle class, saving taxpayers from having to support abandoned women and children. The institutions they created—domestic relations courts and legal aid arms of charitable agencies such as the NDB—were designed to protect the public purse. In a provocative article, Carol Brown argues that around the turn of the twentieth century many men came to view wives and children as burdens, rather than as assets, and there ensued a "class struggle" between "the private family and the public system" over who would bear the costs of support.[10] Indeed, by limiting public liability for poor women and children, antidesertion measures aimed to ensure that middle-class resources would not be depleted by working-class dependents. Class and gender anxieties about workingmen's spending, so prominent in antidesertion rhetoric, thus exposed the disruptive potential of male consumption for both the familial and the social order.

In the context of a debate about the division of domestic money and consumer power between husbands and wives, antidesertion reformers participated in defining the proper uses of state power and public funds.[11] Antidesertion reformers assumed that there existed a relationship between personal spending and social spending. Concerned about irresponsible male consumption, they attempted to ensure that taxpayers would not subsidize married men's personal pleasures. Implicitly, public funds were designated for meeting subsistence needs, rather than for satisfying consumer desires and aspirations.

While arguing that the boundary of working-class men's obligation extended beyond themselves to include wives and children, reformers also marked out the limits of middle-class men's obligation. That boundary, too, would encompass—but not exceed—one's own family. Middle-class familial individualism was thus mirrored in the ideology of the "independent family." When antidesertion reformers intoned that "the family is the cornerstone of the nation,"[12] they meant the "independent" male-headed household. This preoccupation was not quite the same as the earlier notion of the independent citizen as the foundation of the state; it relied primarily not on the productive citizen but on the providing father. An "independent" family was one in which a man provided for his own wife and children; "dependent" women and children were public charges.[13]

Middle-class professionals' fear that taxpayers and charities would be saddled with the responsibility for "other men's children" accounted for the way in which antidesertion measures were designed for poor women only.[14] Public money, antidesertion reformers claimed, should not be used to meet working-class familial obligations. Their definition of the relationship between the family pocketbook and the public purse indicated a belief that dependence and support should define the relations between the sexes, and that the middle-class segment of the population should not be responsible for working-class dependents. The rules governing nonsupport proceedings embodied the fear that workingmen's spending could upset these relations, resulting in illegitimate claims on the public purse and disrupting the economies of both the household and the state.

Antidesertion rhetoric about male spending exposes the familial and social dimensions of the emerging mass consumer society. Antidesertion reformers sometimes sounded like opponents of release and self-gratification through consumption.[15] However, they had no moral objection to consumption per se, provided it was directed to certain ends. They sought to achieve their goals through the use of various state apparatuses—domestic relations courts and welfare programs—institutions that, although contemporaneous developments, are rarely discussed in studies of consumer culture in the United States. In these endeavors, we encounter serious anxieties about male consumption and misspending rather than images of feminine frivolity and extravagance.

WHY BREADWINNERS WENT AWOL

The conviction that desertion reflected men's irresponsible use of their wages solidified over time. In the early years of the twentieth century, many prominent commentators on desertion tended to assume an equivalence between male wage earning and breadwinning; therefore, they believed that unemployment was the main cause of nonsupport. In 1905 Charles Zunser, then an agent for the Committee for the Protection of Deserted Women and Children and later chief counsel of the NDB, cited only two causes for desertion: "defects of the woman" and "the far more important reason . . . bad industrial conditions. Lack of work . . . has driven more men away from their families than any other single factor."[16] As Morris Waldman, the director of the United Hebrew Charities (UHC), recalled, "To take legal measures against such men was considered harsh."[17]

The discovery of desertion, however, stimulated research into its "causes," resulting in a different interpretation.[18] As the social worker Mary Conyngton observed in 1909, "Vivid pictures of the man driven by stress of poverty to abandon his family, finding himself unable to support them" were deemed inaccurate; "the deserter of this kind, if he exists at all, is in a small minority, and . . . ordinarily the man who abandons wife and children is influenced by frankly selfish motives."[19] Charles Zunser changed his earlier opinion about the connection between desertion and unemployment, and by 1931 he was convinced that economic hard times kept men at home, instead. Men were less likely, he argued, to take up with other women when unemployed, and he predicted that the Depression would cause some deserters to return to their families: "In hard times 'other women' are expensive. It feels good to come back to the real wife who has a home and often credit from local tradesmen to tide over a bad economic spell. . . . In hard times, the old wife will have to do."[20]

As the normative meaning of manhood changed in emphasis from producer to provider in the context of an emerging consumer capitalism, charity workers detected a new form of "welfare cheat." The old specter of the able-bodied yet idle man, who refused to join the ranks of sturdy producers, was joined by the specter of the employed man who chose to spend his wages on himself rather than on his family. The welfare fraud that antidesertion reformers claimed they had discovered was perpetrated by the man who could provide but refused to do so, thereby leaving his wife and children burdens on the public purse.

The shift in explanation away from unemployment signaled the recognition by antidesertion reformers that male wage earning and breadwinning were not equivalent: men's personal consumption could disrupt the connection between the two. The search for alternative explanations for men's failure to provide resulted in lists of what could be characterized as "gender disorders." They amounted to a lack of "manliness" in husbands and fathers and inadequate "womanliness" in mothers and wives. In reformers' minds, the two disorders were related: a man with an insufficiently feminine wife was likely to desert; a woman whose cowardly husband left her might lose her womanly virtues. Manliness was defined as responsible providerhood; womanliness as efficient housekeeping and physical attractiveness.

Antidesertion reformers believed that men who abandoned their wives and children lacked the "manliness" necessary to lead a proper family life. Jonah Goldstein, a domestic relations court judge, believed that "the man who deserts his family is hardly worthy of the name 'man.'" A deserting father did not have the "instinct" of manhood, Max Herzberg of the UHC asserted, and was the opposite of a real man—a "coward." C. C. Carstens agreed that deserters were "peculiarly cowardly"; Walter Liebman exclaimed that they were driven by "a strange mixture of folly and cowardice!"[21]

The cowardice of deserting fathers was linked to the cowardice of a soldier who deserted in wartime. The persistent use of the term "desertion" to cover nonsupport underscored the connection between obligation to one's country and the law of support. Relying on the military resonance of the term, Judge Goldstein declared that "desertion is AWOL." One reformer speculated that men who married during World War I in order to evade military service (that is, men who entered into "slacker marriages") were likely to desert their families.[22] In fact, the military branches were concerned with both types of desertion; they assisted the NDB in tracking down nonsupporting, "deserting" servicemen. Like the nurturing tasks of motherhood, which were viewed not only as a private duty but also as a service to the state, a man's obligation to support his family was part of his duty to his country.

The theme of male "self-indulgence" appears frequently in the antidesertion literature. The term indicated not that men failed to work but rather that they spent their wages on their own pleasures. The family deserter, remarked the social investigator Lilian Brandt, is an "irresponsible, ease-loving man" who feels "justified in making arrangements for his own comfort which do not include his wife and children."[23] Morris Waldman declared that "self-indulgence" in the husband was the main factor contributing to desertion, while A. S. Newman, the superintendent of a Jewish aid organization, characterized the cause of desertion as male "selfishness, licentiousness, self-indulgence and a lack of a sense of duty."[24] Such "weak-willed" men were likely to withdraw their support from their families, "usually for the purpose of having a good time on Saturday night," to "spend money in saloons," and generally to seek their own "enjoyment."[25]

"Cowardly husbands" and "shiftless fathers" who allegedly defrauded the charities evoked different anxieties than did the able-bodied unemployed of the nineteenth century. Deserters were assumed to have incomes, and the movement to prosecute them reflected anxieties about working-class men's access to cash wages. Antidesertion reformers defined a man's use of his wage as a social, rather than a personal, matter, one that involved simultaneous obligations to his family and to society. A "shiftless father" treated his wage as his individual property, to be spent on his own pleasures—drink, gambling, "other women"—thereby reneging on his civic duty to support his family.

Antidesertion reformers were attempting to make working-class male consumption responsible. Their efforts paralleled those of settlement house workers and other social reformers to encourage men to participate

**"He is dressed like a dude
and looks so pretty"**

The 26 August 1911 issue of Collier's *depicted the deserter as self-indulgent and unmanly in an article on the domestic relations court.*

in family-oriented leisure pursuits rather than in all-male activities. Shared social time was thought to bind a man closer to his family, making desertion less likely. Joanna Colcord, for example, worried that "the American tendency for the man to get his recreation apart from his family, in saloons and social clubs," contributed to desertion, particularly when such all-male socializing gave husbands an opportunity to compare their own situation with that of their unmarried companions.[26]

Immigrant men came in for particular criticism. Antidesertion reformers theorized that the transition from the repressive old country to the land of liberty and abundance had unleashed male irresponsibility. Morris Waldman decried the way immigrant men mistook "liberty for license."[27] Another reformer complained, "They take the American freedom and liberty in a different light from which it has been given."[28] The lawyer and social worker Bernhard Rabbino described the immigrant deserter's presumed state of mind: "This was America, the Land of Freedom. No more oppressive religious obligations. No more chafing 'Dont's.' Life must be lived to the fullest, material enjoyment must reign supreme. . . . The self-denials of the past were to be amply balanced by the self-indulgences of the present."[29]

Although historians now recognize that women played a key role in the way immigrant families took up American habits of consumption, antidesertion reformers assumed that immigrant men led in adopting new lifestyles.[30] The reformers believed that men's more rapid acculturation in turn contributed to their dissatisfaction with marriage. According to Earle Eubank, "Americanization" for immigrant men meant "a taste for brighter lights, fancier clothing, more stirring amusements and less confined life." *Collier's*, a popular magazine, illustrated the story of a deserted Jewish woman with a cartoon of her nattily dressed husband, equipped with gloves, hat, and cane. "He is dressed like a dude and looks so pretty," read the caption.[31] In contrast, immigrant wives were portrayed as dowdy. Eubank linked immigrant men's material desires to their presumed preference for native-born women. "Plain, hard-working Francisca or Gretchen," he observed, "cannot compare in style with their modernized counterparts in the cities of America."[32] Morris Waldman agreed that "the new environment affects the immigrant husband and wife differently; the former is more open to its influence."[33]

Social reformers offered contradictory interpretations of male consumption. Generally, they interpreted it as self-indulgence. However, they sometimes saw it as signaling a worthy desire for acculturation and a better, more American standard of living.[34] Waldman thought that an immigrant man's Americanization partly lay in the achievement of new and better standards of consumption: "The husband is employed in some shop or factory in the vicinity of Broadway, and so is brought in contact with cleanliness and respectability. In most cases it is cheaper for the man to have his noonday meal in a neighboring restaurant . . . infinitely better cooked and better served than at home. The man becomes accustomed to his separate plates and his cloth napkin—unheard of luxuries at home. The aesthetic sense is aroused. . . . The husband's standard of living has risen above that of his wife."[35]

In other contexts, an aesthetic appreciation of table settings and tasty food might be seen as a sign of refinement. Waldman fondly remembered Solomon Lowenstein, the superintendent of the Hebrew Orphan Asylum, as having a "love for beautiful possessions—he was always to be found with the latest luxury gadget, be it a traveling kit, a cigar lighter or a bathrobe" and a "Sybarite's instinct for gracious living ranging from the gourmet's appetite for Marseillesian bouille-baisse to a dessert of exotic tropical fruits." Lowenstein's "feminine" tastes earned him the moniker "gentleman" from his fellow social workers, including Waldman, who also lauded Lowenstein for his "self-abnegation," "subordination of bodily comfort and security to the needs of the community," and "dedication to duty." Underscoring Lowenstein's "virility" in serving the community, Waldman characterized social work as fraught with danger, as a "hazardous occupation."[36] Lowenstein's luxury consumption was the well-deserved reward for a manly provider who not only headed his own household but was also a brave leader in the Jewish community. Waldman and his colleagues condemned, however, working-class men's purportedly fancy tastes as the self-indulgence of cowards. The working-class man would have to provide for his family before he could indulge in personal consumer pleasures—while the professionals who enforced this principle were able to do both.

RESPECTABILITY AND REBELLION

It is tempting to read antidesertion rhetoric as mere middle-class prejudice against working-class men. Reformers perhaps misinterpreted as selfishness the departure of men frustrated with low wages and periodic unemployment and ashamed that they could not live up to deeply felt breadwinning obligations. Recently, historians have offered evidence that working-class men did indeed define successful manhood as supporting their families. Alice Kessler-Harris argues that over the course of the nineteenth century the locus of working-class men's gender identity had shifted slowly away from production and toward providerhood.[37] The loss of control over the work process, accelerated by techniques of scientific management and the degradation of skill levels, undermined the old touchstone of working-class manhood—the pride of the skilled producer. Workers were developing an "instrumental attitude" toward their jobs, one that looked to the wage and what it could buy in the market for satisfaction and identity, rather than to the workplace.[38]

The link between income and manhood, moreover, was crucial to the twentieth-century campaign for the family wage. Whereas in the nineteenth century the family wage had been viewed as a just reward for and ratification of a man's craft competence, in the twentieth century it became the reason to work and an end in itself. In the process, the family wage shifted from being a demand based on notions of class justice to being a demand based on gender privilege, with middle-class reformers and labor unions using it to undermine women's position in the labor market and to shore up men's position at home.[39] The tendency to emphasize breadwinning as the key to successful manhood was thus increasingly embraced by both "respectable" working-class men and middle-class men.

Some leaders of organized labor who demanded a family wage for male workers also lent their support to the antidesertion campaign. James O'Connell, president of the International Association of Machinists, insisted that organized labor and social workers shared common ground on the issue of desertion: "It is not generally understood that organized labor aims at any reform or any high standards of family ethics. This is indeed a great mistake." As evidence, he pointed out that he had, "in hundreds of cases, been able to run down wife-deserters and men who neglected their families and . . . compel them to return to their wives and their children or in case of their refusal, to strike their names from the rolls of membership of the Association."[40] Labor unions often assisted the NDB in locating nonsupporting men.

Immigrants as well as native-born workingmen strove to attain the status of sole breadwinners for their families. Many immigrants who intended to settle permanently in the United States attempted to meet the gender expectations of their new surroundings. Once they decided to stay, as the historian Ron Rothbart shows, male Poles, Lithuanians, Slovaks, and Hungarians adopted the identity of breadwinners; they demanded a family wage so that they and their dependents could "live like Americans."[41] Susan Glenn argues that Jewish immigrant men also embraced the breadwinning ideal. It had already been gaining in ideological significance in eastern Europe, but conditions there made it impractical for the vast majority. Even in the United States, most working-class Jewish men could not actually support a family alone, but they reallocated the family labor to match available opportunities and reconceptualized the meaning of work. Jewish immigrants replaced the eastern European "breadwinning partnership" with an arrangement in which men and their older children went to work, while wives stayed at home. Wives continued to take in boarders, engage in petty commerce in their neighborhoods, and "help" their husbands in small businesses. But the new arrangement rendered wives' income-earning activities invisible and highlighted their role as "dependent" consumers.[42]

Some clients of the NDB did proclaim their allegiance to the breadwinner ethic and felt ashamed that they could not live up to their own notion of respectable manhood. The unemployed Mr. Minsky, for example, told his wife that he was "no man" and then "went away to seek his fortune." Rachel Minsky welcomed her husband when he returned home and sought the United Hebrew Charities' help in finding a job.[43] Even men who left their wives for "other women" did not necessarily abandon the breadwinner ethic. Daniel Gordon, for example, admitted that he was a bigamist: "It is true that I now find myself in [the] deplorable plight of having two wives and two children by each of them, and that I am living with my second wife and the youngest of the children." Torn by his obligations to the two families, Gordon found himself "between the devil and the deep blue sea." He pleaded: "[My first wife] ought to realize that I cannot come back to her because if I did, I would be derelict in my duty to my second wife and children who are even more helpless than she is. . . . I earn very little and . . . my average weekly earnings do not exceed $30. I'll leave it to any person to decide, how a laborer of my earning ability can support two families."[44] Gordon had gotten himself into a pickle, but he maintained a sense of duty and protectiveness toward his current family consistent with the breadwinning ethic. He contradicted reformers' characterizations of self-indulgent men by shouldering the responsibility for providing for his second family.

However, the NDB files also document a strain of resistance to the breadwinning ideal. Deserted women—perhaps playing to their audience of social workers, lawyers, and judges—supplied information that underscored men's refusal to provide in terms that confirmed reformers' suspicions. Numerous women claimed that even before leaving, husbands controlled their own paycheck and spent it as they liked. Wives described their nonsupporting husbands as "high livers," "sports," "big spenders," and gamblers, who frequented "teahouses and speakeasies," poolrooms, cabarets, and coffeehouses.[45] "He is not much of a man," declared one wife of a gambler.[46] One woman reported that her husband stayed away when he had money and returned without it; another complained that her husband "drinks and gambles—and after getting his wages [he] absents himself for days."[47] Men picked up their wages, drew money out of savings accounts, and sold valuables just before leaving their families.[48]

In contrast to Daniel Gordon, some deserters who left their wives for other women were rebelling against breadwinning itself. One deserter reportedly told his wife that he would "go to a lady friend of his who has a farm, where he could be supported"; yet another told his wife that "he wished he could find a woman, young or old, with a good deal of money, who would become attracted to him and give him her money." Deserted wives reported that their husbands left "looking for a woman with money" or that "other women" "kept" their husbands.[49]

Men's rebellion against supporting their families could be open and defiant.[50] Some husbands taunted their wives with reports of their high earnings and displayed their purchases gleefully. Mr. Siegal indicted himself in the eyes of the NDB and of the wife he deserted in a letter that he wrote to her: "I have a good home and a [new] wife. . . . I am kissing her while I am writing this letter, and I am very glad that I am far away from you. When I married this wife I got $500. She comes from a rich family. She is buying and I am buying a lot. . . . I am dressed in diamonds and jewelry." Another deserter, incarcerated for nonsupport, wrote unrepentantly to his wife, "As long as you live I will not give you the pleasure or the honor [of selling] my car," which she wanted to dispose of to raise money for household expenses.[51] A Mr. Katz responded sharply to a support order by telling the judge, "[Just] try and make me do it."[52]

Even as the breadwinner ethic spread and solidified, it apparently generated resistance. Indeed, the same consumer culture that legitimated workingmen's demands for a family wage also provided a site for resistance to the prescriptions of middle-class reformers. The men whom wives called "high livers" might have participated in the bachelor culture flourishing in urban centers in the early decades of the century. Historian George Chauncey observes that men of this subculture "forged an alternative definition of manliness that was predicated on a rejection of family obligations" and that was "hostile to the constraints of marriage." Such men congregated in the very pool rooms and gambling dens mentioned by deserted wives.[53]

These men were what working-class people called "rough," in contrast to the "respectable" man who dedicated himself to supporting his wife and children and "struggl[ed] manfully to keep his family together." Historian Sherri Broder observes that in Philadelphia neighborhoods, including the Jewish neighborhoods, working-class people defined themselves as respectable in part by repudiating the rough and by uniting in defense of their own standards of proper behavior, which included a commitment to the breadwinner ethic.[54] The readers of the *Forward* who responded to "The Gallery of Missing Men" with helpful tips for the Desertion Bureau, the men and women who informed NDB agents about the behavior and whereabouts of deserters, and the neighbors who testified against deserters in court all participated in defending their own sense of proper manly behavior. Antidesertion reformers, in fact, relied on the overlap between working-class and middle-class conceptions of manhood to carry out their work.

Although men from diverse ethnic communities populated the bachelor culture and the ranks of the rough, there may have been a distinctive element in Jewish deserters' resistance to breadwinning. Jewish immigrants from eastern Europe had access to alternative, competing ideals of manhood. Although the oft-cited example of the scholar supported by his wife was not common in practice, it existed as an ideal that legitimated wives' participation in supporting families. This ideal, along with the more typical breadwinning partnership, competed with the "enlightened" model of male breadwinning and female dependence endorsed by western as well as eastern European maskilim. Some deserters appear to have been torn between allegiance to the breadwinner ethic and a sense that there was nothing wrong with a wife supporting the family. Mr. Spector, for example, acknowledged that "I know it is my Duty to support" but then went on to contend that his wife was working, so why should he be expected to support her and the children?[55] Other, less conflicted men simply demanded that their wives support them and deserted when the women could not or would not do so.[56]

The breadwinner ethic that such men rejected was part of a modern form of male dominance that replaced older, patriarchal systems.[57] In theory, modern marriage offered husbands economic power over dependents and the comforts of domesticity in exchange for breadwinning. Apparently, not all men found the modern marriage bargain attractive. (As one man sought by the Desertion Bureau pointed out, he could get a "woman from the streets" for much less than it cost to support his wife and children.)[58] In contrast to middle-class men, working-class husbands may have found that their wages did not provide much leverage over their wives.

Curiously, the very middle-class reformers who targeted desertion seemed to agree that marriage was an unattractive proposition for men, especially working-class, immigrant men. Social workers' unflattering portraits of deserted women stood in marked contrast to the vivid descriptions of the pleasures that enticed men away. Unlike the thirty-seven incarcerated men who blamed their desertion on the "mad whims" of their wives, antidesertion reformers were relatively unconcerned about female extravagance. Instead, they worried about the wives whose housekeeping and personal style lagged behind the "American standard."

Keeping house according to middle-class American standards, attending to one's appearance, being sexually available, and assuming a posture of dependence were all necessary if a woman wanted her husband and his paycheck to stay home. Deserted wives were suspected of having "a disinclination to marital intercourse" or of suffering from "sexual anaesthesia."[59] Michael Francis Doyle of the Society of St. Vincent de Paul attributed desertion to the failure of married women to preserve their looks: "The wife loses her attractiveness after a few years of marriage and trouble, she becomes untidy and lacks neatness," so the husband departs.[60]

Housekeeping, like sex, was viewed by antidesertion reformers as part of the marriage bargain. They cited domestic "inefficiency" and a woman's inability to create an attractive and peaceful refuge at home as disincentives for male breadwinning. In Progressive Era budget studies, domestic "efficiency" was defined as the ability to attain an "American standard of living." A family's standard of living was measured not only by the family's income but also by the way in which a wife allocated it.[61]

Solomon Lowenstein suspected that deserted women lacked adequate training in the "domestic sciences," resulting in "the unattractiveness of the average tenement home" and "the unpalatable, ill-cooked food" served in it. C. C. Carstens attributed "half-excusable" desertions to "a dirty home, neglected children, and meals that furnish no nourishment." Perhaps speaking from the conviction that the way to a man's heart is through his stomach, Charles Zunser suggested that to decrease the incidence of desertion, "married women should be induced to attend cooking schools. Where this is not possible it would be well to send voluntary workers to the homes to instruct the women in the culinary art." Probation officer John J. Gascoyne agreed: "Lessons in cooking I find are most valuable and then, too, the matter of having the home clean and the children neatly attired, when the husband is about to return from a hard day's labor is important."[62] Antidesertion reformers recommended that deserted women be taught how to make the home more attractive to their husbands than cafés and other women.

Immigrant women received more than their share of criticism for failing to Americanize their domestic habits and personal appearance. The social worker Kate Claghorn pictured the foreign-born woman as "a plain, hard-working, slow-thinking domestic drudge," far less attractive than the "more sophisticated, better-dressed" American woman.[63] The president of the NDB, Walter Liebman, recounted the story of a man who had tried, unsuccessfully, to "Americanize" his wife: "She could not depart from the slovenliness of her home and her person. Result—desertion."[64] Zunser recommended that eastern European Jewish women immigrants attend "a series of lectures in Yiddish on how to make a home attractive and how to manage the baby," the assumption being that these tasks needed to be relearned in America.[65]

A lack of deference on the part of a wife, antidesertion reformers feared, might also sap a man's will to provide. Joanna Colcord, the superintendent of the New York Charity Organization Society (COS), warned that women should guard against "a tendency to dominate or try to control."[66] Morris Waldman found it "alarming" that some deserted women were older than their husbands and thus were not subordinate in the family age hierarchy.[67] "The theory is," explained Lilian Brandt of the COS, "that if the wife is decidedly older she assumes the leadership, to a certain degree, with the result that the husband's sense of responsibility remains embryonic."[68]

Even though many involved in the antidesertion movement were aware that women made crucial contributions to the household income, they nevertheless worried that wage earning among wives might contribute to male negligence. Wifely dependence was viewed as a stimulus to male breadwinning and hence, ironically, as protection against destitution through desertion. Joanna Colcord believed that an "overefficient" woman risked desertion by impinging on male territory: "Many a non-supporter got his first impulse in that direction when his wife became a wage-earner in some domestic crisis." She advised that a woman should adopt an attitude of feminine helplessness when her husband lost his job—she should sit down and cry until he finds a new one. Probation officer John J. Gascoyne advised that "if the probation officer learns that the wife goes out to work by the day, his first effort should be to gradually put a stop to the same."[69] "If a woman becomes a wage-earner," Earle Eubank explained in his 1916 study of desertion, "the husband's feeling of responsibility for providing for her may be lessened. . . . The woman, in turn, from the fact of being economically independent, may be led to assert her independence in ways which will in themselves be provocative."[70]

Reformers' statements revealed what would be a lasting tension between viewing deserted women as victims and stigmatizing them as guilty parties. The *American Hebrew*, citing the findings of a New York Bureau of Public Welfare statistician, made clear the implication that deserted wives were not good wives: "The wife who is sympathetic, considerate, affectionate, home-loving and cheerful is rarely, if ever, deserted."[71] A widow was not responsible for her plight, but it was not easy for charity workers to admit that a deserted woman was abandoned through no fault of her own.

An odd assumption underlay social policies regarding desertion: men would leave their families if they could. Reformers believed that many men, if they thought charities or the state would provide for deserted women and children, would view it as an opportunity to gain their "freedom." The same people who extolled marriage and the family offered little sense of why men would want to stay, beyond a feeling of duty. Recall the comparisons made between tasty restaurant food and unpalatable home-cooked meals, between dating stylish sophisticates and living with a domestic drudge, between an uninviting home and the camaraderie of cafés and saloons. Tinged with distaste for abandoned wives and perhaps even envy for the carefree life they imagined deserters enjoying, reformers' outraged denunciations of self-indulgent men betrayed their own ambivalence about the very marriage bargain they were promoting. Such attitudes would legitimize personal spending on leisure consumption for middle-class men by the 1930s and develop into a powerful rebuke to conventional domesticity after World War II.[72] On some level antidesertion reformers seemed to agree with the sentiment expressed by the thirty-seven resentful prisoners: marriage was no bargain for men.

The assumption that marriage was burdensome for men, and therefore that opportunities to escape would be seized eagerly, rested on a devaluation of wives' contributions to families, often in the form of unpaid labor. The devaluation of deserted women's unpaid household labor was also implicit in their exclusion from the mothers' pension program. Pensions were granted to widows on the principle that motherhood is a service to the state, one that benefits society, the nation, and the "race," and hence deserves compensation. Although desertion was often said to have dire consequences for the state—damaging future citizens by purportedly contributing to juvenile delinquency—deserted women's maternal contribution to society continued to be treated as a private duty not eligible for public compensation.

The thirty-seven outraged letter-writers also disregarded the value of their spouses' labor, characterizing their wives only as frivolous spenders, not as household workers and managers. They appealed to *Forward* readers for gender and class solidarity. Their complaints might have resonated with respectable working-class Jewish men, who increasingly adopted the view that they, and not their wives, were family providers. Although men portrayed themselves as overburdened breadwinners and their wives as dependents, desertion itself made visible the continuing importance of Jewish women as bread givers.

Bread Givers: From Desertion to the National Desertion Bureau

Information is wanted of CHAIM LERMAN, *30 years of age, 6ft. tall, slim, blonde hair, grey eyes, bony, arrived in this country in 1920 from Alaska, chauffeur by occupation, also moving expressman, who left his wife, Rebecca, who has a crippled foot, and their infant . . . from their home in this city on March 5th, 1928, since which time he has neither communicated with the family nor contributed a single penny towards their support, as a result of which the family is destitute. Woman is unable to work and help herself, and family's plight is terrible. Kindly communicate with Charles Zunser, 67 W. 47th St., N.Y.C.*

—Submitted to the Sunday World, *26 February 1929*

In a notice to the *Sunday World*, the National Desertion Bureau (NDB) represented Rebecca Lerman's case as one of destitution "as a result of" her husband's desertion.[1] The notice resembles other advertisements that told of families becoming "a burden upon the community" or "completely dependent on the charities" as a consequence of desertion. The advertisements picture women and children as helpless dependents, whose economic plight stemmed from abandonment by the male breadwinner. But there are silences in such notices and, in Rebecca Lerman's case, misinformation.

Rebecca Lerman was a "bread giver."[2] Her tall, blond-haired, gray-eyed husband had "never supported adequately"; throughout her marriage she had depended on her own income to get by. Even as the NDB was representing her as "unable to work," Rebecca was earning wages. She wrote many distraught letters to the bureau complaining of the difficulty of managing on her meager pay. Previous records of her contact with charitable institutions suggest that her poverty predated her husband's desertion and was not simply a "result" of it. Nor was her application to the NDB a direct result of her husband's departure: she did not apply until six months after he left. At her opening interview with the bureau, Mrs. Lerman stated that her work was irregular but did not mention her occupation. Throughout her contact with the NDB, no one ever asked what she did for a living, although details of her husband's occupation were specifically solicited.[3] A few months after the notice was inserted in the *Sunday World*, Rebecca Lerman ceased contact with the bureau. Her case resumed only when she reapproached the NDB in 1935 in order to meet the requirement of the Emergency Home Relief Bureau (EHRB) that she search for her husband as a condition of receiving assistance. There is no record of any contact with charitable agencies in the intervening six years, suggesting that Mrs. Lerman had managed during that period on her (steadier) work.[4]

The stories that antidesertion reformers told focused on male breadwinning: the lack of a male breadwinner was said to cause the poverty of deserted families, and the retrieval of a male breadwinner was the recommended solution. In their concern with men as family providers, antidesertion reformers represented women and children as dependents. They tended to suppress what they knew from day-to-day contact with deserted wives and children: women were family providers, too. Deserted women's experiences as "bread givers," rather than simply the loss of a male "breadwinner," also shaped their involvement in the antidesertion system.

In the United States, as in eastern Europe, working-class Jewish families relied on multiple earners: wives and children as well as husbands. Periodic unemployment and low wages undermined men's ability to provide for their families on their own. Deserted women tended to be sympathetic toward their unemployed husbands. Rosa Feder, for example, responded with understanding when her husband left to find work. She asked the NDB to place a personal notice in the *Forward* asking her husband to come home and mentioning that the children were crying. When he returned, she "was overjoyed and fully forgave him" for disappearing.[5] As Sherri Broder observes, working-class women typically believed that it was enough for a man to try to provide, whether or not he was entirely successful.[6]

While they understood that men could not be the sole breadwinners for their families, Jewish wives expected that husbands would respect their control of the household economy. In eastern Europe and in their new home, Jewish wives played the role of "baleboste," managing the income and expenditures of the household. The complaints of deserted wives centered on male consumption that undermined the baleboste's control over domestic spending. Wives felt that their husbands' earnings, aside from a small amount of pocket money, should be put toward the household, even if it was not enough to support the family. This was more than simply a matter of dollars and cents; it was a matter of respect for the wife. Often deserted wives paired their complaints about their husbands' financial behavior with other examples of disrespect, ranging from verbal insults to physical abuse. One woman objected to her husband's attempt "to be the boss" at home, where she clearly felt he should not rule.[7] Jewish wives evaluated their husbands less on their success in achieving the status of sole breadwinner than on their attitude toward wife and family.

Deserted wives' expectations for support from their husbands were shaped by the availability of other sources of income. They almost never claimed a right to be supported entirely by their husbands. Usually, they framed their claims in terms of need. "If I would be healthy enough I would not care so much about hims coming home," declared an ailing laundress in a typical statement, "but I aint able to support myself and the children."[8] Most deserted women entered the written record when they applied for welfare assistance, so the emphasis on need is unsurprising. However, the NDB's chief counsel, Charles Zunser, spoke in terms of both needs and rights. While he aimed to prevent deserted families from becoming public charges, he also saw his job as upholding "the woman's right to man's support."[9] Zunser's words were rarely echoed by his clients. Deserted women's actions, as well as their words, indicate skepticism about the likelihood that they could depend on male breadwinning.

This chapter explores why women came into the antidesertion system. Evidence from my sample of 300 case files of the NDB from 1911 through the 1930s suggests that deserted women used the bureau for a variety of reasons. Loss of a job, low wages, irregular work, illness, or the demands of young children or invalid parents brought women into the antidesertion system as much as did desertion itself. Many deserted women sought their husbands' financial support as a sort of "unemployment insurance," "disability pay," or "family leave." It is customary to think of married women's paid employment in this era as a supplement to male breadwinning or as a stopgap measure for times when men were unable to earn adequate wages. For many deserted women, however, the order was reversed: they turned to male support as a backup for a labor market that offered few opportunities for independence to women, much less for women with children.

Deserted women resorted to the antidesertion system when they faced a crisis in their family economy. Clients of the NDB normally were referred by another social agency and entered the legal system only after they had sought financial relief from one or more charitable institutions. The case files portray a complex and repetitive process in which a typical client might begin her involvement with the antidesertion system when she sought some form of public or private economic assistance; she might be sent to the NDB (which did not provide direct financial relief) and then go to court after the bureau located her husband. If, as was usual, the husband failed to pay on the court order, the deserted woman might approach a charity for relief when she reached another financial crisis, and the cycle would begin again.

The factors that brought deserted women into the antidesertion system were more complex than most reform rhetoric suggested. Certainly, desertion was a factor in most cases, but it was not necessarily the only or the most immediate reason why women sought financial and legal assistance. In many cases, deserted women did not become clients of the antidesertion system until long after the desertion had occurred, some waiting years to register a complaint. Other women sought assistance when they themselves wished to leave their husbands or had already left home, fleeing domestic violence. A range of circumstances other than desertion alone precipitated clients' applications to the NDB.

CONTINGENCIES

Most of the NDB's clients did not apply for assistance immediately after their husbands left. The length of time between a man's desertion and his wife's application to the NDB can be determined with some accuracy in more than two-thirds of the cases I studied.[10] Only 7.8 percent of the applicants sought assistance from the bureau a week or less after their husbands had deserted, and only 19 percent within a month. Just over 60 percent waited three months or more before approaching the NDB, and 40.7 percent took six months or more. Almost one-third (29.9 percent) sought assistance more than a year after their husbands had left. Clearly, more than desertion brought these women to the NDB. Often they applied only after the husband's departure had been compounded by a second blow to the family economy.

When clients of the NDB lost their husbands, they lost a wage earner, but often not the sole or even primary breadwinner. In 1911, the year of the NDB's founding, the U.S. Immigration Commission published a survey of Russian Jewish families that found that only about 20 percent of the husbands and fathers in New York City earned enough to be the sole supporters of their families.[11] The histories of clients' household economies prior to desertion are difficult to reconstruct from the case files because such information was not collected systematically. However, anecdotal evidence from scores of NDB case files suggests that even prior to desertion many women could not depend on their husbands alone to support the family. Women frequently reported to the bureau that their husbands had "never supported adequately," in some cases because the men earned too little and in others because they did not contribute what they earned to the household.[12] As in many Jewish families, the household income had been gathered through the efforts of multiple breadwinners, including children—especially daughters—and mothers.[13]

A man's desertion often did not plunge his family immediately into destitution. In families with children over the age of fourteen, with mothers who earned, or with financially able and willing kin, the husband's departure was less disastrous than in families where mothers were occupied with caring for small children. Even then, if child care were available, in the form of either a day nursery or a family member, a mother of small children might be able to ease the loss of her husband's contribution by reentering the labor market, armed with the experience she would have likely gained in her working life before marriage. However, many women, faced with low wages, underemployment, and the double burden of household support and domestic labor, eventually found it necessary to turn to the charities for help.

In many cases, the second blow to the family economy was to the woman's own status as a wage earner and breadwinner. Like other Jewish wives, many applicants to the NDB had a history of income-producing work that continued into marriage. Historians of Jewish immigrant women have established that although wives generally withdrew from their girlhood employments when they married, they did not cease earning. The economic activities of Jewish wives and mothers were notoriously underreported in the census and other surveys, leading to the erroneous impression that married women were family dependents. The statistics—that only 8 percent worked for wages and only 3 percent did homework—severely underestimate their income-earning role.

Women's most common source of income was taking in boarders: in 1911, fully 56 percent of Russian Jewish households in New York had boarders. Between a quarter to a third of Russian Jewish men were in business for themselves, and their numbers were increasing.[14] Wives of such men often worked in the business, too, whether in a small shop or peddling on the street. Pawning household possessions, occasionally vending homemade products, and trading services and goods within neighborhood and kin networks of exchange all added to married women's contributions to the household budget.

A number of deserted women based their sense of entitlement to support on their own contributions to the family income during their marriages. Eva Kaye, who resented her husband for not contributing enough of his wages when he lived at home, argued that he should be made to support her in part because "all during her married life she has worked, taking in washing and things like that . . . even during her pregnant period she had been working."[15] Yetta Taber felt that her husband owed her some support because "she always worked with her husband and enabled him to make a success of his business—but he never gave her a salary."[16] Similarly, Dorothy Beale, who had worked in her husband's garment shop during her marriage until her eyesight deteriorated, complained that she had worked for him all those years "without any salary" and clearly felt that she had earned her keep.[17]

Wives increased their income-producing activities when they were deserted. Censuses of women wage earners throughout the first three decades of the twentieth century revealed that those who lost their husbands had a labor-force participation rate about three times that of married women with husbands.[18] But these women worked in a segmented labor market; women's work was underpaid and insecure, and there was no accommodation for working mothers' double burden of wage work and child care. If women entered the labor market or increased their participation in it after being deserted, frequently the conditions they encountered there brought them to the charities and the NDB.

Many breadwinning mothers applied to the antidesertion system when they lost their jobs. Ella Sirkle, for example, applied to the NDB a full fifteen years after her husband's desertion. She had separated from her husband in 1922 because he was not coming home two or three days a week. With the help of an attorney, they drew up a separation agreement whereby Mr. Sirkle, a radio repairman and electrical company employee, agreed to give his wife $5 a week toward the support of their three small children and newborn baby. He made support payments for three weeks and then disappeared. In 1937 the bureau was finally asked to intervene. The correspondence in Mrs. Sirkle's case file recounts her explanation for the delay: "She claims that she never made very serious efforts to locate him because she felt that she would always be able to support herself and the children and she enjoyed being independent. It was only after Mrs. Sirkle was unable to obtain further employment that she made any effort at all to locate Mr. Sirkle."[19]

During her husband's absence, Ella Sirkle was employed as a photographer's assistant and a clerical worker. Few applicants to the NDB had such white collar jobs, however, and although other deserted wives shared her desire to remain independent and free of their husbands, few could manage for long. Close to 90 percent of the women whose occupations are mentioned in the case files held blue collar jobs. About two-thirds did either garment work (at home or in a factory) or domestic labor, the two most common occupations.[20] Domestic labor included such chores as taking in laundry, scrubbing floors, washing windows, general housework, and preparing meals, including for boarders. In the 1920s and 1930s, opportunities for this type of work were declining. The demand for laundresses dropped, and boarders became fewer as immigration was reduced and living quarters for single people became more readily available.[21] Domestic laborers rarely had steady or full-time work, and garment workers faced seasonal slowdowns and layoffs.

Women's applications to the NDB often followed the patterns of their employment. When they were laid off, got sick, or experienced a drop in their wages, they sought support from their husbands. When they could manage on their own earnings, they withdrew from contact with the bureau or called off the search. Ida Ravich, for example, was deserted by her husband in 1932 but did not begin searching for him until she lost her job five years later. Two months later she was working again; so she wrote to request that her case be closed.[22] Penny Miner was deserted by her husband in 1926 while she was pregnant. She continued to work until the child was born and then started nonsupport proceedings against her husband. Following a few years of periodic work and unemployment during which her NDB case continued fitfully, Penny ceased her efforts to secure support from her husband. From 1933 to 1938, her NDB case file lay dormant. When she reopened her case at the bureau in 1938, Penny explained that she had not taken legal action for the past five years because "she was working and earning enough to take care of her own needs and those of her child."[23]

Work-disrupting illness led some women to seek spousal support. After an eight-year hiatus in her contact with the NDB, which had been initiated during her third pregnancy, Rosa Brown reapplied for help in securing support from her husband. She had recently been hospitalized and explained that "she did not seek him all these years because she was working—now she contends that she is ill and must have his support."[24] During ten years of inactivity in her NDB case, Beryl Felton worked as a dress operator, supporting herself and her child. After an unsuccessful operation from which she did not fully recover, Beryl found "her earning power . . . impaired" and hence renewed her effort to secure support from her husband.[25]

Deserted women struggled not only with periodic unemployment but also with the difficulty of living on a "woman's wage" when employed. Their predicament stemmed from a labor market that operated on the assumption that female workers did not have dependents to support and that husbands subsidized married women's earnings.[26] Deserted women with children sought spousal support to provide the missing supplement. The case files are peppered with comments suggesting that women applied to the NDB because they simply could not manage on what they earned. Janitress Mandy Abel found herself "absolutely unable to get along on her present income."[27] Trudy Wasserman wrote to the NDB about her missing husband: "I hope you will be successful in locating him at an early date as my salary is not sufficient to support my six year old son and myself."[28] Rebecca Lerman went into greater detail: "I have a $18.00 gas bill & rent of $10 both on me at the same time to pay *all* out of my $14.00. Besides my weekly necessities of groceries & oils & powders for baby; and now she needs clothes. It seems as though I would go insane the way the expense to live keeps looming ahead. . . . I can't even make ends meet or catch up with the load of everything on me & all on a thin pay envelope of $14.00 a week & get less than that when baby is ailing & I am forced to stay out to care for her."[29]

Rebecca Lerman's letter highlights yet another impediment deserted women faced when they tried to manage on their own earnings: the "double burden" of wage work and child care. The demands of young or ill children influenced women's wage-earning opportunities as well as their need for assistance or spousal support. The pattern of activity in Gerda Rieman's case was tied to her circumstances as a working mother. Although her NDB case spanned the years 1916 to 1931, it was active for less than four years: from December 1916 to October 1917, briefly in August 1927, and from December 1928 to August 1931. When her husband deserted, Gerda had two toddlers to care for and needed financial assistance. As soon as the children were old enough to be admitted to a day nursery, she went to work and moved into a low-cost home for working mothers with children. When her sons were too old to continue living in the home and she had to move into an apartment, she found that her "very low" earnings were insufficient and briefly reopened her NDB case in August 1927. In December 1928, Gerda was out of work and "anxious" to find her husband in order to make him provide support.[30]

Children were not the only family members with claims on deserted women's domestic labor and income. Women often took care of elderly or ailing parents. Deserted women responsible for a dependent parent found managing without a husband's support especially difficult. Sarah

Green applied for assistance in securing support from her long departed husband when she found herself "in a condition of despair, having nothing to live upon, and an invalid mother to look after, beside her child." Her husband was located and ordered by the court to make regular payments toward the support of Sarah and their child. However, when her husband failed to pay, Sarah did not pursue the matter. Three years passed until her case was reopened with this note: "She has not obtained anything at all under this order, from her husband, but as she has been keeping herself, she did not trouble. She now finds, however, that she is not able to work any longer, and therefore requests that efforts be made to compel her husband to send to her the amounts ordered by the Court."[31]

Women who turned to the antidesertion system as a way of supplementing their meager incomes and supporting their families found that they were taking on yet another job. The work involved in locating a husband, serving him with a warrant, and prosecuting him could be time-consuming, adding yet another task to the demands of wage earning, housekeeping, and child care. When faced with a conflict between going to work or to court, women like Penny Miner refused to jeopardize their employment. When Penny finally obtained steady employment after a few years spent pursuing her husband, she withdrew from the NDB, explaining that she could not now "afford to give time in order to institute Family Court proceedings."[32] Annie Baker, who was referred to the NDB when she applied for relief to supplement her income from a part-time job, attributed her failure to follow through with the bureau to the interruptions in her work that the antidesertion process required: "She was running from one agency to another and back to DRC [domestic relations court] and as her work was beginning to suffer she ceased contact."[33] Rebecca Lerman, who complained bitterly about the inadequacy of her wages, nevertheless refused to jeopardize them in order to pursue her husband for support. When she informed the bureau that she could not participate in a stakeout for her husband that conflicted with her work schedule, she wrote that "I cannot afford to take time off from work. My job means bread & butter & a roof over my head for me. The loss of my job would mean the loss of my baby & home & great sorrow to me."[34]

Some women, finding that they could not manage both taking care of young children and holding down a full-time job, did decide to place their children in an orphanage or in foster care. Indeed, antidesertion reformers found that desertion accounted for between 20 and 25 percent of the children in New York City's orphanages.[35] The difficult decision to part with her children was made easier for a deserted woman by the knowledge that the placement would be temporary, lasting only until the woman could "get on her feet."[36] For example, Dora Weldon, overwhelmed by unpaid bills and a nonsupporting husband at home, "wanted to have the children committed to an institution so that she could go to work, to pay off the debts."[37]

When a Jewish deserted woman applied to an agency to have her children placed, she was referred to the NDB either in lieu of placement or as a way to reimburse the child-placing institution. Harriet Krol was referred to the NDB by the Jewish Children's Clearing Bureau (JCCB), which reported that "she has asked for a Jewish home for placement. She is not able to take care of the children at the present time because she has no money. . . . She stresses the necessity of immediate placement for the children, in order that she may go out to work."[38] Some women turned to the JCCB or the Hebrew Orphan Asylum as a way of getting by and preferred boarding out their children to searching for their husbands. Lena Cohn, who was referred to the NDB by the JCCB, "did not wish [the NDB] to take further action against her husband, her only concern being proper placement" of her child.[39]

Millie Golden, having difficulty caring for her child while working full time, applied to have her daughter placed out by the JCCB. She became frustrated when the JCCB repeatedly responded by sending her to the NDB, instead. Millie, who worked as a waitress in a hotel, reported that "the guests at the place she was working complained because her child was so unruly, and as a result she was asked [by her employer] to . . . make arrangements for her [daughter's] placement, and return to the position alone. . . . She is thoroughly disgusted and tired of being discharged from every position because of the child. . . . She has repeatedly asked the J.C.C.B. to assist her in placing the child." Millie temporarily resolved her child-care situation by turning to her friends. A female friend agreed to care for the child over the winter if Millie contributed to the cost of room and board.[40]

Millie Golden was not alone in having her own network to draw on when her husband deserted. Friends, neighbors, and kin all came to the aid of deserted women. Clients reported to the NDB that they had been "assisted by friends" or "dependent on friends."[41] Others were "actually dependent upon neighbors";[42] one was found "living on collections made by tenants" of hcr building.[43] Deserted women turned to relatives, including parents and siblings—an "old widowed mother" or "a sister . . . in poor financial circumstances."[44] Alternatively, women turned to a familiar resource for meeting emergencies: the neighborhood pawnshop. One woman whose husband had been gone for seven months before she applied to the bureau reported that "she has sold all her belongings to get along thus far."[45] Mrs. Mankowitz provided a list of items she had pawned in order to get by, including "1 Accordian . . . 2 Bronze Ornaments . . . 1 Over Coat . . . 1 Table Cloth . . . [and] 1 Ladies Pocket Knife."[46]

The problem with all these responses to the loss of a husband's financial contribution was that they were not permanent solutions: there were only so many possessions available for pawning; neighbors were willing enough to help during an emergency but would not provide long-term support; and relatives of working-class women usually had limited means.[47] The poor sister mentioned above, for example, soon found herself "unable to keep [the applicant] and the child any longer."[48]

Deserted women found their children to be the most dependable source of additional income. Women with working-age children were able to do without their husbands' support for longer than were women with minor children only. Clients of the NDB who applied more than six months after their husbands' departure were more than twice as likely to have children aged fourteen or older than were women who applied within a month after being deserted. This was true even though the former group had slightly more minor children.[49]

The importance of wage-earning children to the maintenance of deserted women's families is not surprising, given their often significant role even in families with both parents present. Fully 74 percent of American-born daughters aged sixteen or over in Russian Jewish families worked for wages, contributing an estimated 89 percent of their wages to the household budget. Forty percent of younger daughters, aged fourteen and fifteen, also worked for wages. The income of daughters, primary when fathers were unemployed, was no less important when their fathers were earning: in families in which both fathers and daughters worked, they contributed an equivalent amount to the household budget (about one-third each). Sons also made contributions to the family income, but they tended to earn wages less often than daughters and to give less of their wages to the household.[50] Children of working age in early twentieth-century Jewish families clearly were not simply dependents of a male breadwinner.[51]

Children, whose dependence on a deserted woman could bring her into the antidesertion system, could also provide the alternative support that kept her out of court. The pattern of contact with and withdrawal from the NDB was in many cases influenced by the labor force participation of children, as well as of their mothers. Rhea Frank, for example, pursued her husband only so long as her children were under working age. She applied to the NDB just two months after her husband left her with four minor children to support by doing dressmaking at home. However, she subsequently suspended contact with the bureau almost entirely when her oldest daughter reached working age and went to work in a dental-supply house.[52]

A child's unemployment was often the second blow to a deserted family's economy that brought them into the antidesertion system after a period of managing without a father and husband's contribution. For eleven years (1922–33), Gladys Hart, her son, and her daughter "through their own efforts manage[d] to eke out a livelihood," but when her children joined the unemployed during the Depression, she turned to the NDB.[53] Since daughters far outnumbered sons in cases of children contributing to a deserted family's support,[54] a daughter's unemployment or marriage was often the occasion for a deserted woman's application to the NDB. Vera Kalish, whose husband left her for the last time in 1930, was assisted by her daughters. In 1934, "when she lost her income through unemployment and marriage of several of the children, she then began to seek [Mr. Kalish]."[55] Masha Rabin's husband left her in 1924, but she did not apply to the bureau until her combined household income dropped six years later. She and her daughters had all worked, none earning enough alone but together maintaining the family; "now one daughter is married, the woman in poor health & the other girl not making enough money to support both herself & her mother."[56]

Many deserted women came to the NDB either after experiencing yet another economic loss or after exhausting short-term resources. They turned to the NDB much as poor people turned to the charity system—as a way to tide them over a hard spell, a period of unemployment, or illness, or to manage in old age.[57] Most clients of the bureau were also involved in the welfare system as applicants to private and public agencies. The NDB drew its largest group of clients from such agencies' referrals.[58] The traditional reluctance of poor people to use the charities may have contributed to the length of time that it took many deserted women to become NDB clients.[59]

Antidesertion reformers attempting to determine the correlation of desertion with unemployment often declared that there was none.[60] But in light of the evidence concerning clients of the bureau, unemployment emerges as a significant factor—unemployment not of the husband but of the wife. Labor market conditions shaped the reasons women came into the antidesertion system, providing antidesertion professionals with the cases that became their statistics. Antidesertion reformers could not, in fact, measure the incidence of desertion, since they had no way to do so. They could only count the cases that came to their attention, those entering the system because the women involved needed financial assistance.[61] Unemployment, underemployment, low wages, and the burdens of the "double day" were all implicated in these cases.

When we consider that single mothers' position in the labor market affected their use of the NDB, the lack of a strong correlation between periods of high unemployment and rates of application to the antidesertion system may become more explicable. As Joanne Goodwin has demonstrated, single mothers' need for relief fluctuated far less than did that of men or of two-parent families. This reflected the cyclical nature of men's unemployment, which rose and fell with patterns of recession and recovery in the economy as a whole. Single mothers' more constant need for relief reflected their structural position in the labor force as low-paid, marginal, and unpaid workers.[62] The continuity in single mothers' precarious economic circumstances, regardless of general economic recession or recovery, may explain their fairly constant need for assistance and the related steadiness in the rate of applications to the antidesertion system.

USING THE SYSTEM

The most obvious reason women entered the antidesertion system was economic need. But they also came to the NDB for other reasons. Some applied when they found out that their husbands had contracted bigamous marriages after deserting them or that their own marriages were bigamous.[63] Others came when they discovered that they were being unilaterally divorced by their husbands from another state; the women hoped that the NDB would help them contest the divorce.[64] Some applicants wished to find their husbands in order to divorce them. Esther Keller, for example, told the NDB that she "has an opportunity to marry again and unless she obtains her freedom she will have to struggle all her life in the factory."[65]

Then there were women like Chayah Levitsky who had left their husbands. Chayah initially came to the NDB "for the record" to make sure that she would not be considered a "deserter," not in order to secure support from her husband, which she believed he would treat as a "joke." However, she eventually did pursue a domestic relations court order for support. Like many other applicants in her position, Chayah had no desire to reconcile with her husband; she wanted the support paid while living apart from him. She had suffered "kicks and beatings" during her marriage and had turned to the NDB for help in escaping the abuse.[66]

Miriam Peltzer applied to the bureau for similar reasons. She had left her husband, a rabbi, after he had beaten her with a candelabra—the most recent and severe incident in a pattern of assaults for what Miriam believed was "no cause at all." Rabbi Peltzer—called by his mother-in-law a "bum," a "thief," and a "Dillinger"—claimed that his marital problems were caused by the interference of his wife's parents. Peltzer also accused his wife of deliberately embarrassing him by letting water run over in the kitchen and bathroom, buying unsalted meat, and purchasing things on the Sabbath. Her departure from home and her tale of abuse, he asserted, were just additional attempts to embarrass him; her bruises, he claimed, came from a fall down the stairs. Neighbors and a local police officer verified Miriam's story, however, and the NDB believed her, too.[67]

Ever since it had opened its doors in 1911, the NDB had encountered cases of this sort. Battered wives came to the bureau claiming that they had "deserted" their husbands and seeking assistance in arranging separate support. None of the debates surrounding the creation of the anti-desertion agencies had led their personnel to anticipate that they would be called on to intervene in instances of domestic violence. But it is not surprising that women who chose to leave abusive marriages turned to the NDB for assistance. There was no organization that focused specifically on the problem of wife abuse.[68]

Social agencies and community organizations also perceived the NDB as an appropriate place to refer a Jewish battered woman. They shared the impression that the bureau was in the business of regulating male behavior. The Jewish Big Brothers, for example, referred Sadie Spector to the NDB because her husband was "cruel and abusive" to her, although he was "supporting her adequately." Sadie admitted that as far as she knew, her husband gave all his wages to her. She requested that the bureau compel her husband "to desist insulting her & beating her & children" and, intimating incest, "behave himself with his daughter"; otherwise, she wished to make arrangements for separate support.[69]

Battered wives who attempted to enlist the aid of social agencies often expressed the desire to secure an arrangement for separate support. To battered women, separate support seemed a way to leave their abusive husbands while retaining a chance for economic survival. In New York, particularly in the Jewish community, battered women knew that the NDB specialized in compelling men to support their families. Without an anti–wife abuse organization to turn to, these women framed their problems in terms Progressive Era reformers could understand, as instances of desertion.

Not all the battered women who contacted the NDB had left their husbands. Wife abuse was reported in almost 20 percent of the cases in my sample,[70] but women were the deserters in only 18 percent of those cases. In other words, less than one-fifth of the battered women in my sample actually left their husbands. In over half of all the cases involving wife abuse, the men were the ones who left, and in almost 30 percent the men were at home but not contributing adequate support.[71]

It is hard to sort out what inspired battered women to seek outside intervention in their marital conflicts when they came to the bureau to complain about inadequate support from their husbands. Conflict over control of the man's paycheck may have been the context for violence,[72] and women complaining of nonsupport may have been attempting to stave off further abuse by having the NDB regulate their husbands' household contributions. Involving the bureau could have been an attempt to alter the marital power relations that contributed to both the abuse and the nonsupport.[73] Tillie Orbach, for example, complained that her husband insulted her, beat the children and had recently given her a black eye, was a drunkard, and did not support her properly. When asked whether she wanted the bureau to prosecute her husband for support, arrange for separate support, or attempt a reconciliation, she replied that she wanted it to compel her husband "to behave himself & give support."[74] Other battered women wanted the bureau to make their husbands leave home.[75]

Battered women generally did not wish to avail themselves of the service that the NDB and the domestic relations court prized the most: arranging reconciliations. But neither did most deserted women. The NDB consistently offered and often strongly urged women to reconcile with their husbands, should the men be located and contacted by the bureau. But almost none of the NDB's applicants expressed a desire for reconciliation. The few who did were mostly wives of unemployed men who had left to find work.[76] In the vast majority of cases, however, desertion occurred in the context of an unhappy marriage and was indeed a unilateral "poor man's divorce."

Rather than reconciliations, what most applicants to the NDB wanted and needed was resources, especially money but also child care. This is why most of them applied first to the welfare system and why many of them first reported the desertion when they reached a financial crisis, not necessarily when their husbands left. When clients needed money because they were unemployed, ill, burdened with small children, underpaid, escaping abuse, or without wage-earning children, the welfare system sent them to find a man.

Deserted women resisted attempts to divert them into the antidesertion system. Lillian Fogel, for example, deliberately changed her name when applying to the United Hebrew Charities a second time so that her record as a deserted woman would not be recognized. She believed that her family would be "much better off" without Mr. Fogel.[77] Stella Blum was referred to the NDB after attempting to secure relief by posing as a widow; another woman insisted that the bureau cease looking for her husband, even if it meant that she would lose her child-care assistance.[78] A client who originally applied to the United Jewish Aid Societies three years after her husband's desertion and was referred to the NDB complained that it did "nothing for poor people";[79] another refused to provide information, "on the ground that since we are not assisting her, we need not annoy her."[80]

As new and less stigmatizing forms of financial assistance became available in the 1920s and 1930s, deserted women attempted to take advantage of these alternatives to traditional charity and exhibited greater resistance to becoming entangled in the antidesertion process. The desire of clients to receive direct assistance from the welfare system, rather than be diverted into a long search and prosecution of their husbands, became more obvious after the mothers' pension program was opened to them in 1924. This was a form of public assistance that did not share the stigma of charity, or at least not to the same degree. Deserted women who needed affidavits stating that they had searched for their husbands for a number of years,[81] simply wanted the NDB to facilitate their applications. When a zealous bureau worker actually located the husband of one applicant for a mothers' pension, she responded angrily that he had "killed" her chance of getting it.[82]

Similarly, when going on relief became a more common experience during the Depression, Jewish deserted women applying to the Emergency Home Relief Bureau also went to the NDB, intending simply to meet the EHRB's eligibility requirements. Charles Zunser observed that these clients generally did not prefer spousal support to relief: "Often applicants to the EHRB came unwillingly to the NDB and were reluctant to give information; sometimes they distorted the information, so that a true picture was not represented." Confirming that desertion was not the immediate cause of such families' need, he observed: "Many of them had made social and economic adjustments without the deserter's presence in the home, before the depression overtook them, and some are frankly indifferent or averse to the search."[83]

The aversion of some clients to searching for their husbands may have stemmed in part from skepticism about their chances of securing support—skepticism that was well founded. For example, Judy Finkel, whose husband was ordered by the court to give her regular support, claimed that he could not be trusted to pay.[84] A woman who eked out a living for her family by taking in foster children, working in a charity workshop, and doing housework, and who was sometimes reduced to living on coffee and bread, nevertheless doubted that reuniting with her husband would improve her lot. He had moved out of state and expressed a willingness for her and the children to join him; he promised to support them in his new home. However, she declined: she "feels that since she has never known any security when living with her husband, she cannot possibly consider the step which would deprive her of the security that she now has."[85]

Given the choice between earning their own incomes and relying on the promise of spousal support, other women opted for the former. When Gussie Mazer was legally separated from her husband after years of conflict over household finances, her alimony award came with the rider that it would be reduced if she worked for wages. She went to work.[86] When it was suggested that Zelda Rose give her job with the Works Progress Administration to her husband on his promise to support her and their child, she refused, stating that she doubted he would come through.[87] To many women who had experienced insecurity and financial conflict in their marriages, a regular paycheck or relief stipend—no matter how inadequate—seemed more reliable than the slim chance of securing spousal support.

These women bore little resemblance to the image of helplessness and dependency evoked in public representations of deserted women. In the year that the NDB was founded, *Collier's* magazine described a Jewish woman's encounter with the antidesertion system. She was "a little Jewish girl, a pale, black-eyed Jewish girl . . . [who] looked about helplessly like some frightened, timid forest thing . . . so lost, so bewildered . . . eyes widen[ed] with helpless pain," who could not hold up her trembling hand and had to be led out of court because she could not comprehend the directions she was given.[88] This article, like the notice in the *Sunday World* seeking Rebecca Lerman's husband, presented deserted women as "helpless" and passive objects.

The deserted wife

The helpless, imploring deserted wife, as depicted in Harper's, *30 May 1908.*

It is clear that women who applied to the NDB were far from passive. Coming from complex family economies that depended on women's contributions, working-class Jewish wives responded to desertion by drawing on a range of resources. Both before and after applying to the bureau, they struggled to piece together a livelihood from their own and their children's labor, from the pawnshop and local creditors, and from networks of neighbors and kin. Clients who had been battered by their husbands actively sought to escape the abuse. Applying to the NDB represented but one strategy among many that Jewish women in New York employed in pursuit of their own and their children's economic and physical security.

Social welfare and legal professionals' familial ideology and class biases influenced the solutions available to deserted women who found themselves unable to manage any longer on their own resources. Family reformers designed the antidesertion system with the goals of securing male support in order to reduce the relief rolls and of reconstructing "broken" families. Yet they encountered clients struggling with a hostile labor market, a sexual division of labor that assigned caretaking to women, and male violence in the home. These were not the problems as antidesertion reformers had defined them. In fact, the reformers' family wage ideology only aggravated women's weak labor market position and their economic and physical vulnerability in marriage. As the next chapter suggests, clients' skepticism about gaining economic security through the antidesertion system was warranted, given the inability of the courts to deliver on the promise of male breadwinning.

chapter 5

Desertion and the Courts

The purpose of the proceedings is not to adjust domestic relations but to prevent abandoned wives and children from becoming public charges.
—People ex. rel. Heinle v. Heinle *(1921)*

At the abandonment trial of Harry Linowitz, the husband of a National Desertion Bureau (NDB) client, Judge Malone expounded from the bench that "he was thoroughly in sympathy with the movement to stamp out the evil of family desertion, and that no deserter coming before him need expect mercy." Judge Malone spoke not as the voice of an autonomous, self-referential body of law, but rather as an instrument of a social policy clearly preoccupied with relations of gender and class. He explained his stern attitude toward Linowitz in terms that echoed the arguments of antidesertion reformers: "The drain upon the taxpayers is growing heavier because of these deserters who shake off their duties and obligations and thrust their children upon an already overburdened community."[1]

The first part of this chapter examines the legal basis of nonsupport proceedings and judicial interpretation of the statutes governing desertion cases. The legal system was interested primarily in containing dependency in the family by enforcing the financial obligations of family members to one another. This is not a matter of hidden motivations: the economic rationale behind antidesertion laws was openly expressed in judges' rulings. The antidesertion system was designed for social control, especially (though not exclusively) for the control of men.

Dreams of social control, however, are rarely fully realized in practice. The second part of this chapter measures the success of the antidesertion system against its promise to regulate male breadwinning. Drawing on evidence from my sample of 300 case files, I evaluate both the NDB's efforts to locate and prosecute deserters and the courts' ability to make providers out of runaway husbands. My findings suggest that the dream of stabilizing the social order by regulating families was indeed difficult to translate into practice.

THE LEGAL FRAMEWORK

The domestic relations court was primarily a mechanism for relieving the public of the support of poor dependents. Reflecting the financial motivations for its establishment, the court was given jurisdiction over proceedings involving "all persons charged with abandonment or non-support of wives or poor relatives."[2] Regarding nonsupport of wives and children, it specified proceedings under subdivision one of section 899 of the New York Code of Criminal Procedure, which defined "disorderly persons" as "persons who actually abandon their wives or children, without adequate support, or leave them in danger of becoming a burden upon the public, or who neglect to provide for them according to their means."[3]

Although the statute appears to mandate that husbands share their class status with their wives—by supporting them "according to their means"—in fact the courts almost always ruled that this alone was not sufficient basis for a complaint. As Judge Hazard observed in 1930 in *Case v. Case*, "Rather curiously all the numerous cases bearing upon the paragraph seem persistently to construe it as if the word '*or*' was '*and*.' "[4] Building on the decision in *Case*, another judge acknowledged, "I am aware of the fact that the disjunctive 'or' is used in this section," but "an act should not be characterized as criminal unless it offends the public. . . . The act of a man in neglecting to support his family in accordance with his means is not, in and of itself, criminal in its nature because it involves a difference between the husband and wife in which the public is not interested."[5]

On the eve of the creation of the domestic relations courts, a string of decisions made clear that decisions under the "disorderly persons" law (and the almost identical section 685 of the Greater New York City Charter) would be concerned less about a just distribution of resources within the family than about limiting the obligations of taxpayers to poor women and children. They agreed that "the statute was not enacted for the settlement of matrimonial differences"[6] and that it was not intended "to enforce the performance of marital obligations and duties, beyond what was necessary to protect the community against the unnecessary imposition of the support of a man's wife and children."[7] This is how the "disorderly persons" statute continued to be construed.[8]

The statute, which allowed for complaints by a destitute woman or a welfare agent, was thus part of the "family law of the poor." If a woman had any property or possessions that the charities believed she could sell,

The Brooklyn Domestic Relations Court, 1922. (Milstein Division of United States History, Local History and Genealogy, The New York Public Library, Astor, Lenox and Tilden Foundations)

she could not bring a complaint in the domestic relations courts. Destitute women and children were not entitled to more than would remove them from the relief rolls. Since men were not required to support "according to their means," children and wives were not entitled to share the economic status of their fathers and husbands.

A case in point is Malka Bloom, who applied for charitable assistance when her husband deserted her and her four minor children in 1926. Embarrassed and distressed by her need for charity, Malka eagerly pursued her complaint against her husband in the domestic relations court, with the legal aid of the NDB. She succeeded in obtaining a support order for $20 per week, a little less than a third of her husband's weekly earnings. When she later learned that her husband's salary had increased to between $90 and $95 a week, she sought to have the support order increased; but she was told that the court would not entertain her complaint because, although making ends meet on $20 was difficult for her and the four children, she was no longer a public charge and her husband had fulfilled his obligation to the public.[9]

In contrast, women who sued for alimony or child support in a New York supreme court, itself an expensive process, faced no arbitrary upper limit—they could receive an order for as much as the court decided a man could afford. Furthermore, women who sued in the supreme court were not subjected to home visits to monitor their housekeeping and mothering skills, as were women who resorted to the domestic relations courts. The two classes of women and their children had access to two different systems of family law: the common law and the poor law.

The underlying concern for containing dependency in the family found in the poor law system of family liability operated in the other, smaller set of cases heard in the domestic relations courts: those applying to the support of poor relatives. The principle of family liability reversed the gender and parent-child relationships typical of desertion cases. Children were ordered to support parents in most poor relatives cases, but a wife could also be required to support her husband.

Domestic relations courts were in effect poor-law courts, created to handle an impoverished economic class with the goal of protecting the pocketbooks of the middle-class. They perpetuated what Jacobus tenBroek has labeled the "dual system of family law," which placed the poor on a different legal track than the family of means. As tenBroek observes, the "family law of the poor" was less concerned about the allocation of private property in the family than about the use of public funds, and it treated all familial resources as a shared pool rather than as individual possessions.[10]

The domestic relations court operated within the framework of the poor law, enforcing economic obligations among various kin relationships. Although most of its cases involved regulating male breadwinners' responsibility for wives and children, the court could also order wives to support husbands, children to support parents, and, after 1921, grandparents to support grandchildren.[11]

On 21 June 1934, Jacob Dinsky, a fifty-eight-year-old unemployed tailor, appeared in the domestic relations court as a petitioner represented by the NDB. Claiming that he was destitute, Mr. Dinsky requested that the court order his wife and two of their six children to support him. The judge listened as Mr. Dinsky told how his wife had taken away his clothing store and all his assets. Yetta Dinsky, his fifty-four-year-old wife, denied that the business ever rightfully belonged to her husband, and she asserted that while she was in a precarious financial position, her husband seemed to have plenty of money to spend on other women. The judge, believing that Mrs. Dinsky was lying, ordered her to pay $9 a week toward her husband's support and two of her adult sons to pay $4 a week between them.[12]

It would be difficult to find the rationale for Yetta Dinsky's obligation to support her husband in histories of family law and of women's legal status. At common law, marriage was conceived of as an arrangement in which female subordination and service were exchanged for male protection, including economic support. Yetta Dinsky was a married woman entitled by common law to her husband's support, a mother whose dependence was ideologically presupposed, yet she was ordered by the court to take up the role of breadwinner for her husband. In the words of the New York Court of Appeals, "As between the wife and the state, the support of the husband is primarily the responsibility of the wife."[13] Although the rhetoric surrounding the creation of the domestic relations court promoted the ideal of reconstructing families consisting of children, dependent mothers, and responsible breadwinning fathers, ultimately the court's mandate to save public funds outweighed any normative conception of marriage as a gendered exchange of female service for male protection. The family law of the poor, guided by considerations of class, thus could result in decisions for which histories of women and family law have left us unprepared.

In addition to the case of Yetta Dinsky, the NDB handled at least two other cases that illustrate the way in which normative conceptions of gendered obligations could be set aside in the family law of the poor. Each of the two families, including the fathers, was instructed by a welfare agency to locate and prosecute a daughter. In these cases, the state labeled young women deserters and attempted, by withholding public funds, to create families in which women were responsible for the support of men and children for parents and siblings.[14]

The domestic relations court was, Raymond Moley observed, "largely a collection agency."[15] Although its objectives were often described with lofty rhetoric about repairing family life and reconciling disaffected spouses, the court was primarily interested in the material aspect of marriage as it affected middle-class taxpayers. Other kinds of domestic cases, such as wife-battering, received no hearing unless accompanied by nonsupport.[16] The "court of domestic relations" was thus as much a creature of class relations as of gender relations.

CHASING DESERTERS

If the court was a collection bureau, the NDB was one of its agents. The NDB provided the legal system with a steady supply of Jewish deserters. Cumulative evidence from bureau case files points to both the successes and failures of its vigilant antidesertion work.

Antidesertion reformers complained that laws and courts were of little use when deserters had disappeared. A missing man could not be prosecuted; first, he had to be found. The NDB attacked this problem with vigor. Its staff's careful documentation of the location process evokes the pleasure of detection. Indeed, some accounts of tracking down and apprehending deserters read like installments in a serialized detective novel. Following up a clue provided by a client, NDB assistant secretary Samuel Edelstein provided one such account on 23 September 1931:

> Called at the Puritan Hotel—183 Bowery, and made a discreet investigation. The day clerk told me he knows nothing about the deserter—neither under the name of K— or L—. He referred me to the night clerk who enters upon his duties at the Hotel at 6 P.M.
>
> From one of the patrons of the hotel, whom I followed out, I ascertained the deserter does stop at the hotel. My informant examined the man's photo, and assured me it is a striking resemblance of one of the guests.
>
> He told me I would get little co-operation from the clerks and suggested I rent a room for the night and watch the guests as they arrive, as the photo of the deserter is a very good likeness of the man he has in mind.

I called at 6 P.M. and rented a room. The day clerk was already gone, and I was unknown to the night clerk. At about midnight a man came in who resembled the deserter's photo, but he seemed to be rather too stout for the description, and so, not feeling certain I decided to wait until morning. I followed the man to the room, and found he occupied #18. My room was a few doors away from his, and therefore, I watched it.

At 8 A.M. I left my room and awaited the man's appearance in the reading room. At 8:30 he appeared and I followed him to a restaurant, from there on his way to his job on Spring St.

By that time I felt certain the man was the deserter. I insisted upon his arrest, although he at first denied his identity.[17]

Not all location reports were this dramatic, but the bureau had reason to be proud of its detective skills. It drew on the investigating staff of hundreds of agencies around the country (and around the world, if necessary); tracings provided by the postmaster; information supplied by the State Department, the military branches, and licensing agencies; and clues provided by clients, neighbors, relatives, employers, unions, and readers of a wide range of newspapers. Every week the NDB reached many thousands of *Forward* readers, some of whom wrote messages to the bureau revealing deserters' whereabouts. Despite increasing urbanization and geographical mobility in the early decades of the twentieth century, the relatively high degree of occupational and residential concentration of Jews in major cities seems to have made it hard for Jewish men to evade the notice of the communities to which they fled.

That NDB workers might have derived satisfaction from the location process would not be surprising: it was the most successful facet of their work. The bureau located 76 percent of the husbands in the cases in my sample. Seventy-one percent of this group were found in the state of New York and 29 percent out of state. Some of these "locations" were relatively simple, especially if the men were still at home or in touch with the wife. Nevertheless, by tracking down most of its clients' missing husbands, the bureau successfully removed a major barrier to effective enforcement of desertion laws.

The NDB hoped to persuade located husbands to support their families and, ideally, to reconcile with their wives. But persuasion almost never worked, and the bureau usually resorted to legal coercion. The majority of husbands in my sample who were located in New York landed in the domestic relations court. However, less than one-fourth of those found out of state were extradited and tried for abandonment.

Securing extradition under the Child Abandonment Law of 1905 continued to be difficult, even for women with tenacious NDB lawyers as their advocates. Charles Zunser pestered district attorneys who responded reluctantly, if at all. District attorneys refused to extradite husbands who had abandoned pregnant wives (even after the child was born); fathers whose families were not imminent public charges; deserters who had gone to California; and fathers who sent any money, no matter how meager, after leaving home. Even when a district attorney agreed to extradite, he often refused to pay for the fugitive's transportation to New York. Deserted women themselves had to come up with the fare and thus gamble their own scarce funds on the slight chance of future child support.[18]

More than one-fourth of those extradited never went to trial, either because the wife failed to appear in court (confirming district attorneys' fears that women would not follow through) or because the man jumped bail. All but one who stood trial in the court of general sessions were found guilty. The man found innocent deserted again immediately after the trial. Most of those found guilty were required to post bond, were paroled, and typically disappeared again. Henry Hornstein was the only convicted deserter who paid substantial child support. He first spent eleven months in the penitentiary before being released on parole. Then over the next four years he made child support payments. Although his payments decreased in frequency and amount over time, the NDB could claim success in this case.[19]

Only two out of the NDB's sixty-eight out-of-state locations in my sample resulted in substantial financial assistance for a deserted woman.[20] The obstacles to extradition and prosecution—the reluctance of district attorneys and wives, the shortage of transportation funds, and the repeated disappearances of husbands—rendered the NDB's efforts to use the Child Abandonment Law of 1905 largely fruitless. Yet the NDB persisted, involving agencies all over the country in the search for runaway fathers, apparently never doubting that these efforts were worthwhile.

Fewer obstacles stood in the way of prosecution in the domestic relations court. In contrast to the district attorney's office, where abandonment cases competed for attention with homicides and burglaries, the domestic relations court specialized in hearing charges of nonsupport. An army of judges, probation officers, investigators, clerks, and delegates from New York City's welfare agencies populated the court, all determined to make deserters pay. Unlike most complainants, NDB clients also had lawyers to represent them.

A woman could not simply file a complaint at the domestic relations court and then, once process had been served on her husband, return on the date of the hearing. First, she had to wait. Millie Oliver complained to the NDB that, "after leaving your office last week, I went to [the] Domestic Relations Court in an attempt to get a warrant. . . . After waiting 4 hours, I became exhausted, and went home ill."[21] Reportedly, so many women showed up at one branch of the court on a single day that "the lobby was not large enough to accommodate all the would-be petitioners and the overflow spilled over upon the lawn."[22] On finally reaching a court officer's desk, the weary client found that before her complaint would be accepted, she would be subjected to an investigation. After a preliminary interview, a probation officer investigated her home conditions. If her husband was available, the probation officer listened to his side of the story and then held a conference to reconcile the couple. When reconciliation failed, the officer collected reports from agencies involved in the case and prepared a statement for the judge. The form sent to the NDB by the court reveals the kind of information investigating officers solicited. It asked for comments on four aspects of the complainant's life: "capacity of woman as a housekeeper," "quality of woman as a mother," "habits and characteristics of the man and wife," and "general standards of the family."[23]

Until 1933, when the law was changed to mandate preliminary investigations in all cases, most complaints were not fully investigated. There were simply too few officers assigned to the court. In 1920, for example, less than one-third of the complaints were investigated; by 1932, the proportion had declined to 10 percent.[24] Representatives of social welfare agencies stationed at the court filled in the gap, providing judges with a third party's assessment of the couple's conflict.

Once a woman completed the preliminary interview, she could enter her complaint. Then process—a summons or a warrant—was issued.[25] There were not enough warrant officers, so the court normally passed the responsibility of serving process on to the complainant. She was to find her husband, grab the nearest police officer and show him her certificate of warrant, and have her husband arrested. If a client was lucky, the NDB might help her serve process. Usually, however, clients were expected to do the job themselves. Women were instructed to stake out their husband's haunts—places of employment, union halls, lodges, cafés, and the like. If a woman did not succeed in serving the warrant before it expired, she had to go back to the court to renew it. The legal system thus depended quite directly on women's unpaid labor. Wage-earning clients such as Penny Miner decided that the time required to pursue their husbands would be better spent earning a paycheck.[26]

When the day of the hearing finally arrived, an NDB client met a bureau attorney at the court. Occasionally a husband also brought a lawyer. A representative of an interested social welfare agency might join them at the hearing. The judge, after 1933 wearing civilian clothing, questioned the entourage.[27] He (or, rarely, she) measured the couple's claims against the report provided by the investigating officer.[28] Husbands typically claimed that they were unemployed or not earning enough to pay support. A wife might complain about abuse; her husband might counter with charges of harassment.

A wife had to prove that her husband could afford to pay support. The NDB could provide the critical testimony, as it routinely contacted employers while searching for a deserter. In some cases, cooperative employers provided the bureau with detailed, week-by-week accounts of wages paid to the husband. If a woman could not prove that her spouse was working, her case was dismissed or adjourned until she could offer sufficient evidence. During the Depression, judges may have been more inclined to believe men's claims of unemployment.[29] In August 1930, for example, Judge Leonard McGee chose to disregard the NDB's statement that a Mr. Gross was earning between $40 and $45 per week as a furrier. Bureau attorney Fannie Rosen reported that "Judge McGee then again made a recitation of his knowledge of bad economic conditions and told me that we will have to produce proof that the man earns sufficiently to comply with the order, before he can take action."[30]

Judges took women's earnings into account when setting a support order. When Magistrate Henry Goodman set Irwin Rosenfeld's order at $15 per week in March 1925, Deborah Rosenfeld stated that she would not take less than $20 a week, a sum she believed her husband could well afford. The judge refused her demand, replying that since Deborah was regularly employed, she ought to be satisfied with the $15 order.[31] A judge who could not compel a man to support his family might instead recommend that the wife find employment. A Mrs. Abramovitz, who had supported her two children since her husband left in 1920, came to the domestic relations court after losing her job and attempting to throw herself under a subway train in 1929. The NDB despaired of finding her husband, who "associated with Emma Goldman and Bergman [*sic*] and practically deserted his wife for the cause of anarchy." Although Judge Maurice Gottlieb could not order her missing husband to pay support, he "took a personal interest in her and secured work for her."[32] In another case in which the husband could not be found, a judge suggested that Betty Riskin make a complaint against her father-in-law, who apparently was shielding his son. However, the court ultimately refused to entertain her complaint because "the law imposes upon her the duty of working and supporting her own child."[33]

When women took legal action to secure support, they risked retaliatory violence from abusive husbands. After returning home from a court hearing in February 1918, David Sirkin beat his wife for several days and then left home again. When Risa Sirkin next attempted to serve him with a summons at his mother's house, he assaulted her there once more. Until 1933, domestic relations court judges could not issue orders of protection when women such as Risa Sirkin complained of abuse. Although approximately 50 percent of the domestic cases that formerly had come before the lower criminal courts involved wife abuse, those cases were left behind in the regular magistrates' (or police) courts when the new, "socialized" courts were established in 1910.[34]

At first the NDB shared the court's policy of shunning domestic violence cases. Occasionally in the 1910s, they would try to talk to a batterer, but if he supported adequately, the NDB would not press the issue.[35] In the 1920s, the bureau vacillated in its approach to women who left abusive men. Sometimes it clung to its primary mission of reconstructing families as economically sufficient units; at other times it responded to the requests of battered women by assisting in arranging separations.[36] The case of Bessie Geller illustrates the evolution of the NDB's response to women who left abusive husbands. Bessie Geller, the mother of one child, was a client of the bureau for fifteen years, from 1914 until 1929. She left home the first time after her husband, Izzy, a tailor, beat and choked her and threatened to shoot her. Over the next six years, Bessie left her husband many more times and came to the bureau for help. In 1920, when Bessie's occasional jobs as a cook dried up and Izzy refused to contribute an adequate portion of his substantial paycheck to household expenses, the NDB finally decided to take the case to the domestic relations court.

On 23 April 1920, Bessie Geller's complaint was put on the court calendar for a hearing on 30 April, one week later. Mrs. Geller complained to the NDB about the week-long delay, and the bureau, moved by her history of abuse, protested to the domestic relations court. "The Domestic Relations Court is too rigid," complained Monroe Goldstein, then the bureau's chief counsel, and he asked, "Was [Bessie Geller] to stand the neglect and abuse until next Friday?" "The case," he contended, "is not alone one for adjustment but presents grounds for protective treatment for the wife and son." Goldstein urged that, in light of numerous other similar cases, the court should consider a way to provide immediate "first-aid" for battered wives. Goldstein's complaint to the domestic relations court indicates that the NDB's staff was beginning to take wife abuse seriously enough to raise the issue with their colleagues in the antidesertion movement.

In Bessie Geller's case, the court proceeded as usual, making an order for support and relying on the NDB to reconcile the couple to living together. However, the bureau instead arranged a temporary separation and over the next decade alternated between helping Bessie Geller to leave her husband and bringing the couple back together again. In 1929, the NDB broke its otherwise firm policy of not appearing in the supreme court and helped the Gellers get a divorce.[37]

Women who sought to escape abusive marriages ultimately changed the perspective of professionals at the NDB. In 1932, when reform of the domestic relations courts was on the legislative agenda, Charles Zunser publicly advocated a bill that would allow the court to order a husband to support a wife who left in response to his violence and to issue orders of protection that would effect marital separations.[38]

Despite the fact that Charles Zunser and his allies were successful in changing the court's jurisdiction in 1933 to include orders of protection against violent men, judges continued to treat the issue lightly. In the case of Rebbetzin Peltzer—whose husband beat her with a candelabra in 1935—bureau lawyers advocated an order for separate support. However, Rebbetzin Peltzer received little sympathy from the domestic relations court judge who heard her case. He ordered Rabbi Peltzer to pay the meager sum of $4 a week toward the support of his wife and child but did not issue a protection order against Rabbi Peltzer. Instead, he ordered Mrs. Peltzer not to bother her husband.[39]

Beyond their primary charge of regulating male breadwinning, judges had considerable latitude. They could choose to ignore complaints of abuse or attempt to protect female complainants.[40] After 1933, they could order a wife to improve her housekeeping. Judges could also order either party to undergo a psychiatric or physical exam. During a hearing in February 1928, Lazar Woolf accused his wife, Ceil, of running a house of prostitution. The judge ordered both parties to undergo a medical examination. When Ceil indignantly refused to comply, she was told that "if she

[did] not submit to a medical examination, she [would] have no standing in court."[41]

In such complex marital disputes, the judge could play a pivotal role. However, the caseload was so great that it is doubtful that the justices expended the kind of fatherly care that Bernhard Rabbino had envisioned. Magistrates rotated in and out of the Manhattan and Bronx domestic relations courts on a fortnightly basis; only Brooklyn had an almost full-time judge.[42] Thus, only three judges sat in the New York domestic relations courts at any one time. In 1930, they held 16,724 arraignments, and it is not surprising that by 1932 they were complaining that their vacations had "come close to the vanishing point."[43] The overworked justices apparently kept their minds focused on the main business of the court, issuing support orders. Even after the court gained a psychiatric clinic in 1933, judges made referrals for examinations in less than 1 percent of their cases.[44] Similarly, judges made little use of their expanded jurisdiction after 1933 to hear cases of domestic violence. In 1936, for example, they heard complaints of abuse in only about 1 percent of their cases.[45]

In most cases, the justices hewed close to their mandate of enforcing male breadwinning in order to prevent abandoned wives and children from becoming public charges. Typically, they issued an order for the husband to support for one year and placed him under supervision or on probation.[46] A judge could send a particularly recalcitrant nonsupporter to the workhouse for up to one year. A man adjudged to be a disorderly person could be required to post bond, which would be applied toward support if he absconded. At his discretion, a judge could reduce the amount of a support order if a man's earnings declined and, usually at the request of the wife, could have a man released from the workhouse early.[47]

Probation occupied a large portion of the court's work. Judges used the workhouse sparingly because "in jail [men] are liabilities and very often their families become a burden upon the public."[48] Antidesertion reformers also recognized the uselessness of rendering a man unemployable by sending him to jail. Periodically, they attempted to convince the Board of Estimate to require deserters in the city workhouse to earn a small sum that could be sent to abandoned families. However, all attempts to create a program of forced breadwinning failed. Most convicted deserters were therefore released on their promise to pay a fixed sum weekly through a city agency to their wives. Probation officers were assigned to monitor men's compliance with support orders.

Once again, the system relied on deserted women's unpaid labor. Probation officers carried staggering loads; in 1920, one probation officer was responsible for an average of 173 men per month, in addition to conducting preliminary investigations.[49] In their reports to the mayor, judges kept up a crescendo of alarmed complaints about the harried condition of probation officers, who reportedly felt like mere "truck horses" and suffered nervous breakdowns from overwork. Often the most an officer could do was periodically ask a probationer whether he was still supporting his family—and then take the man at his word. "Frequently," one report admitted, "petitioners are the ones who keep Probation Officers informed of the arrears."[50] In other words, deserted women themselves did the work of supervising husbands on probation.

A woman discovered whether or not her husband was complying with a court order when she made her weekly pilgrimage to a city collection agency. The Department of Public Charities collected and dispensed support moneys until 1919, when this responsibility shifted to "alimony bureaus" attached to the Manhattan and Brooklyn courts. Women living in the other three boroughs faced a burdensome trek each week.[51] On arriving at an alimony bureau, they often found that no money had been left for them. In 1920, the total of ten clerks at the two alimony bureaus handled 9,000 accounts, a workload that translated into long waits for deserted women. The court's report for that year described the inconvenience and pandemonium of the collection system:

> Compelling the deserted wives to call in person for their support occasions the expenditure of carfares, loss of wages and repeated visits, for quite often the money is not paid regularly and several visits are required to secure the funds which are so sorely needed. It also results in such confusion and noise at the Alimony Bureau that it is almost impossible for the small staff to do their work accurately, and in addition to the terrific nervous strain under which they labor frequent errors in the receipt and payment of moneys are made.[52]

The NDB's clients were more fortunate than other deserted women. They, too, were burdened with the task of compensating for overworked probation officers and alimony bureau clerks, but the NDB could sometimes lighten their load. At the direction of the court and with the couple's consent, support payments were sometimes made through the NDB rather than the alimony bureau. The NDB also badgered delinquent men and urged probation officers to take action. In addition, the NDB continued to track down men who absconded after appearing in court. Given the additional assistance that NDB clients received, one would expect them to have been more successful in collecting support than most complainants.

Yet the evidence from my sample of 300 case files suggests that even with the NDB's help, the legal system ultimately failed in its mission of regulating male breadwinning. Eighty percent of the men located by the bureau in the state of New York were ordered by the court to support their families and placed on probation. Most made a few remittances, then stopped paying, and had to be hauled back into court for violating a support order. Of the men in my sample who were ordered by the domestic relations court to support their families, 72 percent appeared in court more than once. David Kerr held the record, with sixteen nonsupport hearings over a period of six years.[53] The bureau's lack of success does not necessarily indicate that Jewish men were exceptionally recalcitrant, since the courts reported similar difficulties in exacting compliance from deserters of all backgrounds. The domestic relations court consistently held more rehearings than first-time arraignments, and as the years passed, the rearraignments piled up. By 1936, the court was conducting more than four times as many rearraignments (69,498) than new cases (15,141).[54] Half of the men in my sample who appeared in court only once did so because they subsequently absconded so effectively that the bureau never located them again. Most of the other half had wives who did not persist beyond the first hearing.

Despite their apparent inability to compel husbands to pay, the domestic relations courts claimed to be collecting large sums each year. It is difficult to evaluate such claims: the number of accounts represented by each sum was not specified; nowhere was the amount collected measured against the total amount ordered to be paid; and the portion of each sum consisting of defaulted bonds was never reported. Annual reports of the courts typically attempted to convince the mayor and the Board of Estimate that the system was worth maintaining and expanding because it reduced the welfare burden on the city. Amid the usual boosterism, however, the 1920 report included some figures in passing that may shed some light on the profitability of the system. About one million dollars had been collected for 9,000 accounts.[55] This breaks down into $111 per account, or about $2.14 on average per family per week. Subtract from that the carfare and lost earnings of the wife when she visited the alimony bureau, and the benefits of the system for her virtually vanish.

The NDB's clients witnessed the failure of the system in their own cases. The steps that followed an in-state location—the serving of process, domestic relations court hearings, probation, and sometimes jail—resulted in only four men in my sample paying (however unevenly) for the full year required by a support order and one man paying for six months. Three other men located in New York but *not* taken to court also made payments for at least six months. If a husband had the means to pay, his predisposition to support, rather than legal coercion, seems to have decided the outcome. The NDB's record in successful out-of-state cases strengthens this impression: in one case, the husband paid only after being extradited, tried, and found guilty; in the other, the located man was never extradited or tried but nevertheless made support payments for three years. If we add together the NDB's successes in both groups of cases, its record appears to have been truly abysmal. Only ten of the 300 cases resulted in support being paid for at least six months. All that work for a 3.3 percent success rate!

How can the persistence of the antidesertion system be explained in the face of such failure? Antidesertion reformers campaigned for stiffer abandonment laws and for domestic relations courts with the claim that these measures would save public funds. The improved legal system, they argued, would shift the burden of supporting poor women and children back onto male breadwinners. The NDB claimed that it would remove Jews from the public charity rolls and thus protect the Jewish community's reputation. It promised to reduce the expenses of the Jewish charities as well. Historians are accustomed to suspecting that social reformers' altruistic rhetoric hid what were at root financial motives. But what are we to make of a reform movement that openly declared its economic motives while reaping so little financial gain? Antidesertion reformers may have been convinced by their own rhetoric or unable to admit failure; the institutions may have become self-perpetuating and the personnel invested in their own positions and importance. But perhaps the antidesertion movement is symptomatic of a tendency of welfare reform in the United States more generally, the tendency for the state's financial efficiency itself to become the most powerful public policy rationale.

The NDB and the legal system failed to live up to their promises. An astonishing amount of effort and resources went into prosecuting men who almost never resumed their breadwinning responsibilities. Yet the system continued in the face of this dismal record, and prosecution of nonsupporters became a permanent component of public policy for poor women and children. Already in its first few decades of existence, the antidesertion system seems to have become a "family policy trapped in its own rhetoric."[56]

Deserted Women and Social Welfare Policy

To be sung with the melody of Clementine

In an office, in an office,
In the great metropolis;
We are doing fancy case work,
Tell me what you think of this:

Once we were plain social workers
Stationed here to give relief;
Now we juggle therapeutics,
We will tell you all in brief.

We do not look at dispossesses,
Gas electric bills ignore;
And your troubles with your landlord
Don't intrigue us any more. . . .

He left his wife for another,
And his children quite a few;
It's a fixation on his mother,
There is nothing we can do. . . .

Your case now has become too chronic,
Your problems too involved we see;
There remains but one solution—
And you go to H.R.B.

—Lyrics found in an NDB case file

In the early 1930s, someone at the National Desertion Bureau (NDB)—probably Charles Zunser—left new lyrics for the song "Clementine" in a case file.[1] By then, the lyricist observed humorously, social workers in private charities—once there "to give relief"—had taken up "therapeutics." Hence many deserted women were going to the "H.R.B." (Home Relief Bureau) for a "solution" to their economic problems. The Emergency Home Relief Bureau (to use its full name) promptly returned them to the legal system. Jewish deserted women received the same directions as before the Depression: Go back to the NDB.

Progressive Era Jewish reformers wanted to protect their community's reputation, to stave off immigration restriction, and to ensure that immigrants Americanized properly. Responding indignantly to what they perceived as male irresponsibility, they took up the cause of Jewish women jilted by self-indulgent men. They also aspired to reducing the numbers of Jewish women and children dependent on both state and community charities. They claimed that the NDB's work resulted in a decreased proportion of deserted families dependent on the Jewish charities.[2] However, as my evaluation of NDB case files indicates, any reduction in the Jewish charities' caseload probably did not reflect the return of male breadwinners to deserted families. Rather, as this chapter will demonstrate, charities kept deserted women at bay by turning requests for assistance into complaints of nonsupport and by redirecting potential welfare recipients to the legal system.

The NDB's clients typically entered the antidesertion system when they faced a financial crisis. The often long and futile process of pursuing their husbands for support did little to meet the immediate economic emergency—frequently a dispossess notice from the landlord. Many deserted women turned to welfare agencies for help. At least one-third of the women in my sample received direct financial assistance from either a public or a private agency, or both.[3] Amounts ranged from a $2 emergency grant from the United Hebrew Charities (UHC) to a $55-per-month mothers' pension from the Board of Child Welfare. Regular and substantial pensions were rare; most assistance took the form of small emergency grants or more regular, but still small and short-term, supplements to women's and children's earnings. Thus, even the minority of deserted women who received welfare were generally not dependent on it. Their "dependence" on welfare, like their "dependence" on their husbands, was contingent on other factors in their family economy.

The sources of financial assistance and the role of private and public agencies changed over time in regard to deserted women, but three features remained constant. First, despite public rhetoric about female dependence, all agencies expected mothers to work for wages. Second, both private and public agencies expected older children and relatives to contribute support to the deserted family. Third, welfare agencies conditioned assistance on women's active cooperation in the search for and prosecution of their husbands. As the primary responsibility for poor relief passed from private to public agencies in the 1930s, this policy devised by the charities in the early years of the century became an integral part of government aid programs.

The NDB also held steadily to its mission, but after 1931 its referrals increasingly came from the public welfare system. The transition exposed the already close ties between the NDB and the state. In fact, Jewish agencies' proud claim to "take care of our own" depended on this connection to the state. In turn, government welfare agencies used the bureau and the antidesertion system as a means of deflecting deserted women's claims on the state.

THE CHARITIES

Before the Depression, private charities provided some direct assistance to deserted women. Of the women I studied who received aid prior to the 1931 establishment of the Emergency Home Relief Bureau, 92 percent were assisted by private charities. Whether or not NDB clients received monetary relief, at least several agencies were involved in virtually every case.[4] The charities used a variety of terms to describe their nonfinancial involvement in clients' affairs: women and their children were "under supervision" or "under observation"; an organization was "interested" in a family or a case was "active" at an agency. These terms covered a range of activities, including investigating a client's home conditions, searching for her husband, asking relatives to contribute to her support, intervening in familial conflicts (sometimes at the request of a family member), and making referrals to employment and child-care services. The main sources of support continued to be the labor of the women themselves and of their children.

The Jewish charities fully expected women to work for wages. Case workers commended clients who persisted in menial jobs despite clearly inadequate earnings. "All people . . . think highly of her," the United Jewish Aid Societies of Brooklyn (UJAS) commented approvingly about one domestic worker. "She is quiet and a conscientious and hard worker. . . . Even when [her husband] was home she had to work very hard to support the family."[5]

The words "heroic," "respectable," "worthy," and "deserving" appear in reports about poor mothers who worked to support themselves and their children, indicating the charities' approval of clients' wage-earning efforts. Monroe Goldstein recommended a factory worker to the UJAS as a "very worthy person" who has "struggled along with a view to making both ends meet."[6] Another client, "one of the numerous cases of a poor shop girl who worked and kept the husband in college and, upon his graduation, [was] deserted," also "struggled along heroically . . . in an endeavor to be self-supporting." By "working hard to support" her child, she earned praise as a "very good and respectable woman [who] certainly deserves any assistance."[7]

When women applied for financial assistance, they were frequently referred to employment agencies, such as the YWHA Employment Bureau, to unions, or to specific employers. Social workers found places for children in day nurseries and orphanages so that mothers of young children could take jobs. Clients often approached the charities with requests for such child-care services, but occasionally women who wanted financial assistance resisted social workers' arrangements. Sylvia Bernstein, the deserted wife of an allegedly wealthy bootlegger and the mother of three young children (an infant, a three-year-old, and a six-year-old) wanted the Jewish Social Service Association (JSSA) to pay her rent in June 1927 because she was about to be evicted. The JSSA heard from another agency that Sylvia was "very lazy" and not deserving of charity. The JSSA did give emergency aid to Sylvia, who impressed them as "attractive" and "intelligent." But her social worker was frustrated by her insistence on caring for her children herself: "She is a devoted mother. However, she refuses to do anything for herself. When we suggested that she place her children in a nursery and go to work she balked, saying she would never consent to this."[8]

The charities expected women to be both "good mothers" and wage earners. A "good and respectable" client was willing to cede some child care to others in order to go to work, but eagerness to do so could reflect negatively on her commitment to mothering. At the suggestion of a judge, Ida Stern, a garment worker, asked the Jewish Children's Clearing Bureau (JCCB) to place her children in an institution. In her social worker's view, Ida's ambition to start a small millinery business once the children were placed might have been "a good plan for her to get on her feet," but it was not necessarily in "the best interest of the children." The social worker's report continued: "Her attitude toward the children is not unselfish enough. She is high strung and claims that upon her return from work she has neither the physical nor the mental strength to devote herself to her children. All she wants then is rest and freedom from worry."[9] Social workers also considered certain types of work inappropriate for mothers. The JCCB refused to place Millie Golden's child because "the woman is doing work [waitressing in a hotel] for which she is not fitted, and . . . the JSSA should make some arrangement about the woman's work so that she could keep the child with her."[10]

Since the JCCB was primarily concerned about the "best interest of the child," it may have been more critical of women's wage earning than the charities, which were interested in keeping women off their rolls. Yet charity workers were also ambivalent about whether good mothering could include working to support one's children. They suspected women who wanted to work of being inadequate mothers. For example, in one disparaging report about a client, a JSSA social worker commented disapprovingly that the woman "always expressed her desire to work instead of attending to household duties. She would leave the children in a nursery and the home was very much neglected."[11]

Apparently, worthy clients had to walk a fine line: they had to be willing to take a job, but not want it too much; they had to be amenable to using child-care services, but without unseemly eagerness to do so. The difference was a matter of attitude, rather than of outcome. The distinction arose from the tension between social workers' ideal of dependent motherhood and their ideal of family independence. While holding onto the hope that retrieval of the husband would resolve this tension, social workers doled out just enough aid and advice to help the family survive in the meantime.

There is some evidence that families with a husband and father present received more than did deserted women. In some cases, the charities simply gave enough relief to tide a man and his family over until he was well or reemployed. However, they sometimes made a larger financial commitment. The JSSA, for example, expended substantial funds on Isidor Mazik, a habitual gambler who periodically deserted his family. His wife, Ruth, had been complaining to various agencies, including the NDB, of nonsupport and other conflicts with her husband since January 1928. In August 1933, the JSSA decided that the solution lay in establishing a business for Mr. Mazik. They invested $600 to start a cleaning and pressing store for him. Over the next few years, the JSSA occasionally supplemented his earnings and made additional investments in the business. Nevertheless, Isidor incurred many debts (apparently, some from gambling) and in 1936 mortgaged the store to cover them. The JSSA bailed him out, cleared up his debts, and invested more money in the store. In December 1936, after meeting Mr. Mazik's financial emergencies several more times, the JSSA finally decided that the store could not be salvaged. Isidor deserted again. Ruth spent at least the next eight years pursuing her husband through the domestic relations court and occasionally applying to the Department of Public Welfare for home relief.[12]

No woman in the cases I studied received the kind of investment made by the JSSA in Isidor Mazik's future. In rare cases, the amount expended by a charity on a deserted family may have equaled that spent on him. But a deserted woman would have received the money in a series of small sums intended to meet immediate needs. Ambivalent about the effects of mothers' paid employment, social workers treated deserted women's wage work as an expedient to be pursued until the "normal" (male) breadwinner could be returned. Requiring women to exhaust all their resources before becoming eligible for relief, the charities then maintained deserted families at the edge of destitution. The charities did not offer deserted women the kind of chance for permanent independence that they intended for Mr. Mazik.

When calculating whether a woman could survive without relief, charity workers routinely assumed that working children's wages would be used for family support. The charities found children jobs and discontinued aid when children were employed.[13] When one applicant protested this policy, claiming that "my daughter needs her wages for her self," the UJAS nevertheless figured in the daughter's earnings and deemed the family income "adequate" without assistance.[14] Social workers criticized older children who did not contribute to the family budget as exhibiting "irresponsibility and lack of adjustment,"[15] terms also used to describe nonsupporting husbands. Relatives of both the husband and wife were expected to contribute, too.[16] Clients understood that the charities requested information about relatives in order to keep the cost of support within the family. According to the UHC, Hinde Antler "refused to give information regarding her brother's residence, and stated that should we find her brother is able to give [assistance] the United Hebrew Charities will not help, and for this reason will not give us his address." Social workers labeled women such as Hinde "uncooperative" and denied them aid.[17]

"Uncooperative" women defined their own needs and how the charities could best meet them. Social workers criticized determined clients such as Joyce Silverberg, who "came to us only in a crisis and always with her own set plan. Our impression of her is of an intelligent, but high strung, overaggressive person, who has a strong need to wield complete control over a situation."[18] Joyce and other women like her usurped and challenged social workers' expertise. Unwilling to bend to case workers' prescriptions for their personal lives, less-than-pliable clients risked being refused the assistance they wanted.

Above all, cooperating with the charities entailed active participation in the location and prosecution of husbands. Women who did not collaborate energetically enough with the NDB were denied relief and cut from the charity rolls. This policy remained consistent over time. In July 1914, the UHC reported about one client who had missed an opportunity to serve her husband with a warrant: "We have not granted relief (although it might be necessary) because of the woman's failure to cooperate with your Bureau."[19] In December 1921, the NDB informed the UHC that it had not received "proper cooperation" from a client who claimed to be ashamed to arrest her husband. On this basis, the UHC discontinued assistance.[20] In March 1933, the JSSA closed a case "because of the woman's attitude"—she had resisted the agency's plans to reunite her with her husband.[21]

Social workers suspected clients of "collusion" or "pauperization" when they seemed reluctant to pursue their husbands. They believed, for example, that Rita Rothman was guilty of both. Rita's husband, who had taken another wife in Chicago, was extradited to New York in 1913 on the charge of child abandonment. Rita, who had worked washing clothes and had received intermittent aid from the UHC, had fallen ill and could no longer work. She told the judge that she was not particularly eager for her husband to return home. "Well," the judge queried, "I can put him in jail for five years, but you would not like to see him in prison then would you?" Rita's reply—"No, I would not"—indicated that she was "thoroughly pauperized." Not following through with the prosecution was one sign that she was unconcerned about "imposing" on the charities; another symptom of both "pauperization" and "collusion" came in a report from Mr. Rothman's "bitter" sister in 1923 that "[Rita] always insisted that she had no use for him and does not want to live with him; that she knew all the time where he was and could at any time reach him, and that even now she knows perfectly well where he is; that on many occasions she expressed herself to the effect that she does not want to know where the man is and if the U.H.C. would learn the fact that she knows where man is, they would refuse to aid her." Perhaps Rita already knew what the UHC was forced to concede a few months later—that "the chances are that Mr. Rothman will not be able to support the family."[22]

The eagerness of charities for husbands and fathers to support families receiving relief led to the hasty discontinuation of aid when men promised or were ordered to pay. In March 1929, the UJAS stopped assisting Nora Fineman because her husband promised to send money. But by May, he had sent nothing, and Nora returned to the UJAS with a dispossess notice.[23] Overly optimistic social workers interpreted any payment from a husband as an indication that he would continue supporting his family. In 1927, the JSSA discontinued aid when one husband agreed to pay $10 per

The United Hebrew Charities Building at Second Avenue and 21st Street, a gift from the wealthy Loeb family. (Courtesy NYC Municipal Archives)

week for his wife and three children. He paid a total of $20 over the next four months. The NDB observed that the family was experiencing "great hardships," but that "since [the wife] has received some money from her husband, the charities have quite naturally refused to give her any further assistance."[24]

The state and federal governments, not repentant husbands, finally relieved the charities of the responsibility for meeting the financial emergencies of deserted families. During the Depression, Jewish charities abandoned the Peter Stuyvesant Pledge—the promise that the Jewish community would take care of its own poor—and shifted most of their clients to public relief programs. Impoverished deserted women on the charity rolls before the Depression were transferred to public assistance once it became available in 1931.

In sometimes heated debates, Jewish social workers struggled to define a new role for themselves.[25] The growing prestige of psychology and psychiatry and the professionalization of social work (accelerated in the 1930s by the Jewish School for Social Work) influenced the new role of Jewish agencies. Economic assistance for immigrants, the chronically ill, and the aged became specialized functions, distinct from family services. Family case workers became counselors and offered their services to the middle class as well as the poor.[26]

The experiences of deserted women with the Jewish charities reflected the change. Without responsibility for general relief of the Jewish poor, the charities relaxed the rules and occasionally provided funds to women who slipped through the cracks of the public system. "Supervising" clients remained within the purview of the charities, but increasingly a referral to public welfare seemed to suffice. Clients noticed the change. One woman, refused aid by the JSSA and referred to the Emergency Home Relief Bureau, played to social workers' new view of themselves in an attempt to gain additional economic assistance. In 1935, she sent her daughter to the JSSA to complain about being unhappy at home. The social worker reopened her case but soon reclosed it, upon discovering that the girl was "only interested in finances."[27]

One Jewish family agency that changed little with the expansion of public welfare was the NDB. As they were created, government programs incorporated the antidesertion strategies developed by the charities. Mothers' pension boards and New Deal agencies made aid to deserted women conditional on their cooperation in pursuing husbands for support. The NDB increasingly served public agencies rather than private charities, thereby strengthening its ties to the state.

MOTHERS' PENSIONS

The first moment when needy NDB clients might have shifted from primarily private to public sources of financial assistance was in 1924, when deserted women became eligible for mothers' pensions. However, the formal inclusion of deserted women did not significantly affect the proportion of NDB clients drawing on private charities. In the years between the opening of the pension program to deserted women and the inauguration of Depression-related programs, charities were still the providers in 91 percent of the instances in which NDB clients in my sample received relief. An examination of the approximately two dozen cases in which bureau clients applied for a mothers' allowance reveals some reasons for the negligible impact of the pension program on deserted women.

Fear of encouraging "shiftless" fathers to abandon their families resulted in the exclusion of deserted women from the New York mothers' pension program from its inception in 1915 until 1924. In that year, pensions were extended to deserted women whose husbands were effectively "dead" to them. Following the recommendation of the state attorney general and the New York Commission to Examine Laws Relating to Child Welfare,[28] the legislature passed a bill providing that

> an allowance may likewise be granted, in the discretion of the board of child welfare, to any mother whose husband has absented himself for five successive years then past without being known to such mother to be living during that time and without furnishing means of support during that period for her child or children. Proof of such fact, satisfactory to the board of child welfare, shall be filed with such board which shall include an affidavit of the mother, duly executed, showing that diligent search has been made by her to discover the whereabouts of such husband and no such evidence has been found.[29]

In 1926, the requisite period of the father's absence was shortened to two years, but case reports indicate that some deserted women were still required to provide evidence of a five-year absence and search even after that date.[30]

When a woman applied to the Board of Child Welfare for a pension after 1924,[31] she was sent to a location agency, such as the NDB, to the domestic relations court, or to the district attorney. If her husband was located, she was denied a pension. The NDB's skillful detective work could thwart its clients' hopes for mothers' pensions. The bureau's inability to enforce support orders meant that women whose husbands were located usually received neither spousal support nor a mothers' allowance.

Sophie Venner was stymied by the bureau's remarkable detective work. In 1931, Sophie applied to the JCCB to have her children committed; her application was refused, she said, because she was considered "a good mother." She went to the Department of Public Welfare, which recommended that she apply for a mothers' pension from the Board of Child Welfare. The board asked her for an affidavit from the NDB to validate her claim that her husband had disappeared. The NDB reported the results of its search in the affidavit: the bureau had learned through a Cleveland agency that a local shopkeeper had seen Sophie's husband in the store on several occasions. The shopkeeper reported that Mr. Venner was unemployed and had no permanent address, since he moved constantly to evade unpaid landlords. This was as far as the bureau's search had gone, since Sophie said she wanted to go to Cleveland herself to confirm the identification of her husband before he could be scared off by an agency investigator. After expressing concern about transportation money, Sophie withdrew from contact with the bureau. Apparently, she never went to Cleveland.

Sophie Venner's first pension application was rejected on the basis of the NDB affidavit that reported the alleged sighting of her husband. In 1938, she tried again to apply for a pension,[32] and the Board of Child Welfare sent her back to the NDB because on her own she could not prove that she had been searching diligently for her husband. The bureau took steps to institute another search, beginning with the publication of a notice with her husband's picture. Sophie expressed her frustration in a letter to the NDB:

> In my opinion, and judging from past experience, publicity has been fruitless. Legally my husband does not exist since he has not been heard from in the past eight years. In addition my son . . . will reach his tenth birthday on July 9, 1938. Therefore I think it is about time you allowed me the pension to which I am entitled for the years remaining until my son's sixteenth birthday, and discontinued this useless dilly-dallying, evasion, and pretended concern for my husband's whereabouts before he, my son, becomes of age and therefore "ineligible."

Reminding Sophie that she had been the recipient of the bureau's "*free* service," an offended Samuel Edelstein wrote a sarcastic reply and closed her case. From his perspective, he had made a "good faith" attempt to find Mr. Venner, while Sophie had seemed reluctant to locate her husband and, finally, ungrateful for his efforts on her behalf. From Sophie's perspective, the NDB's service was far from "free": it had cost her a pension and represented a lost opportunity to supplement substantially her irregular income from occasional domestic work and homework (assembling powder puffs).[33]

The "location" of Sophie Venner's husband thwarted her application for a mothers' pension and offered no chance of receiving support from her husband, since he was never contacted directly. But applicants whose husbands were indeed located and prosecuted often found themselves in the same position. Anna Carnovsky, who applied for a pension in August 1938, was rejected in September 1939 after her husband was located through the combined efforts of the NDB and the Board of Child Welfare. Mr. Carnovsky was extradited to New York, jumped bail, and disappeared again. Anna received neither a pension nor support from her husband.[34]

Given the obstacles deserted women faced, it is not surprising that very few of them received mothers' pensions. Indeed, even after deserted women became eligible for pensions two years after their husbands disappeared, they remained only 2 or 3 percent of pension recipients.[35] Although the NDB staff's location techniques undermined some of their clients' applications, it may have been even more difficult for deserted women to prove the length of a father's absence and of location efforts without an NDB affidavit. The requirements that hedged in deserted women's access to mothers' pensions appear to have created an effective de facto bar to their inclusion in the program.

New York was the only state that specified in its mothers' pension law that "aid is restricted to an amount not exceeding the cost of institutional care."[36] Some NDB clients may have heard that mothers' pensions were intended to substitute less expensive home care for institutional care of children. One woman used this argument in an attempt to convince the bureau to help her get what she termed a "desertion pension." Six of her eight children were in the Hebrew Orphan Asylum. "Can't you see," she urged the NDB, "if I could get the children home and have them give me some allowance, I think it would be cheaper for the city to do that."[37]

Mothers' pensions in New York City, as elsewhere, were too low to provide adequate support for a fatherless family. Even before the expansion of eligibility criteria, when the recipients of mothers' pensions were widows, more than half worked for wages. Despite the rhetoric advocating full-time mothering that surrounded the creation of the program, the policy of the Board of Child Welfare was to encourage recipients to work for wages. In 1919 the board established an employment bureau in cooperation with the State Industrial Commission in order to find work for pension recipients, with the goal of moving them off the rolls.[38]

The Board of Child Welfare also expected older children to use their wages for family support and included children's earnings in budget calculations to determine the size of a pension. One of the few NDB clients to receive a pension, Polly Katz survived with her three children on a monthly pension and the earnings of the oldest daughter. Polly was an ideal candidate for a pension: her husband (and his $10,000 savings account) had disappeared without a trace six years before she applied to the Board of Child Welfare. The NDB had been entirely unsuccessful in locating him, and it supplied an affidavit to that effect. A year and a half after the affidavit was submitted, Polly Katz began receiving a pension. Her family's income in 1935 consisted of $25 per month from the Board of Child Welfare and the $12 per week earned by her eighteen-year-old daughter. Thus, her daughter's wages—not the pension—provided the main support of the family. The sum was not adequate—even though, according to the Board of Child Welfare, Mrs. Katz was an "excellent manager"—and Polly asked the Department of Public Welfare for a supplement.[39]

Despite the upper limit on aid, the New York City Board of Child Welfare did grant some of the most generous allowances in the country. The deserted woman who managed to get past all the obstacles to receiving a pension was relatively fortunate. She could receive up to $60 a month by 1931[40]—that is, as long as she continued to pursue her husband. Dina Milkman was one of the fortunate few: she received a monthly allowance of $55 in 1927 for her four children five years after her husband had disappeared without leaving any clues. The Board of Child Welfare investigator insisted that Dina keep returning to the domestic relations court to renew the warrant for her husband's arrest. In 1932, she was still making periodic trips to the NDB and the domestic relations court, "despite the fact that there has been no word of [the] man in many years."[41] Although Dina Milkman had to engage in this futile exercise, she did receive a significant sum on a regular basis for a number of years and thus enjoyed a degree of economic stability rare among the NDB's clients.

Most Jewish deserted applicants to the New York City Board of Child Welfare were redirected to the NDB and domestic relations court and never received a pension. The Board of Child Welfare utilized the legal procedures and institutions created by antidesertion reformers to defer or deny deserted women's applications for mothers' pensions, basing its policy on the reformers' argument that the responsibility for support properly rests with the husband, not the public.

This pattern may not have been unique to New York. Comparisons with other states suggest that when antidesertion reforms preceded or coincided with the creation of pension programs, deserted women faced similar obstacles. In Pennsylvania, pension legislation including deserted women was passed in 1913; domestic relations courts were established in 1914; and the next year, in 1915, deserted women were struck from the roster of eligible recipients. Deserted women received comparable treatment in Illinois. There, domestic relations courts were created almost simultaneously with the passage of mothers' pension legislation. Deserted women were quickly dropped from the list of eligible recipients, as a "distinct state machinery was developed by the local state to address deserted and other non-supported women," writes historian Joanne Goodwin. She adds that "those groups of single mothers who were politically vulnerable were eliminated from eligibility and directed toward the Court of Domestic Relations and the poor relief office."[42]

By creating separate boards to allocate mothers' pensions, rather than assigning the responsibility to the courts, the framers of the New York program intended to remove the stigma of poor relief from aid to women with dependent children. But when pensions were extended to deserted women, the antidesertion system of courts and agencies became an adjunct of the Board of Child Welfare, bringing mothers' pensions into closer relation with the poor law system of family liability. During the Depression, this linkage of public welfare with the antidesertion system—including the NDB—continued.

HOME RELIEF

During the Depression, the government became the primary source of relief for NDB clients who received financial assistance. The shift was dramatic. Before the creation of the Emergency Home Relief Bureau (EHRB) in 1931, less than ten percent of the welfare recipients in my NDB sample received aid from a public agency. After the establishment of the EHRB and other New Deal programs, 87 percent of them did.[43] Administrators of relief programs in the 1930s were astonished by the number of people classified as "unemployable," including mothers of young children, who applied to agencies set up for the unemployed.[44] These applicants included deserted women who had been poor long before the Depression. The new programs offered them a fresh economic avenue, but one that was paved with familiar policies.

During the Depression, the EHRB further incorporated differential policies for women based on marital status into public assistance rules and procedures. Created in 1931 by the Wicks Act, the New York City EHRB was funded by a combination of local disbursements, state contributions provided under the Temporary Emergency Relief Administration, and, after the creation in mid-1933 of the Federal Emergency Relief Administration, by federal monies. While work relief set up under the Wicks Act provided recipients with cash wages, home relief remained as in-kind grants (food, clothing, fuel, etc.) until pressure from clients and some administrators resulted in a shift to cash grants in 1934. New York City's relief rolls soared during the Depression, peaking at one-sixth of its population.[45] Faced with an overwhelming demand for assistance, agencies sought once again to reduce the numbers on relief by turning responsibility over to families. The EHRB did this by utilizing the domestic relations court and the family liability sections of the poor law.

The EHRB's regulations followed the family liability provisions of the Public Welfare Law regarding obligations of support among husbands, wives, grandparents, stepparents, and children. When a legally responsible relative was unwilling to support, the EHRB sent the applicant for relief to the domestic relations court.[46] By special arrangement, Jewish applicants were referred to the NDB. If the applicant was unwilling to go to court, EHRB policy instructed that "the case should be rejected or closed."[47]

Deserted wives had to contend with this and other coercive strategies that distinguished them from single, widowed, or divorced women. They faced the official reluctance of the EHRB to provide separate relief grants for husbands and wives. Furthermore, they risked losing their legal settlement in New York City—an eligibility requirement for relief recipients—if their husbands were located, on the principle that a married woman's domicile followed that of her husband. In a gesture toward enforcing breadwinning responsibilities, the EHRB indicated that it would recommend dismissal of Works Progress Administration (WPA) workers who deserted their families. Since only one person per family could hold a WPA job, this theoretically allowed deserted women whose husbands were fired the chance to apply for WPA employment. However, as the case of Zelda Rose (the woman who was urged to cede her WPA job to her husband) demonstrates,[48] the policy preference for male breadwinning placed deserted women's WPA positions at risk when their husbands returned.

The EHRB discontinued relief to a deserted woman when the court issued a support order; it did not wait to see whether her husband actually paid. When Tessie Unman's husband was released in May 1936 from the penitentiary, where he had served five weeks for refusing to post bond for failing to pay on a support order, the EHRB told her that she had to report his release to the NDB or become ineligible for relief. Tessie complied and, with the blessing of the NDB and a support order from the court, agreed in

June 1936 to reconcile with her husband and set up a new home with him and their three young daughters. The NDB reported these arrangements to the EHRB, which discontinued Tessie's relief on the basis of the support order. But Tessie's husband did not comply with the order, leaving her with neither relief nor support.[49]

Applicants realized their vulnerability under EHRB policy and asked the NDB to protect them. Lila Carlebach greeted the news that her husband had been located in New Jersey with concern that if Mr. Carlebach were ordered to provide support, home relief would be discontinued. She believed that his contributions would be irregular at best and that home relief was a more dependable source of income. She discussed her concern with an NDB worker, and the bureau agreed to intercede on her behalf with the EHRB.[50] Dora Leitner had secured "countless orders" for her husband to support her and their daughter and found that "because of these court orders, which [the] man never obeyed, [she] had great difficulty getting on the rolls of the EHRB." When she finally managed to get home relief, Dora continued to feel vulnerable to charges that she had not cooperated sufficiently in prosecuting her husband. When she learned that the NDB had told the EHRB that she had failed to provide a photograph of her husband, Dora pleaded that "an issue should not be made of this to injure her standing with the relief." The EHRB did reduce Dora Leitner's relief allowance when her husband was ordered to provide her with $6 per week. He paid only $4 irregularly, and Dora soon found herself unable to pay the rent. She complained to the NDB, and Charles Zunser enlisted the help of Mr. Leitner's probation officer in having the EHRB restore $2 of the relief allowance.[51]

The EHRB's policies effectively gave husbands power over their wives' eligibility for assistance. Occasionally a vindictive man would use this power to punish his wife. Dora Leitner, who unsuccessfully applied for a mothers' pension before going on home relief, believed that her husband intentionally thwarted her application. In May 1935, she complained that "he reports to the court just to prevent her from becoming eligible for a Board of Child Welfare pension." Later that year, when Mr. Leitner promised to provide support, a judge released him over the objections of both the NDB and Dora Leitner. Mr. Leitner made only one contribution of $5, and "he told [Dora] at the time that he will make just one payment 'enough to take her off home relief.' Her [EHRB] allowance was cut off." Mr. Leitner also reported to the EHRB that his wife had money in the bank. Discovering on investigation that no such bank account existed, Charles Zunser wrote the EHRB that Mr. Leitner "was probably motivated only by a desire to have you discontinue his wife's allowance." For any number of reasons—to secure support from her husband, to demonstrate her trustworthiness to the EHRB, or perhaps to exact revenge—Dora reported to the EHRB that she had caught her husband working for a fur company after he had applied for home relief.[52]

Another instance of the power a nonsupporting husband could exert over his family's affairs was the case of Harriet Krol, who applied to the Jewish charities for placement of her children so that she could go to work. According to the Jewish Children's Clearing Bureau, in a report corroborated by the JSSA, Harriet "was being assisted by the Home Relief Bureau but they closed her case when they discovered that her husband was working, earning $15. a week. Mr. Krol came to the [EHRB] precinct reporting that he was supporting his family from his earnings and that his wife was taking relief on false pretenses. Mrs. Krol reports, however, that he failed to give her the money which he told the Home Relief Bureau he was allowing her. Her assistance from the Home Relief Bureau was discontinued."[53] In a trend toward greater flexibility in private agencies than in public welfare policy, the JSSA provided Harriet Krol with emergency funds.[54]

The EHRB's attitude toward husbands extended to children as well. The EHRB assumed that older children would use their wages for family support, and it required relief recipients to locate and prosecute children who violated this presumed norm. The EHRB was also more likely to refer children than mothers to WPA jobs. In the cases I studied, twice as many sons and daughters as mothers were assigned to the WPA. Deserted women stopped receiving relief when the EHRB deemed a son's or daughter's wages from the WPA or other employment to be adequate for the entire family.[55]

However, the assumption that children would apply their earnings to family support was not always correct. Tsipporah Applebaum, for example, was reluctant to give the EHRB her twenty-year-old son's address because, she claimed, when he lived with her he had "treated her cruelly and indifferently. He threatened to beat her, broke dishes at home, and never spoke to her." Nevertheless, the EHRB insisted that her son be located, assigned him a WPA job, and discontinued aid on his promise to support his mother. He gave her only a tiny sum, and, at its last contact with her, the NDB reported that Tsipporah was destitute, "liv[ing] on coffee and bread," and afraid to antagonize her son.[56] While Tsipporah Applebaum's experience with her son may have been unusual, the EHRB's equation of wage earning with providing was not.

The EHRB made the cooperation of parents in pursuing missing work-age children a condition of relief. Eddie and Elsa Getz were referred by the EHRB to the NDB for assistance in tracking down their twenty-one-year-old daughter, a dancer, in order to compel her to support her parents and her brothers. Following a similar referral, Alex and Shena Backman applied to the NDB for help in locating their twenty-six-year-old daughter, a stenographer, again in order to compel her to support her parents and her brothers. Both families were reluctant to pursue their daughters and ultimately withdrew from contact with the NDB. Based on their failure to cooperate with the NDB, the EHRB denied their requests for relief.[57]

Welfare assistance, during the Depression as before, remained conditional on a client's willingness to engage in intrafamilial litigation. The "means test" for deserted women entailed more than proof of destitution; it required that deserted women demonstrate their desire for male support over and over again—each time that they applied for aid. It was difficult for women to escape the "deserted" category once they had been placed in it. The Social Service Exchange, by keeping track of all applications to social agencies (including the domestic relations court), made it unlikely that women could pass as widows once they had been identified as deserted. One NDB client did try to outwit the system by changing her name, but the United Hebrew Charities found her out.[58] Divorce and remarriage had to be documented carefully before a woman could change her marital status in the eyes of the welfare system. Fruma Dibner applied for a mothers' pension as a widow and mother of five after her husband of nine years died. However, her application was rejected because she could not prove that she had divorced her first husband, who had run off to Canada several years before she remarried. Although Fruma considered herself a widow, according to the pension board she was still a deserted woman, now tainted by the suspicion of sexual immorality and fraud.[59]

The label "deserted" determined the way social agencies treated women many years after there was no hope of securing a husband's support. Ora Chaim's husband "just wandered off" in 1922; he was mentally ill and had never been able to hold a job. Ora survived by doing housework, despite her disabled leg, and with the help of her children. In the 1930s, several of her applications for relief and for a mothers' pension were rejected because, according to the EHRB, she had not made a sufficient effort to find her husband. In 1954, after Mr. Chaim had spent at least six years in a state hospital and then disappeared again, the Department of Public Welfare contacted the NDB about Ora, at that time sixty-eight years old and still deemed a "deserted woman."[60]

In the 1950s, the Department of Public Welfare, not the Jewish charities, was handling Ora Chaim's case. On the whole, New York's Jewish community welcomed the expansion of public welfare in the Depression under the aegis of the New Deal, seeing it (like mothers' pensions in the earlier years) as the realization of the Jewish principle of *tzedakah* (justice). As public agencies increasingly relieved the community of the responsibility for taking care of its own poor in the United States, case workers in Jewish family agencies increasingly lent their counseling services to middle-class Jews. Jewish philanthropies shifted their programs to focus on ethnic continuity and assistance to Jews abroad.[61]

Charles Zunser's successor, Jacob Zukerman, remained proud of the contribution Jews had made to social welfare—the NDB was "the only organization in the world specializing in the field of family desertion." However, he presided over a substantially different agency, one no longer focused simply on poor deserted Jewish women. Shortly after Ora Chaim's final referral, the NDB adopted a new name, the Family Location Service, to reflect its changing mission. In the post–World War II period, the desertion bureau increasingly lent its tracking services to new groups: refugees seeking relatives in the United States, parents looking for runaway teens, and non-Jews. Although still affiliated with the Jewish Federation (successor to the JSSA), the desertion bureau's cases no longer came primarily from the Jewish charities. Instead, the Family Location Service supervised nine employees of the New York City Department of Welfare who handled the public welfare cases of clients "of all faiths, of all races and religions."[62]

Jacob Zukerman parlayed his experience at the NDB into a position as a family court judge. By the time he ascended to the bench, the domestic relations courts had been through several waves of reform, each seeking to realize the ideal of "socialized justice." In 1933, the courts shifted from criminal to civil jurisdiction, a reform hailed as a "radical change." Advocates of the change claimed that the domestic relations court would cease to be a "poor law agency" and become a modern "welfare agency." Cases would no longer be brought only by "the people"—a stigmatizing legacy of the poor law—but rather by petitioners (not complainants) against respondents (not defendants). A psychiatric clinic, the power to intervene in cases of abuse, and the authority to award temporary child custody would make the court "one of the greatest social laboratories in the world."[63]

Yet much stayed unchanged after the 1933 reform. The court retained an arbitrary upper limit on support orders; it maintained close ties with welfare agencies, which could still initiate cases in order to unload dependent wives, children, and poor relatives; it continued to use sanctions normally reserved for criminal actions; and it declined to intervene to stop domestic violence unless accompanied by nonsupport. It was still associated with the poor and not the middle class.[64] As one recently de-classed ex-wife of a businessman told the NDB, "[I] wouldn't want to come in contact with the type of women who go to those courts."[65] The domestic relations court continued to merit the moniker "Welfare Court."[66]

Since the construction of a distinct desertion policy by private charities early in the twentieth century, "private" and "public" responsibilities and social and familial obligations had been intimately linked. The interpenetration occurred at the levels of both community and family. The Jewish charities' role in building the antidesertion system belied the claim that until the Depression, Jews had taken care of their own. The use of state power already had been integral to the desertion policy of private Jewish charities for at least two decades. New public assistance programs followed the charities, making instrumental use of poor people's intimate relations by incorporating family support into the economy of welfare policy.

The Legacy of Antidesertion Reform

The world of Jewish antidesertion reformers now seems remote. Yiddish readers no longer scan "The Gallery of Missing Men," clucking disapprovingly. Americans worry about "welfare" rather than "charity," and when they do, they rarely think of the Jewish poor. The participation of Jewish and other ethnic charities in laying the groundwork for the American welfare system has largely been forgotten. Stories of National Desertion Bureau investigators and wives tracing by hand postmarks on letters from husbands, expending shoe leather in tracking men, staking out their haunts, and flagging cops on the beat to serve warrants seem antiquated in our technological age. Yet the legacy of the Progressive Era antidesertion campaign is still with us.

"Deadbeat dads" have replaced deserters as the nemesis of welfare reformers. "Wanted" posters alert the public to men derelict in their familial duties.[1] Their victims are cast as children, not women. Paternalism toward women on welfare has all but disappeared, replaced by resentment toward "welfare mothers" who are purportedly cheating the taxpayers. Women applying for welfare are directed to wage work, without the ambivalence that complicated Progressive charity programs. Nevertheless, heterosexual marriage continues to be seen as a solution for poor women's and children's poverty.

A brief survey of developments since the 1930s reveals some of the avenues through which antidesertion reform's legacy persisted. The linkage between law enforcement and the welfare system embodied in the domestic relations courts developed into a permanent feature of the U.S. welfare state. Driven by periodic outcries against "welfare cheats," measures to locate and prosecute absent fathers were resurrected time and time again as the welfare state developed, despite periodic reports that antidesertion programs were not cost effective.

The antidesertion legacy lived on in the Aid to Dependent Children (ADC) provisions of the 1935 Social Security Act and in their implementation. In its early years, ADC continued the pattern established by mothers' pension programs of underfunding deserted women.[2] In New York City, home relief—which became the general assistance program of the Department of Public Welfare—continued to be the main source of public aid to deserted women, including clients of the NDB. Studies by the Bureau of Pension Assistance in the early 1940s found that deserted women faced greater hurdles than did widows or divorced women. Deserted women were required to prove that their husbands had truly abandoned them, and then the location efforts were begun. Fear of encouraging desertion, and of thereby opening ADC to political attack, continued to shape the way the welfare system treated deserted women. According to the public policy historian Blanche Coll, location of a father could mean "automatic denial of ADC, the welfare agency reasoning that support was his responsibility, not the public's."[3]

In the 1940s, a wave of legislative initiatives again aimed to solve the problem of extraditing deserters. Three times early in the decade, a bill to make it a federal crime to leave the state in order to avoid child-support payments was introduced in the U.S. Senate; in 1947, another bill was introduced to impose civil remedies for desertion and nonsupport; in 1948, Congress passed the Fugitive Felon Act; and in 1949, New York passed the Uniform Support of Dependents Law, becoming the first state to do so.[4] In 1950, disregarding statements by Bureau of Public Assistance officials disparaging the effectiveness of antidesertion measures, Congress passed NOLEO (Notice to Law Enforcement Officials), which Coll describes as "the first statutory signal of growing disfavor with ADC." The legislation required state welfare agencies to "provide for prompt notice to appropriate law-enforcement officials of the furnishing of aid to dependent children in respect of a child who has been deserted or abandoned by a parent."[5] A decade later, the secretary of health, education, and welfare, Abraham Ribicoff, ignored the advice of his consultant on public welfare, George Wyman, who said that collecting support from absent fathers was a "hopeless task"; in 1961, Ribicoff sent a set of recommendations for welfare reform to President John F. Kennedy, with "more effective location of deserting parents" at the top of the list.[6]

In amendments to the Social Security Act of 1967, 1974, and 1975, lawmakers spurred by resurgent suspicion of "welfare cheats" again attempted to solve the problem of extradition. The 1974 and 1975 provisions set up a parent locator service, resurrecting through a federal-state partnership the private services offered by the NDB in the Progressive Era.[7] In 1979, New York began adding income-withholding provisions to all court-ordered support assignments, and federal provisions for automatic wage-withholding were adopted in the Family Support Act of 1988.[8] In 1992, it became a federal crime to evade support obligations owed for a child

THESE FATHERS ARE BEHIND IN THEIR CHILD SUPPORT.

They gave birth to a democracy. A system of government based on human rights. The same system ironically that now allows for millions of children to go without adequate health care. Or food. Or a decent place to live.

It seems inconceivable that these conditions would have lived up to our forebearers' ideal of liberty and justice for all. Who knows. Judging by these statistics, maybe that concept died along with them. Consider:

– One in five American children lives below the official poverty level. (The majority are from rural and suburban communities.)

– In immunizing infants against polio, the United States ranks behind 16 other nations.

– 23 nations have lower infant mortality rates than the United States.

– Approximately 2.5 million American children were reported abused or neglected last year.

– An estimated 5.5 million American children don't regularly get enough to eat.

Many of these kids don't do well in school. (You try and concentrate when you haven't eaten all day.) As a result, when they grow up, they're less able to compete for good jobs. Which leads to higher unemployment. And, along with it, increased welfare and crime.

But believe it or not there is some good news in all of this. We can do something about it; there is a way to break this cycle. And it starts by adopting a plan devised by the Children's Defense Fund. One that ensures every child a Healthy Start, a Head Start and a Fair Start.

1. A Healthy Start. Children need basic health care to grow into healthy, productive adults. Yet many families simply cannot afford it. Congress has voted to extend health care to all poor children by the year 2002. But what about those who get sick in the meantime? Clearly, these children cannot wait for basic health care.

2. A Head Start. Quality preschools, child care and Head Start programs give children a tremendous boost in school. The president and Congress already have expressed support for these programs. Now they must put their money where their mouths are. Only by getting children ready for school can we begin to achieve other national education goals.

3. A Fair Start. Poor children need a level playing field to succeed. Should we be the only industrialized nation not to ensure families a minimum level of economic security? We can, through jobs, refundable tax credits for families with children and stronger enforcement of child support laws.

All told, these investments will prevent thousands of child deaths and save millions of dollars in later medical, education and welfare costs. We cannot afford not to make these investments. For '92, we must commit to putting children first. And, at the very least, guarantee every child a Healthy Start, a Head Start and a Fair Start. Because the way to move our nation ahead is to keep our children from falling behind. *To join our campaign to Leave No Child Behind, call 1-800-CDF-1200.*

Kids can't vote. But you can. **THE CHILDREN'S DEFENSE FUND**

In this advertisement, the Children's Defense Fund defines child support broadly and as a national responsibility. (Children's Defense Fund)

living in another state.[9] Since the replacement of AFDC with TANF in 1996, such measures continue to accumulate at the federal and state levels.[10]

Over time, any expectation that support enforcement would allow women to be full-time mothers disappeared. Although charities had in practice expected wives and mothers to earn wages, they retained a rhetorical commitment to maternal care for children. Even that rhetoric is gone: wage earning for mothers and support collection were explicitly wedded in the Family Support Act of 1988.[11] Continuing prosecution of absent fathers thus implicitly recognizes the lack of opportunities for women to earn a "family wage" on workfare or in the labor market at large. Given the history of antidesertion reform, a male "family wage" also seems an unreliable basis for guaranteeing the welfare of women and children.

The complex prosecutorial machinery developed by antidesertion reformers and extended by later policymakers could not make breadwinners out of men who were either unable or unwilling to provide. Nevertheless, welfare reformers since the Progressive Era have looked to the bonds of marriage for a solution to women's and children's poverty. Vice President Dan Quayle's famous quip that marriage is "the best anti-poverty program" echoed an assumption underlying antidesertion campaigns since the early twentieth century. Presidents and policymakers have offered prescriptions for "encouraging marriage," including recent proposals to redirect welfare funds toward programs that would "promote and encourage marriage more aggressively among low-income people." In the twenty-first century, states are encouraging poor women to marry for money, offering to pay "marriage bonuses" to welfare recipients who tie the knot.[12]

If the antidesertion system failed to enforce male breadwinning, why did it survive for so long? It did not succeed in meeting the goal of "family preservation" or even—given the expensive system of courts and agencies—saving public funds; but perhaps it served other, largely symbolic, purposes. Certainly, early twentieth-century Jewish family reformers intended antidesertion activity to symbolize their responsible stewardship of the immigrant working class. The language of the New York State Commission on Relief for Widowed Mothers, which drafted the state's mothers' pension legislation, suggests that deserted women's initial exclusion from eligibility and subsequent deflection into the courts served to fend off fears that direct state provision to women would encourage family breakup and welfare fraud. During the period covered by this study, legal and welfare reformers seem to have entertained few doubts about the ultimate success of the antidesertion system in meeting its familial and financial goals. But after the 1930s, politicians repeatedly disregarded the advice of policy analysts who found that child-support enforcement programs had been largely ineffective. On the level of symbolic politics, however, advocating antidesertion measures may have been useful in demonstrating legislators' own abhorrence of fraud, their own devotion to conventional "family values," and even their own manly responsibility. By implicitly contrasting themselves to "deadbeat dads" enjoying the high life at the taxpayers' expense, legislators can represent themselves as dependable custodians of the public purse.

The antidesertion system did deflect many women's claims away from welfare agencies and toward the courts, thus delaying, disrupting, or forestalling altogether the granting of aid to deserted applicants. Moreover, these tactics served as a signal to poor women that their own and their children's welfare was dependent on their personal relationships to particular men. The Jewish antidesertion campaign was a message to immigrant women that they should expect Jewish husbands to be family breadwinners. But apparently, most clients of the NDB had not fully adopted the American expectation that men were to be the sole household providers. The frequently lengthy delay between their husbands' departure and their contact with the bureau suggests that they continued to view themselves and their daughters as "bread givers" also responsible for family support. They rarely expressed a sense of entitlement to a man's support, either because they had realistic expectations of their husbands or because they had not fully internalized a normative American understanding of the marriage bargain. Some women did seek freedom from domestic violence and asked for the bureau's assistance in separating from their husbands. But for most of its clients whose husbands had already left home, the NDB was a "last resort."[13] They exhausted other options before applying to a welfare agency—which then directed them toward a highly ineffective solution to their economic difficulties. Ultimately, deserted women experienced the power of the antidesertion system to shape their lives more than did the men who were its apparent targets.

The Jewish antidesertion campaign began as an attempt to defend the community's reputation and stave off immigration restriction by ensuring that poor Jewish women and children would not become a burden on the American public. By enforcing the obligations of Jewish men to their wives and children, Jewish charities aimed to construct a boundary between the Jewish community and the state. Paradoxically, the Jewish community's efforts at internal policing led to a more intimate relationship with the state. The history of the Jewish antidesertion campaign is a reminder that social policy has had many varied and unexpected origins—including even the reforms undertaken by middle-class Jewish professionals to protect their community. Their role in shaping antidesertion strategies in New York exposes the complex and syncretic roots of welfare policy in the United States.

The Jewish antidesertion story is one strand among many that shaped the way many Americans think about welfare as a matter of "encouraging marriage" rather than of addressing poverty directly. Recalling the history of the antidesertion campaign makes the coincidence of campaigns to reform welfare with anxieties about marriage and family instability more explicable. The history of deserted women's relationship to assistance programs suggests that the bonds of marriage were not a private matter; they were an integral part of the welfare system itself.

Abbreviations

NDB National Desertion Bureau

NDBCF National Desertion Bureau Case Files,
YIVO Institute for Jewish Social Research, New York, N.Y.

Introduction

1. *Personal Responsibility and Work Opportunity Reconciliation Act of 1996.*

2. Written definitions in law and social policies varied; the definition used here reflects the way desertion was defined in practice by the NDB. Women who left their husbands to escape domestic violence were also considered "deserted wives" by the NDB. For more on such cases, see Gordon, *Heroes of Their Own Lives.*

3. Kessler-Harris, *In Pursuit of Equity.* For an analysis of how the gendered imagination is also a heterosexual imagination, see Wittig, *Straight Mind.*

4. Skocpol, *Protecting Soldiers and Mothers*; Gordon, *Pitied but Not Entitled*; Ladd-Taylor, *Mother-Work*; Michel, "Limits of Maternalism"; Mink, *Wages of Motherhood*; Goodwin, *Gender and the Politics of Welfare Reform.*

5. The phrase "relations of rescue" is borrowed from Pascoe, *Relations of Rescue.* For a useful discussion of the gendered politics of rescue, see Rosenberg, "Rescuing Women and Children."

6. Bederman, *Manliness and Civilization.*

7. Glickman, "Inventing the 'American Standard of Living.' "

8. Kessler-Harris, "Gender and the Construction of Culture" and "Gendered Interventions."

9. Ayers and Lambertz, "Marriage Relations"; Oren, "Welfare of Women"; Ross, " 'Fierce Questions' "; Benson, "Living on the Margin"; Stansell, *City of Women.*

10. According to the legal scholar Martha Minow, incorporating welfare law into the conventional trajectory of family law history poses "massive interpretation problems." Minow, " 'Forming Underneath Everything,' " 839.

11. Stone, *Family, Sex and Marriage*; Degler, *At Odds*; Griswold, *Family and Divorce.*

12. Kerber, *No Constitutional Right to Be Ladies*; Basch, *In the Eyes of the Law*; Minow, " 'Forming Underneath Everything.' "

13. TenBroek, "California's Dual System of Family Law." For a British study that touches on the consequences of the poor laws for deserted women, see Thane, "Women and the Poor Law."

14. For the expansion of judges' "patriarchal" power, see Grossberg, *Governing the Hearth.*

15. For a review of the "separate spheres" literature, which often relies on a gendered public/private dichotomy, see Kerber, "Separate Spheres, Female Worlds."

16. For an exploration of the public dimension of the ostensibly private marriage relationship, see Cott, *Public Vows.*

17. Eubank, *Study of Family Desertion*, 34.

18. I used files beginning with the letters A, B, and M. They contain cases prosecuted in the United States, most of them in New York City. The NDB also pursued a much smaller group of "F" cases abroad, which I omitted from my sample for this book. Citations of case files appear with the letter and number assigned to each case by the NDB, followed by the abbreviation NDBCF (National Desertion Bureau Case Files). The Jewish Board of Family and Children's Services, which deposited the files in the YIVO Institute's archive, requires as a condition of its permission to use the files that the confidentiality of NDB clients be maintained. I have therefore changed the names of clients. Most of their real names appeared in the public press, but to meet confidentiality requirements, I have indicated case file numbers in which press clippings appear instead of citing specific articles.

Chapter One

1. Educational Alliance, *Sholom Aleykhem*, 36–38.

2. Jacobson, *Barbarian Virtues*; Bederman, *Manliness and Civilization*; Glickman, "Inventing the 'American Standard of Living.'"

3. Traverso, *Welfare Politics in Boston*, 3–4.

4. Diner, *Time for Gathering*, 49–56. The majority of Jewish immigrants came from the German states in this period, but the nineteenth-century migration also included Jews from Bohemia, Moravia, Slovakia, and Hungary. Eastern European immigrants also came to the United States before the large post-1880 influx (about 41,000 in 1870–80).

5. Cohen, *Encounter with Emancipation*, chap. 6. German Jewish leaders did not respond positively to the new immigrants at first and even contemplated supporting immigration restrictions. However, by the end of the first decade of mass immigration from eastern Europe, German Jews emerged as vigorous defenders of immigrants' rights and opponents of restrictive legislation. See Szajkowski, "*Yahudi* and the Immigrant."

6. Kuznets, "Immigration of Russian Jews"; Robles and Watkins, "Immigration and Family Separation"; Glenn, *Daughters of the Shtetl*, 48.

7. Barkai, *Branching Out*, 199, 210.

8. For a discussion of these metaphors in immigration historiography, see Gjerde, "New Growth on Old Vines."

9. Greenberg, *Jews in Russia*. For my understanding of Jewish marriage in Russia, I am particularly indebted to the pioneering work of ChaeRan Y. Freeze, *Jewish Marriage and Divorce.*

10. D. Biale, "Love, Marriage, and the Modernization of the Jews."

11. D. Biale, "Childhood, Marriage, and the Family"; Freeze, *Jewish Marriage and Divorce*, 30–35.

12. Glenn, *Daughters of the Shtetl*, 12–16.

13. Baum, Hyman, and Michel, *Jewish Woman in America*, 55–56, 65–70, 74; Ewen, *Immigrant Women in the Land of Dollars*, 52–58; Kuznets, "Immigration of Russian Jews," 78.

14. Freeze, *Jewish Marriage and Divorce*, 35.

15. D. Biale, *Eros and the Jews*, chap. 7.

16. The maskil Ayzik-Meyer Dik, for example, worried about the demoralizing effect of commercial endeavors that brought women in contact with male customers. He criticized such women for endangering the moral tone of the Jewish family and promoted the Western bourgeois family ideal of the domestic yet refined wife dependent on a sole male breadwinner. As David Roskies observes, this was the "polar opposite of what actually existed in nineteenth-century Eastern Europe and even in Dik's own household." If Dik's occupation as a writer of lowbrow romances was unusual, his relationship was typical of eastern European Jewish marriages that depended on the contributions of both spouses. Roskies, "Yiddish Popular Literature," 855.

17. The Yiddish writer Y. L. Peretz represented the strand of the Haskalah that turned away from the bourgeois aspirations of the early maskilim. Nevertheless, Peretz was a "fanatical" advocate of male breadwinning and female domesticity. M. Olgin, *Yitzhak Leibush Peretz* (New York, 1955), 14, cited in Adler, *Women of the Shtetl*, 61. As Ruth Adler speculates, Peretz may have been influenced in his critique by the example of his parents: his penurious and often absent father was an itinerant merchant, and his mother operated a notions shop to keep the family afloat. However, in his own life, Peretz exhibited some ambivalence about the kind of marriage he advocated—indeed, about marriage itself. Looking back on his life, with his one divorce and his second—not entirely happy—marriage, Peretz expressed regret that he had not remained a bachelor. Adler, *Women of the Shtetl*, 15–17, 69, 126. Although Peretz himself did not find marriage particularly satisfying, he nevertheless urged other Jewish men to fashion themselves into breadwinning husbands.

18. Parush, *Reading Jewish Women*, 42.

19. Hyman, *Gender and Assimilation*, 69–71.

20. Freeze, *Jewish Marriage and Divorce*, 153.

21. Baker, "Voice of the Deserted Jewish Woman."

22. Freeze, *Jewish Marriage and Divorce*, 233.

23. Stein, *Making Jews Modern*, 170–72.

24. Cohen, *Encounter with Emancipation*, 109.

25. I. M. Wise, *Israelite*, 5 April 1861, cited in Baum, Hyman, and Michel, *Jewish Woman in America*, 29.

26. Diner, *Time for Gathering,* 63, 81–84. For more on the phenomenon of husbands' deserting to the West, see Basch, "Relief in the Premises."

27. Cohen, *Encounter with Emancipation,* chap. 3.

28. Ibid., 121.

29. Moloney, *American Catholic Lay Groups,* 4–6.

30. Wenger, *New York Jews,* especially chap. 6.

31. Jacob Massel, "Inshurens sistem in di ordens," *Tageblat,* 11 March 1911, cited in Soyer, *Jewish Immigrant Associations,* 98.

32. The five organizations were the Hebrew Benevolent and Orphan Society, the Hebrew Benevolent Fuel Association, the Ladies' Benevolent Society of the Congregation of the Gates of Prayer, the Hebrew Relief Society, and the Yorkville Ladies' Benevolent Society. In 1946, the Jewish Social Service Association became Jewish Family Services, which in 1978 took its current form as the Jewish Board of Family and Children's Services. Romanofsky and Rubin, "Jewish Family Service," 245–55.

33. The NCJC became the National Conference of Jewish Social Service in 1919. Rubin, "Conference of Jewish Communal Service," 125–30.

34. Block, "Virtue out of Necessity," 24, 51, 64.

35. Ibid., 40–41.

36. Morris D. Waldman to Prof. Bentwich, 3 June 1950, box 1, folder 2, Morris David Waldman Papers, American Jewish Archives, Cincinnati, Ohio. Sociologist Alfred Kutzik aptly characterized the relationship of immigrant beneficiaries of and participants in Jewish charities to wealthy philanthropists this way: "Philanthropy stratified as it integrated the community." Kutzik, "Social Basis," 371.

37. Goldberg, "Gender, Religion and the Jewish Public Sphere," chap. 1.

38. Bodek, " 'Making Do.' "

39. Letters of 4, 16, and 19 February 1915, box 2, National Association of Jewish Social Workers Papers (I-88), American Jewish Historical Society, Waltham, Mass.

40. Rebekah Kohut, *As I Know Them* (Garden City, N.Y.: Doubleday, Doran, 1929), 38, cited in Rogow, *Gone to Another Meeting,* 133.

41. The NCJW did assist deserted women—for instance, when they arrived at Ellis Island. However, the organization was not a leader in antidesertion activities. For example, in 1911, the year that the NDB was established and after more than a decade of attention to desertion at the NCJC, there were neither papers nor any resolutions on desertion at the NCJW convention. *Sixth Triennial Convention of the Council of Jewish Women,* 11–19 December 1911.

42. Lee K. Frankel, "The Early Days of the Charity," n.d., box 2, Lee Kaufer Frankel Papers (P-146), American Jewish Historical Society, Waltham, Mass; Levine, "Jewish Family Desertion," 114.

43. Bijur, "Report of Committee on Desertions," *First National Conference of Jewish Charities* (11 June 1900), 57.

44. Jews were involved both in the business of prostitution and in antiprostitution

campaigns. However, there was also an antisemitic stereotype of Jewish men as procurers who preyed on innocent Christian girls. Bristow, *Prostitution and Prejudice*; Feldman, "Prostitution."

45. Quoted in R. S. Friedman, " 'Send Me My Husband,' " 9.

46. A. S. Newman, "Discussion," in *National Conference of Jewish Charities* (1910), 102.

47. Jacobson, *Whiteness of a Different Color.*

48. Sherman, "Racial Factors in Desertion," *Family*, October 1922, 145; November 1922, 166, 169; December 1922, 198–200; January 1923, 223.

49. Ibid., November 1922, 170; October 1922, 143; January 1923, 221. In blatantly racist terms, Sherman also applied this view to African Americans who had long been in the United States, arguing that emancipation had deprived them of the civilizing oversight of white men and implying that greater association with the example of white Americans would ameliorate desertion among African Americans. Ibid., January 1923, 223.

50. Regarding Slavic women, Sherman commented that "owing to their ignorance of American custom and of the English language, the women can find places [as domestic servants] only among middle-class Jews and Germans, so that their experience in the homes of others does not give them a great deal of insight into Anglo-Saxon institutions." Ibid., November 1922, 167.

51. Document dated 28 April 1903, folder labeled Desertion 1902–1909, box 115, Community Service Society Collection, Columbia University, New York, N.Y.

52. *National Conference of Jewish Charities* (1910), 104–5.

53. Most of the NDB's clients married after immigrating to the United States. Of the 300 NDB cases I read, I could determine the place of birth for 271 wives (80 percent abroad, 20 percent in the United States) and 280 husbands (80.7 percent abroad and 19.7 percent in the United States). The place of marriage is recorded in 281 of the cases (17.8 percent prior to emigration, 82.2 percent in the United States).

54. Waldman, "Family Desertion" (1905–6).

55. *National Conference of Jewish Charities* (1912), 116.

56. Certificate of Incorporation of National Desertion Bureau, 26 June 1914, Incorporation Papers (I-154), American Jewish Historical Society, Waltham, Mass.

57. "Mrs. Miriam Zunser, Author, Playwright," *New York Times*, 12 October 1951.

58. I am indebted to Charles Zunser's relatives Harriet Fraad, Rosalyn Baxandall, and Emily Wortis Leider for sharing their memories of him with me. For more on the Zunsers, see Leider, "Postscript."

59. Samuel Edelstein to Judge Jacob Panken, 20 August 1934, box 1A, folder June–October 1934, Jacob Panken Collection, Tamiment Institute Library, New York, N.Y.

60. Quoted in Auerbach, "From Rags to Robes," 255.

61. See Auerbach, "From Rags to Robes"; Drachman, *Sisters in Law.*

62. Cahan, *Bleter fun mayn leben*, 490–96. According to another account, copy for

the "Gallery" was vetted by the Educational Alliance's Legal Aid Bureau before the NDB was established and took over the responsibility of submitting copy for the column. Waldman, "Family Desertion" and "Discussion" (1910), 90–91, 98.

63. A. S. Newman, "Discussion," in *National Conference of Jewish Charities* (1910), 98–99. Whether charity workers were aware of it or not, the Talmud provided support for their strategy in a rabbinical recommendation that nonsupporting fathers of toddlers should be subject to public humiliation: "Make him stand [in public] so that everybody can see and hear him, and have him proclaim himself to be less sensitive than a raven, for a raven looks after its young, but this man does not look after his children and is unwilling to assume financial responsibility for them." This recommendation from Rav Hisda is an exception to the general Jewish prohibition against shaming a person in public. It appears in a debate over whether or not fathers are responsible for the maintenance of children under the age of six. *Talmud: Steinsaltz Edition*, 10:113.

64. Waldman, "Family Desertion" (1912), 67, 77, 92.

Chapter Two

1. Conyngton, *How to Help*, 148, 150.

2. Patterson, *America's Struggle against Poverty*, 20–34.

3. O'Neill, *Divorce in the Progressive Era*; May, *Great Expectations.*

4. Rabbino, *Back to the Home*, 146, 154.

5. It is difficult to know the actual scope of desertion. Deserted women might report themselves to be widows, unmarried, or married. A deserted woman might take a new husband without the legal requirement of a divorce from the husband who left and might describe herself simply as married. On the other hand, mutual separations might be termed desertions, depending on the perspective of the surveyor. Cultural attitudes toward separation and desertion might also shape the way women label themselves and how others understand their status. For example, the statistic usually cited for Jewish desertion comes from the U.S. Senate's 1911 *Report on the Condition of Woman and Child Wage-Earners in the United States*, which shows a higher rate of desertion and widowhood among Jewish (24 percent) women than among Italian women (12 percent). (See R. S. Friedman, "'Send My Husband to Me,'" and Glenn, *Daughters of the Shtetl*, 261.) However, it is possible that the prominence of desertion as an issue discussed in the Jewish press and community might have led to Jewish women more readily describing themselves as deserted.

In any case, as many historians have pointed out, Progressive reforms were not necessarily responses to the appearance of new problems or radically changed conditions. Certainly, many people were poor in the centuries before poverty was "discovered," to use James Patterson's term, in the Progressive Era. The process of social problem definition is ideological, and not simply an automatic response to social phenomena. For historians who take this position on Progressive Era problem definition, see Patterson, *America's Struggle against Poverty*; Gordon, *Heroes of Their Own Lives*; Rodgers, *Atlantic Crossings*.

6. Coontz, *Way We Never Were*; Gillis, *World of Their Own Making*.

7. Of course, desertion was not solely a masculine option, but women's fewer economic opportunities beyond marriage and the difficulty of traveling without a man probably made them less likely to abandon their husbands, unless a replacement was waiting in the wings. After 1882 in New York, poor relief officials had the power to compel a husband to support a wife—assuming that they could locate the husband. M. D. Smith, *Breaking the Bonds*; Basch, *Framing American Divorce*; Branscombe, *Courts and the Poor Laws*, 251.

8. Formal training in social casework began in the late 1890s, and its spread paralleled the growth in attention to desertion in the early decades of the twentieth century. Richmond, *Social Diagnosis*, 31–32.

9. *Annual Report of the Charity Organization Society* (1884), 71–72; *Annual Report of the Charity Organization Society for the Year 1887* (1888), 84–85; *Annual Report of the Charity Organization Society for the Year 1888* (1889), 81–82.

10. Taussig, *Fifty Years of Social Service*, 80–81.

11. U.S. Congress, *Congressional Record*, 21 December 1895, 280.

12. U.S. Congress, House, *Report No. 781*, 55th Cong., 2d sess., 1897–98.

13. *Statutes at Large of the United States of America*, 30:1379–80. For more on the gender and family politics of the Civil War pension program, see McClintock, "Binding Up the Nation's Wounds."

14. See, for example, the adoption, in 1903, of a uniform law of bankruptcy, which made family support a nondischargeable obligation; *Statutes at Large of the United States of America*, vol. 32, pt. 1, 798. Congress also exercised jurisdiction over desertion-related issues in Washington, D.C.

15. Richmond, "Married Vagabonds," 108, 109. The paper was first read at the National Conference of Charities and Corrections, New Haven, 1895.

16. Schneider and Deutsch, *History of Public Welfare*, 180–82; Mrs. W. Einstein, "Pensions for Widowed Mothers," 230, 241.

17. Schneider and Deutsch, *History of Public Welfare*, 182.

18. Carstens, "How to Aid," 141. This paper was first read at the New York State Conference of Charities and Correction, November 1904.

19. Breed, "Difference in the Treatment," 80–82, 85–86.

20. Ibid., 84, 90; Carstens, "How to Aid," 140–41.

21. Waldman, "Family Desertion" and "Discussion" (1910), 57, 88.

22. The Cincinnati United Jewish Charities claimed that it did provide funds for the support of deserted families, but only indirectly, through the Ohio Humane Society. Max Senior, president of the UJC, felt that this discouraged the "tendency on the part of Jews to rely upon the charitable organizations" and encouraged them instead to use the law in the form of blue-uniformed Humane Society Officers. Ibid., 85.

23. Ibid., 102.

24. Ibid., 103.

25. Breed, "Difference in the Treatment," 87.

26. Lowenstein, "Jewish Desertions," 144.

27. H. B. Einstein, "Pensions," 131; Schneider and Deutsch, *History of Public Welfare*, 185–86.

28. Breed, "Difference in the Treatment," 79.

29. For more on Jewish involvement in the mothers' pension movement and on Einstein in particular, see n. 16 above and Marcus, *American Jewish Woman*, 84–85; Leff, "Consensus for Reform"; Lubove, *Struggle*, chap. 5; Skocpol, *Protecting Soldiers and Mothers*, 425, 667.

30. Eubank, *Study of Family Desertion*, 61.

31. Colcord, *Broken Homes*, 51, 61, 130.

32. Leff, "Consensus for Reform."

33. Cited in Skocpol, *Protecting Soldiers and Mothers*, 435.

34. Eubank, *Study of Family Desertion*, 22–26; Brandt, *Five Hundred and Seventy-four Deserters*, 10; Wallstein, "Deserted and Abandoned Children"; Liebman, "Some General Aspects of Family Desertion," 201.

35. Tiffin, *In Whose Best Interest?* 103.

36. Skocpol, *Protecting Soldiers and Mothers*, chap. 8; Lubove, *Struggle*, 91–112.

37. Hebberd, Address to the National Conference, 534–35, 541. Hebberd, secretary of the State Board of Charities of New York, was appointed director of investigations for the New York State Commission on Relief for Widowed Mothers, which drafted the pension legislation, and his 1913 speech was reprinted as an appendix to the 1915 Hill-McCue Bill. Commenting on Hebberd's position, the charity worker Mary Breed worried about the example of Illinois, where deserted women had been removed from the pension rolls: "Even so the tide of desertion has not been stemmed and is said to be greater than before the passage of the original bill, which placed deserted women on the same footing as widows." Breed, "Report of the Committee," 1071.

38. *Report of the New York State Commission on Relief for Widowed Mothers*, 21.

39. The New York pension program was finally opened to deserted mothers almost a decade later, but with the stipulation that, in order to qualify, a deserted applicant must first engage in a complex and lengthy search for her husband, to be followed by prosecution if he was located. For more on the implementation of the pension program, see chap. 6.

40. Pound, "Administration of Justice"; Pound, "Individual Interests"; G. E. White, *Patterns of American Legal Thought*, 99–135; M. White, *Social Thought in America*, chap. 5; Grossberg, *Governing the Hearth*, chap. 8; Willrich, *City of Courts*, 96–115; Summers, "Pragmatic Instrumentalism."

41. Waldman, "Family Desertion" and "Discussion" (1910), 93. Technically, according to Jewish law, a divorce is not valid unless acknowledged by the wife—a technicality

that was apparently frequently overlooked. A parallel secular practice could be found in migratory or out-of-state divorces obtained unilaterally by men wishing to free themselves of legal obligations to their wives (who, ironically, could be divorced in some states on the grounds of desertion for not sharing the domicile of their absconding husbands). In an interesting turnaround, in 1983 Jewish women successfully campaigned for a law making the absence of a *ghet* a bar to civil divorce because Jewish men were withholding *ghets* as a way to extort concessions from their wives beyond what was granted in the civil court (i.e., money, reductions in alimony and child support payments, child visitation, and custody). R. Biale, *Women and Jewish Law*, 100.

42. Zunser, *National Desertion Bureau*, 2.

43. *Annual Report of the Charity Organization Society* (1902–3), 47.

44. There was considerable debate about whether abandonment should be a misdemeanor or a felony. See Baldwin, *Family Desertion*; Baldwin, "Most Effective Methods," 566–69.

45. *Annual Report of the Charity Organization Society* (1902–3), 47; Waldman, "Family Desertion" (1912), 51; Zunser, *National Desertion Bureau*, 2.

46. The act reads in part: "A parent or other person charged with the care or custody for nurture or education of a child under the age of sixteen years, who abandons the child in destitute circumstances and willfully omits to furnish necessary and proper food, clothing or shelter for such child, is guilty of a felony, punishable by imprisonment for not more than two years, or by a fine not to exceed one thousand dollars, or by both. In case a fine is imposed the same may be applied in the discretion of the court to the support of such child. Proof of the abandonment of such child in destitute circumstances and omission to furnish necessary and proper food, clothing or shelter is prima facie evidence that such omission is willful." *Penal Code*, sec. 480. The bill as proposed did not include wives because its proponents feared that the legislature would not be willing to punish desertion of a wife severely. Frankel, "Report of Committee on Desertions," 46–47.

47. Waldman, "Family Desertion" (1912), 52.

48. Liebman, "Some General Aspects of Family Desertion," 206–7.

49. *Governors Conference of the States of the Union* (1914), 187.

50. Zunser, "Family Desertion: Some International Aspects," 253.

51. Brockelbank, "Family Desertion Problem"; S. N. Katz, "Historical Perspective"; Harris, "Child Support for Welfare Families." My thanks to Michael Katz for providing me with a copy of Harris's paper.

52. "A Domestic Court," *New York Times*.

53. Rabbino, *Domestic Relations Court*, 5.

54. *New York Senate Document* 30.

55. "Want Special Court for Domestic Woes," *New York Times*.

56. *New York Senate Document* 30, 1352–54, 1418, 1425, 1428, 2438.

57. Ibid., 934, 937, 939, 1421, 3216, 3428, 3478, 3493. Much to the NCJW's cha-

grin, Julius Mayer drafted the requirement that women arrested for prostitution undergo a medical exam. For more on Jewish women's involvement with the Page Commission, see Joseph, "The Nafkeh and the Lady," 101–16. Michael Willrich attributes the founding of the Chicago domestic relations court to the efforts of women's organizations such as Jane Addams's Juvenile Protective Association and the Bureau of Personal Service. Willrich, *City of Courts*, 133–36. Addams's work on the domestic relations court was mentioned by the New York women who testified before the Page Commission. Minnie Low, who founded and ran the Bureau of Personal Service, briefly mentions her connection to the Chicago domestic relations court in the autobiographical statement she wrote for the NCJC in 1916. She also noted that "I have been a member of the Board of Directors of the National Desertion Bureau, I notice by the letterheads, for the past few years, but that . . . is an office on paper only." Minnie Low autobiographical statement, 29 February 1916, box 2, National Association of Jewish Social Workers Papers (I-88), American Jewish Historical Society, Waltham, Mass.

58. *Laws of New York*, 1910, chap. 659, sec. 74; Boushy, "Historical Development," appendix.

59. Gilfoyle, *City of Eros*, 258–59.

60. *New York Assembly Document* 54, 48.

61. Ibid., 46, 50.

62. Rabbino, *Back to the Home*, 34; "Want Special Court for Domestic Woes," *New York Times*.

63. "A Domestic Court," *New York Times*.

64. Waldman, "Family Desertion" (1912), 55.

65. For example, the president of the NDB, which relied on publicizing desertions, argued that family cases in the courts should not be publicized. Liebman, "Some General Aspects of Family Desertion," 210.

66. Private hearings and the separation of male deserters from common criminals may have preserved men's dignity, too. The premise of the *Forward*'s "Gallery of Missing Men" was that men would be mortified if their actions became known.

67. Coontz, *Way We Never Were*, 146.

68. Boushy, "Historical Development," 173.

69. Coontz, *Way We Never Were*, 147.

70. For a specific instance, see A3381, NDBCF.

71. "A Domestic Court," *New York Times*.

72. Rabbino, *Back to the Home*, 120–27.

73. Ibid., 1; Rabbino, "Domestic Relations Court."

74. *Annual Report of the Board of City Magistrates of the City of New York (Second Division) for the Year Ending December 31, 1910*, 7.

75. Rabbino, *Back to the Home*, 38.

76. Rabbino, *Domestic Relations Court*, 12.

77. Ibid., 14.

78. Waldman, "Family Desertion" and "Discussion" (1910), 88.

79. Palzer, *Handbook of Information on Non-support*, 3.

80. Collins, "Proposed Constitutional Amendment," 13.

81. Liebman, "Some General Aspects of Family Desertion," 201.

82. Waldman, "Family Desertion" and "Discussion" (1910), 87.

83. McCormick, *Party Period and Public Policy*, 311–56; Skocpol, *Protecting Soldiers and Mothers*, 261–67.

Chapter Three

1. Metzker, *Bintel Brief*, 110–12.

2. B1620, NDBCF.

3. Heinze, *Adapting to Abundance*, 23, 30.

4. There is no exact English equivalent for the Yiddish term *baleboste*. It is the feminine version of a term derived from Hebrew that translates literally into "master of the house." The closest English phrase would be "mistress of the household" or "household manager." Ibid., chap. 6.

5. Prell, *Fighting to Become Americans*, 10.

6. E. T. May, *Great Expectations*.

7. In the nineteenth century, organized labor promulgated "a new discourse of virtue, replacing a producerist republicanism with a consumerist one." Glickman, "Inventing the 'American Standard of Living.' "

8. M. May, " 'Problem of Duty.' "

9. Recent echoes of Progressive Era antidesertion reformers' arguments, but applied to middle-class men, can be found in B. Ehrenreich, *Hearts of Men*.

10. C. Brown, "Mothers, Fathers, and Children."

11. Claiming to defend the public purse, antidesertion reformers were in fact defining its social meaning as what sociologist Viviana Zelizer calls "special money." The institutionalization of rules governing the use of funds, rules that carry cultural meanings and particular conceptions of the social structure, is a crucial factor in the creation of "special money." Zelizer, "Social Meaning of Money."

12. Rabbino, *Back to the Home*, frontispiece. This aphorism appears with minor variations in most of the literature on desertion.

13. As Linda Gordon notes, there is an ironic contradiction in "the rhetoric that welfare represents deplorable 'dependence,' while women's subordination to husbands is not registered as unseemly." Gordon, "New Feminist Scholarship," 14.

14. For the phrase "other men's children," see Eubank, *Study of Family Desertion*, 34.

15. Cross, *An All-Consuming Century*, chap. 4.

16. Zunser, "Impressions of a Worker," 59.

17. Waldman, "Family Desertion" (1912), 51.

18. Marilyn Friedman comments that such research typically overlooked the significant causes of women's poverty, which lay in the "poverty of feminization," the result of inequities in the economic, legal, governmental, and social systems. M. Friedman, "Women in Poverty," 91–104.

19. Conyngton, *How to Help*, 150–51.

20. "Desertion and Unemployment," 12. Judge Jonah Goldstein agreed: "There are more desertions in good times than in times of economic stress. In times of economic stress, the husband sticks closer to home. Wives are less expensive than lady friends." J. J. Goldstein, *Family in Court*, 165. By 1910, Waldman had also become convinced that male "self-indulgence" was the main factor in desertion. Waldman, "Family Desertion" and "Discussion" (1910), 61, 81.

21. J. J. Goldstein, *Family in Court*, 163; Herzberg, "How the Jewish Charities Are Dealing," 248, 250; Carstens, "How to Aid," 141; Liebman, "Some General Aspects," 204.

22. J. J. Goldstein, *Family in Court*, 163; Colcord, *Broken Homes*, 97.

23. Brandt, *Five Hundred and Seventy-four Deserters*, 45, 63.

24. Waldman, "Family Desertion" and "Discussion" (1910), 61, 81, 96.

25. Baldwin, "Most Effective Methods," 572; *Second Capital District Conference of Charities and Correction* (1914), 1082; Gascoyne, "Judicial and Probationary Treatment," 462; Waldman, "Family Desertion" (1912), 110.

26. Colcord, *Broken Homes*, 47–48.

27. Waldman, "Family Desertion" (1905–6), 53.

28. Affachiner, "Deserted Woman," 24.

29. Rabbino, *Back to the Home*, 29–30.

30. Heinze, *Adapting to Abundance*, chap. 6.

31. Spadoni, "In the Domestic Relations Court," 15.

32. Eubank, *Study of Family Desertion*, 39.

33. Waldman, "Family Desertion" (1905–6), 53.

34. Heinze, *Adapting to Abundance*, 23, 30.

35. Waldman, "Family Desertion" (1905–6), 53.

36. "Solomon Lowenstein," Feb. 1942, box 1, folder 21, Morris David Waldman Collection, American Jewish Archives, Cincinnati, Ohio.

37. Kessler-Harris, "Gender and the Construction of Culture"; Kessler-Harris, "Gendered Interventions," 11–13, 18.

38. Ronald Edsforth describes the attitude of workers who entered factories after the "second industrial revolution": "For them, success could be measured in terms of improved income and the things they could buy with it, and extended leisure time and the pleasure they could derive from it. As they saw it, industrial work was principally a means to this kind of individual fulfillment, not part of a craft tradition that conveyed its own standards of value." Edsforth, *Class Conflict*, 34, 84, 89, 95, 114.

39. M. May, "Bread before Roses," 1–21.

40. *National Conference of Charities and Correction* (1912), 88–89.

41. Rothbart, "'Homes Are What Any Strike Is About.'"

42. Glenn, *Daughters of the Shtetl*, 12–16, 76–89.

43. B1355, NDBCF.

44. B1667, NDBCF.

45. B567, A4171, M8867, A3850, M9567, A4975, M4667, M4067, M7925, NDBCF.

46. M46, NDBCF.

47. A3671, M7139, NDBCF.

48. A6467, M7746, M4968, M5467, NDBCF.

49. M8465, M5567, B567, A4570, B2568, A767, NDBCF.

50. M5567, M2620, M6663, M10567, NDBCF.

51. B1940, M9867, NDBCF.

52. M10355, NDBCF.

53. Chauncey, *Gay New York*, 79–80.

54. Broder, "Informing the 'Cruelty,'" 42; Broder, *Tramps, Unfit Mothers, and Neglected Children*, 55–56.

55. M355, NDBCF.

56. M5267, M2863, M2967, B1867, A8867, A3269, A4471, NDBCF.

57. Gordon, "Family Violence," 464–65.

58. A4630, NDBCF.

59. Colcord, *Broken Homes*, 34, 38.

60. Doyle, "Causes of Family Desertion," 246.

61. M. May, "The 'Good Managers,'" 351–72.

62. Carstens, "How to Aid," 140; Lowenstein, "Jewish Desertions," 144; Zunser, "Impressions of a Worker," 59; Gascoyne, "Judicial and Probationary Treatment," 464.

63. Claghorn, *Immigrant's Day*, 82.

64. Liebman, "Some General Aspects of Family Desertion," 205.

65. Zunser, "Impressions of a Worker," 60.

66. Colcord, *Broken Homes*, 36.

67. Waldman, "Family Desertion" (1905–6), 53.

68. Brandt, *Five Hundred and Seventy-four Deserters*, 20.

69. Gascoyne, "Judicial and Probationary Treatment," 463; Colcord, *Broken Homes*, 154.

70. Eubank, *Study of Family Desertion*, 13.

71. "Statistics on Marital Happiness."

72. Breazale, "In Spite of Women"; Ehrenreich, *Hearts of Men*.

Chapter Four

1. M7389, NDBCF.

2. "Bread giver" here is used to refer specifically to female providers, in the sense popularized by Anzia Yezierska in her novel *Bread Givers* (1925).

3. Only for a brief time in 1919 and then in the mid-1930s did the NDB request information about deserted women's employment. Even then, the appropriate space on the application form was often left blank.

4. M7389, NDBCF. The Social Service Exchange kept a central register of clients' contacts with social agencies. Rebecca Lerman's record indicates that she had numerous contacts with a range of social service institutions up to 1929 and after 1935, but none in the intervening years.

5. M5863, NDBCF.

6. Broder, "Informing the 'Cruelty,'" 37–39, 42–43, 45.

7. M8465, NDBCF.

8. B267, NDBCF.

9. A2852, NDBCF. In this case, there were no minor children at the time Zunser asserted the wife's right to support.

10. Here, "desertion" is defined in its fullest sense, as both physical and financial withdrawal from the family. In cases where the man left home but continued to provide support, the length of time was measured only from the time he ceased to contribute. Similarly, cases of men living with their wives but contributing inadequate support are not included in these statistics.

11. Glenn, *Daughters of the Shtetl*, 66.

12. Cases in which wives complained that their husbands "never supported adequately" include M3210, M5267, M5667, M7237, M10767, NDBCF.

13. Many historians have described women's participation in the early twentieth-century urban Jewish family economy and commented on the inadequacy of male wages for supporting families. They include Glenn, *Daughters of the Shtetl*, chap. 2; J. E. Smith, "Our Own Kind," 393–411; Kessler-Harris, *Out to Work*, 123–28; Ewen, *Immigrant Women in the Land of Dollars*, chap. 6.

14. Glenn, *Daughters of the Shtetl*, 65–76.

15. M1367, NDBCF.

16. M7070, NDBCF.

17. M5667, NDBCF.

18. Stadum, *Poor Women and Their Families*, 69. In government reports on wage-earning women, they were generally divided into three categories: married; widowed or divorced; and single and unknown status. Deserted women probably resembled the second category most—women who had lost their husbands, whether to death or separation.

19. M11567, NDBCF.

20. The relatively high rate of employment by NDB applicants in domestic service is striking, given what historians have written about Jewish women's aversion to and underrepresentation in this type of work. There are several possible explanations. Deserted women, like widows and divorcees, probably had a higher rate of domestic service employment than single women in the Jewish community, as in the general

population. Such women's share in the domestic labor force increased over the first three decades of the twentieth century. Also, in briefer encounters with officials—for example, census takers—Jewish women may not have reported their paid domestic labor because it carried a stigma in the community. However, such information may have emerged in their more extended contact with agencies such as the NDB. For Jewish women's disdain for domestic service, see, for example, Kessler-Harris, *Out to Work*, 127–28; for Jewish immigrants' tendency to deny that wives were working, for reasons of respectability, see Glenn, *Daughters of the Shtetl*, 76–79; for rates of participation of women in domestic service by marital status, see Stadum, *Poor Women and Their Families*, 73.

21. Neckerman, "Family Patterns," 207–8.

22. M11667, NDBCF.

23. M7487, NDBCF.

24. M620, NDBCF.

25. M7671, NDBCF.

26. According to Alice Kessler-Harris's analysis of the meaning of a "woman's wage" in the 1920s, although three-quarters of women workers supported themselves and their families, their earnings were depressed by employers' "idealized image of marriage with its attendant financial subsidy," and debates about women's wages were "haunted by visions of married women subsidized by their husbands." Joanne Meyerowitz similarly observes that women's wages were determined by employers' assumption that "all working women lived in families where working males provided them with partial support." Kessler-Harris, *Woman's Wage*, 29–30; Meyerowitz, *Women Adrift*, 33.

27. M3662, NDBCF. The case notes make it clear that Mrs. Abel had work away from home, but they do not specify her occupation.

28. M6314, NDBCF.

29. M7389, NDBCF.

30. A8767, NDBCF.

31. A3071, NDBCF.

32. M7487, NDBCF. Similarly, Mrs. Maitz stated that she had not met her NDB lawyer at the domestic relations court because "it was impossible for her to keep the appointment at the F.C. as it just happened she obtained some work, which she needed very badly." M5508, NDBCF.

33. M9867, NDBCF.

34. M7389, NDBCF. In another case, an NDB client left a stakeout for her husband before he was sighted because "after a long period of unemployment she [had] obtained some work to be begun today." Later she explained why she had not engaged in further surveillance: "As I have been busy working, and real tired when I am throu, I had no chance to go up and watch the house." A5073, NDBCF.

35. Brandt, *Five Hundred and Seventy-four Deserters*, 10; Eubank, *Study of Family*

Desertion 22–26; Liebman, "Some General Aspects of Family Desertion," 201; Wallstein, "Deserted and Abandoned Children."

36. A4379, NDBCF. The quote is from the case file of a garment worker who reportedly felt that boarding out her children might be "a good plan" for the difficult period following her husband's departure.

37. A4275, NDBCF.

38. M10392, NDBCF.

39. M9767, NDBCF.

40. M8230, NDBCF.

41. M1234, M3967, NDBCF.

42. A4630, NDBCF.

43. A6967, NDBCF.

44. A4630, M4567, NDBCF.

45. M9237, NDBCF.

46. M2622, NDBCF.

47. Neckerman, "Family Patterns," 203. The willingness of neighbors to help in an emergency, though placing limits on their assistance, is exemplified by the case of a candy peddler who contracted pneumonia. While she was in the hospital, her family was "kept up by contributions from neighbors," but upon her return she found that "the good people [did] not want to help her" any longer. B1367, NDBCF.

48. M4567, NDBCF.

49. Among women who applied to the bureau within a month of their husbands' departure, 13.2 percent had children aged fourteen or older, and 75.2 percent had children under fourteen. Among women who applied six months or more after they had been deserted, 27.4 percent had children aged fourteen or older, and 82.2 percent had children under fourteen years of age.

50. Glenn, *Daughters of the Shtetl*, 80, 84, 264 n. 108; Ewen, *Immigrant Women in the Land of Dollars*, 105–6; Eisenstein, *Give Us Bread but Give Us Roses*, 117–38.

51. Younger children did help out—for example, by collecting coal or by helping their mothers with homework—but they did not normally bring home a paycheck until they reached their teens.

52. A4867, NDBCF.

53. M9234, NDBCF.

54. Three times as many daughters as sons contributed to family support in the cases I sampled.

55. M10276, NDBCF.

56. M8465, NDBCF.

57. The pattern of poorhouse use in the nineteenth century followed this tendency. M. B. Katz, *Poverty and Policy*, 86–87.

58. Other sources of referrals were legal and community organizations such as the

family court and the *Jewish Daily Forward.* Some women also came to the NDB on their own initiative, having learned about its existence from friends or the press.

59. Case notes such as "she will not consider accepting charitable maintenance under any circumstances except as an emergency measure" (A5268, NDBCF) or "she is ashamed to apply to the charities" (A3850, NDBCF) suggest clients' initial reluctance to use the charities. In both cases cited here, the women did turn to public assistance when they could no longer manage without it. A social work student studying the bureau in the 1930s observed that "the NDB is frequently used as a last resort." J. Levine, "Jewish Family Desertion," xvii.

60. Charles Zunser, summing up a number of attempts by the NDB to determine the causes of desertion, wrote in 1931 that, "during periods of wide-spread unemployment, there was not an untoward or unusual increase in the number of cases reported to us. . . . We have been through two such depressions—in 1914 and in 1921, aside from the present one. In neither of these years was there an unusual rise. . . . The condition of unemployment prevalent throughout the country for about six months prior to the recent lamentable crash in the stock market, simply did not register itself as far as the Bureau was concerned." "Desertion and Unemployment," 10–11.

61. As Jeanne Levine observed, the existence of desertion became known to antidesertion workers only when it was "associated with some other difficulty" that brought it to an agency's attention. J. Levine, "Jewish Family Desertion," 5.

62. Goodwin, "Gender, Politics, and Welfare Reform," chap. 3.

63. M2869, A282, A496, A4171, B1940, B1667, B1234, M7925, NDBCF.

64. M7487, M10767, NDBCF.

65. B1940, NDBCF. In this case, the NDB held to its policy and refused to help Mrs. Keller obtain a divorce. On the NDB's policy in this regard, see the end of chapter 1.

66. M10067, NDBCF.

67. M10867, NDBCF.

68. Indeed, the issue received little attention in the early twentieth century, even from feminists. Linda Gordon has argued that this silence about wife abuse in the Progressive Era amounted to a "cover-up." Gordon, *Heroes of Their Own Lives,* 21.

69. M3664, NDBCF.

70. Applicants to the NDB were not routinely asked about domestic violence. Since mentions of abuse appear in the case files only if women volunteered information and a bureau worker thought it worth recording, it is likely that the figure of 20 percent underestimates the incidence of violence in clients' families.

71. In some cases, nonsupport followed on abuse when women fought back. Men could use desertion as retaliation. Desertion followed violence in the case of Gilda Abel. According to the case notes, "woman was working & came home late—man scolded her & he beat her—she hit back—so man left." He subsequently left town to evade a warrant issued for nonsupport. M3662, NDBCF.

72. Ross, " 'Fierce Questions,' " 577–602.

73. Linda Gordon observes that "weaker members of family power structures"—women and children—made similar use of child-saving agencies by inviting intervention in familial conflicts. Gordon, *Heroes of Their Own Lives*, 296; Gordon, "Family Violence," 472.

74. M3668, NDBCF.

75. A4379, M2244, NDBCF. Battered women were not the only applicants who wished to use the NDB to regulate men's behavior beyond the contribution of support. Nonsupported women whose husbands still lived at home asked the bureau to intervene in other ways. One woman wanted it to make her husband "treat her better"; another wished it to make her husband keep "more respectable hours." A6367, M7389, NDBCF.

76. For example, one woman whose husband left to find work asked that the bureau place a personal notice in the *Forward* asking her husband to return home and mentioning that the children were crying. When he returned, she "was overjoyed and fully forgave him" for not telling her where he had gone. M5863, NDBCF.

77. B1468, NDBCF.

78. A7668, A6234, NDBCF.

79. A9234, NDBCF.

80. A3381, NDBCF.

81. When deserted women were first made eligible for mothers' pensions in New York in 1924, they were required to prove that they had searched for their husbands for five years, but this was later reduced to two years. However, even when deserted women produced the requisite affidavits, they were refused pensions (B267, NDBCF). Deserted women's experiences with mothers' pensions are discussed in chapter 6.

82. A8112, NDBCF.

83. J. Levine, "Jewish Family Desertion," 22, 51. Zunser cooperated with Levine on her thesis, corresponded with her, and participated in several interviews for the thesis.

84. B667, NDBCF.

85. M7237, NDBCF.

86. B2667, NDBCF.

87. B2568, NDBCF.

88. Spadoni, "In the Domestic Relations Court," 15.

Chapter Five

1. B67, NDBCF. Harry Linowitz was extradited from South Carolina and tried in the court of general sessions in New York City in 1915 and was sent to the penitentiary for one year. He paid a total of $10 in child support in 1917 and then left again, this time for Ohio.

2. *Laws of New York*, 1910, chap. 659, sec. 74.

3. Cases brought under the Child Abandonment Law, when the district attorney successfully secured extradition of the defendant, continued to be heard in the court of general sessions—with open proceedings and formal legal procedure—after the domestic relations court was established. In effect, by crossing state lines, a family deserter crossed into a different legal regime.

4. *People ex rel. Case v. Case* 138.

5. *People v. McAdam* 164.

6. *People v. De Wolf* 133.

7. *Goetting v. Normoyle* 191. See also *People v. Smith* 139 ("The purpose of this section is not to furnish appropriate provision for family support, but simply to prevent the family from becoming a public burden").

8. *People ex rel. Case v. Case* 138 and *People v. McAdam* 164; *People ex. rel. Heinle v. Heinle* 115 ("The purpose of the proceedings is not to adjust domestic relations but to prevent abandoned wives and children from becoming public charges"); *Germer v. Germer* 167. In the two exceptional cases, where the statute was interpreted literally, the destitution of the woman was relevant to the decisions, both written by the same judge. Thus even as Judge Tompkins exclaimed that not to read the statute literally would be "to rate the Municipal pocketbook . . . above the well-being of its wives and children!" he repeatedly stressed the "destitution" of the wife and her children ("that she is not possessed of any property; is living with a sister who is asking board, which she has no means of paying"); *People v. Goodwin* 167 and Tompkins's opinion in *People v. Gross* 161.

9. A5268, NDBCF.

10. TenBroek, "California's Dual System of Family Law"; Minow, "'Forming Underneath Everything,'" 839. See also Lewis and Levy, "Family Law and Welfare Policies"; Weyrauch, "Dual Systems of Family Law"; Harris, "Child Support for Welfare Families."

11. Mutual obligations between grandparents and grandchildren were added to the Greater New York City Charter in 1921. In 1929 the Public Welfare Law extended this statewide and added obligations between stepchildren and stepparents. Branscombe, *Courts and the Poor Laws*, 265. TenBroek wrote his articles as an argument against the last provision in particular, which by 1964 had extended the definition of liable "stepfather" to include virtually any "man-in-the-house."

12. M10167, NDBCF.

13. *Hodson, Commissioner of Public Welfare v. Stapleton* 290 New York Supplement 570 (1936), cited in Abbott, *Public Assistance*, 276.

14. M11174, M11867, NDBCF. These cases are discussed further in chapter 6.

15. Moley, *Tribunes of the People*, 213.

16. Palzer, *Handbook of Information on Non-support*, 4.

17. B2267, NDBCF.

18. A7623 (no extradition for pregnancy abandonment); M7951 (public charge); A7668 (California); M6667 and M7487 (small amount of money sent); A7668 and A6867 (woman asked to pay for extradition), NDBCF.

19. M7951, NDBCF.

20. Those two included Mr. Hornstein and one man who paid without being prosecuted. The latter case is discussed later in this chapter.

21. M11234, NDBCF.

22. *Annual Report of the Domestic Relations Court, 1933*, 21.

23. A39969, NDBCF. In this and several other cases, the NDB appears not to have completed the form, perhaps because investigation of clients was normally done by the referring agency.

24. *Annual Report of the Board of City Magistrates of the City of New York for the Year Ending December 31, 1920*; *Annual Report of the Domestic Relations Court, 1933*.

25. A summons was either mailed to the man or given to the wife with instructions to serve it on her husband; a warrant had to be served directly by an officer.

26. M7487, NDBCF. See chapter 4, text at n. 87.

27. In 1934, as part of the further "socialization" of the courts, judges adopted a policy of not wearing robes. Judges wore civilian clothing in the domestic relations courts until 1948, when all but two donned robes. One could speculate that the readoption of robes by mostly male judges may have helped distinguish their authority from the feminizing connotations of social work. "Justices Reverse a 14-Year Policy," *New York Times*.

28. Although a few female judges joined the domestic relations court bench in the 1930s, the judges were almost all male. There was some debate about whether men or women would make better judges, and whether bachelors would be preferable to married men. See "Judge Anita," *Literary Digest*; "Says Bachelor Is Unbiased," *New York Times*.

29. In Judge Edward F. Boyle's report for 1932, he estimated that at least 75 percent of respondents were either unemployed or only casually employed. *Annual Report of the Domestic Relations Court, 1933*, 17. In 1937, the NDB advised a client that the court would believe reports of her husband's unemployment and would not help her. M11267, NDBCF.

30. B2167, NDBCF. Mr. Gross had in fact admitted the month before to another judge that he earned $40–$45 per week, and his statement seems to have been the basis of Rosen's estimate.

31. M10863, NDBCF.

32. B2067, NDBCF.

33. A6355, NDBCF. Grandparents were only liable if both parents were not able to support their children. Although Mrs. Riskin was unemployed, the judge and the probation officer agreed that she was capable of being a breadwinner.

34. This estimate comes from my survey of the 1,200 family cases in the docket

books of the borough of Richmond for the years 1898–1904 and 1908–9, the only extant and accessible records available.

35. In 1917, for example, Edie Simon applied to the NDB for help in securing separate support from her husband after he had beaten her and stabbed one of their five children. Her husband, Chaim Simon, worked irregularly as a men's tailor but supported the family when employed. After an initial letter to Mr. Simon requesting a meeting, the bureau decided to drop the case. In 1917, it did not yet believe that arranging separations for adequately supported battered wives was their responsibility. M1767, NDBCF.

36. In 1923, when Batya Hirsher left her abusive husband, a butcher, and asked the NDB to arrange separate support for herself and her three children, the bureau responded by sending one of its male investigators to extract a promise that Mr. Hirsher would stop assaulting his wife. Although willing to go to greater lengths to intervene than in the case of Edie Simon, the bureau kept its focus on reconciliation and declined to arrange a separation when nonsupport itself was not part of the wife's complaint. This was a case where the bureau basically continued its earlier practice in regard to battered women who left their husbands. M4545, NDBCF.

37. A843, NDBCF.

38. Zunser, "Family Court Bill."

39. M10067, NDBCF.

40. Even before judges were empowered to issue orders of protection in 1933, they could make staying away from the wife a condition of probation.

41. M2244, NDBCF.

42. This changed in 1933, when these courts became the family division of a domestic relations court system that encompassed the children's court as well. Courts were added that year in Richmond and Queens, and ten justices split their time between the children's and family divisions in the five boroughs. With only one justice sitting in each borough's family division at a time and with caseloads increasing in the 1930s, it is clear that the judges could devote little time to each case. "Domestic Relations Court," *Bulletin of the New York Academy of Medicine*, 68.

43. *Annual Report of the Domestic Relations Court, 1933*, 25.

44. "Domestic Relations Court," *Bulletin of the New York Academy of Medicine*, 75.

45. *Annual Report of the Domestic Relations Court, 1936*, 86.

46. In practice, there was little difference between being placed under supervision or "probationary oversight" and being placed on probation. However, ordinary probation was entered on a man's criminal record, whereas supervision or oversight was not.

47. The sentencing options available to domestic relations court judges are described in Zunser, "Domestic Relations Courts," 1–12.

48. *Annual Report of the Board of City Magistrates of the City of New York for the Year Ending December 31, 1920*, 62.

49. Ibid., 62. When several officers were out sick, the caseload per remaining officer could rise to between 440 and 500 at one time.

50. *Annual Report of the Domestic Relations Court, 1936*, 36.

51. The Bronx domestic relations court, created in 1919, did not have an alimony bureau. Support ordered from that court and from the Richmond magistrates' court were dispensed in Manhattan, while women from Queens used the Brooklyn bureau.

52. *Annual Report of the Board of City Magistrates of the City of New York for the Year Ending December 31, 1920*, 64.

53. Mr. Kerr paid $14 in 1917 and paid on an $8 per week court order irregularly in 1918 and 1919; there was no record of further payments. M7237, NDBCF.

54. *Annual Report of the Domestic Relations Court, 1936*, 86. If anything, this underestimates the number of recurrent cases, since it does not include readjournments in cases in which men promised, but were not actually ordered, to pay. New arraignments include cases previously settled with failed "adjustments" or "reconciliations" arranged by the probation officer or judge, so the proportion of new cases heard was probably lower than the figure indicates.

55. *Annual Report of the Board of City Magistrates of the City of New York for the Year Ending December 31, 1920*, 63.

56. Harris, "Child Support for Welfare Families."

Chapter Six

1. M10567, NDBCF. No author or date is given. The lyrics' contents and position in the case file suggest that they were written in the early 1930s. Charles Zunser reportedly inherited his father's talent for writing amusing verse. He had the most regular access to the files and was remembered as a "brilliant humorist" by Morris Waldman. "Presentation by Morris Waldman at the Fiftieth Anniversary Dinner," box 6, folder 4, Morris David Waldman Papers, American Jewish Archives, Cincinnati, Ohio.

2. The Jewish Social Service Association reported that between 1910 and 1929 desertion cases declined from 10.5 percent to 6.7 percent of its caseload, and the NDB took credit for the reduction. Zunser, "Family Desertion: Some International Aspects," 246.

3. In addition, some women received indirect financial assistance in the form of child care in a day nursery or an orphanage. However, it is difficult to determine from the case files who paid for such services. The woman herself, her husband, relatives, the child-caring institution, a charity, and the city are all occasionally mentioned as bearing the costs, but generally the payer is not specified in the NDB files. Many bureau clients also used medical services, some of which may have been paid for by charities, but the files almost never specify who paid for hospital stays and doctors' bills.

4. Judging by the explicit evidence in the case files, most NDB clients received no

monetary relief from any public or private agency. However, some may have received assistance without it being recorded by the NDB.

5. A6568, NDBCF.

6. B168, NDBCF.

7. M245, NDBCF.

8. M6667, NDBCF.

9. A4379, NDBCF. Bypassing the JCCB, Ida Stern boarded out the children herself.

10. M8230, NDBCF.

11. M7265, NDBCF. In fact, the client did attend to "household duties," though not necessarily her own; she worked as a housekeeper.

12. M7603, NDBCF.

13. Cases include B1867 (UHC found son a job); A7668 (aid discontinued once when the daughter was employed and on another occasion when the son received compensation for an accident); A8067 (expectations that both daughters and sons would support their mother and siblings), NDBCF.

14. A7668, NDBCF.

15. A8067, NDBCF.

16. Cases include M9867 (father-in-law expected to contribute) and A8112 and M10567 (applications for assistance denied because women would not cooperate in contacting relatives), NDBCF.

17. M1567, NDBCF.

18. M10500, NDBCF.

19. B467, NDBCF. Later, the woman did have her husband arrested. He was ordered to provide support, and on this basis her requests for relief continued to be denied. However, her husband did not pay, and eventually the woman ended up on relief.

20. M10863, NDBCF.

21. B2367, NDBCF.

22. B267, NDBCF.

23. A6967, NDBCF.

24. M6234, NDBCF. See also the recommendation in M496, NDBCF, that "all relief should be discontinued" after the man made a single payment of $4; he then disappeared and never sent another payment.

25. Ephraim, "Introduction"; Morris and Freund, *Trends and Issues*, 287–88; Walkowitz, "Making of a Feminine Professional Identity."

26. Kovarsky, "Current Purposes and Goals."

27. B1940, NDBCF.

28. *New York Legislative Document* 88 (1924), 19.

29. *Laws of New York*, 1924, chap. 458.

30. U.S. Department of Labor, Children's Bureau, *Mothers' Aid, 1931*; A3969, B267, M7746, NDBCF.

31. Apparently, the implementation of the law admitting deserted women into the pension program was delayed. In 1925, an NDB client was told that the Board of Child Welfare could not implement it yet. B267, NDBCF.

32. By then, the mothers' pension program had been subsumed under Aid to Dependent Children.

33. A8112, NDBCF.

34. M10967, NDBCF. See also M9867, M10567, NDBCF.

35. U.S. Department of Labor, Children's Bureau, *Mothers' Aid, 1931*, 4.

36. Most states either had a specific cap or no cap at all. Ibid.

37. B2267, NDBCF.

38. Caccavajo, *Guide to the Municipal Government*, 92.

39. M7446, NDBCF.

40. U.S. Department of Labor, Children's Bureau, *Mothers' Aid, 1931*, 17–18.

41. A3939, NDBCF.

42. Goodwin, "Differential Treatment," 18, 20. My speculation about the effect of the antidesertion movement on mothers' pension programs was stimulated by Theda Skocpol's comment to me that the timing of mothers' pension legislation in various states may have been related to the existence of domestic relations courts. I suspect that antidesertion reforms more effectively influenced the scope, rather than the timing, of such legislation.

43. This figure represents all aid extended to deserted women in my NDB sample after 1931 until the end of their case files, virtually all of which trail off before 1940. Occasionally, a file was reopened briefly after that date, when a former client applied for some form of assistance (see the story of Ora Chaim later in this chapter for an example).

44. Coll, *Safety Net*, 30.

45. Schneider and Deutsch, *History of Public Welfare*, 293–342. The EHRB operated until 1937, when it was incorporated into the Department of Public Welfare.

46. The EHRB's praise for the role of domestic relations courts in saving the city money is recorded in *Annual Report of the Domestic Relations Court, 1936*, 40.

47. J. Levine, "Jewish Family Desertion," xiii, 51, 80; *Manual of Policies*, 56.

48. B2568, NDBCF. See chapter 4, text at n. 87.

49. M11067, NDBCF. Mrs. Unman first complained to the domestic relations court in 1929, before her husband left in 1931. In the ensuing years, the couple was in court many times, and the NDB record indicates that in 1945 Mrs. Unman was still being referred to the domestic relations court by welfare agencies.

50. A5268, NDBCF.

51. M10567, NDBCF.

52. Ibid. Although Mr. Leitner did receive home relief a month later, his initial

application was rejected; Dora reported that "because of this several of the man's communist friends called at her home and told her that the man will obtain relief in spite of her and threatened her with bodily injury if she attempts to complain at court again." Mr. Leitner's paramour was also involved in this vindictive cycle, threatening to have Dora's relief discontinued if Mr. Leitner were not released from jail. Dora Leitner was periodically on relief and in the domestic relations court until at least 1946, when she severed her relationship with the NDB. An NDB caseworker responded to her withdrawal by noting that she "appears to be very silly and shallow and mistrusts even [the National Desertion] Bureau."

53. M10392, NDBCF.

54. Ibid.; Sokol, "Financial Resources."

55. For example, A11167, M7237, M11567, M11622, NDBCF.

56. M7237, NDBCF.

57. M11174, M11867, NDBCF. The fact that the daughters were not contributing to the family's support leads to two different speculations. On the one hand, we could take them as evidence that working-class daughters contributed much less consistently to their families' support than historians have assumed. On the other hand, a more likely interpretation is that most daughters did contribute and that these daughters ran afoul of both their families and the law by evading their traditional responsibilities.

58. B1468, NDBCF.

59. A282, NDBCF.

60. A11167, NDBCF.

61. Wenger, *New York Jews*, 155–165, 204.

62. Zukerman, "Role of the Public Agency."

63. *Annual Report of the Domestic Relations Court, 1933*, 28, 32–33. My familiarity with the post-1933 court system comes from reading the Lawrence B. Dunham Papers, Rockefeller Archive Center, Sleepy Hollow, N.Y.

64. *Annual Report of the Domestic Relations Court, 1933*, 34; Zunser, "New Domestic Relations Court." The domestic relations court would enforce alimony orders from a higher court only if the woman lacked the means to proceed in that court (Zunser, "New Domestic Relations Court," 377).

65. This client had once lived on upper Fifth Avenue with her husband and had been a volunteer "social worker" at Beth Israel Hospital. M11234, NDBCF.

66. Comments by both the NDB and the district attorney using this term can be found in A3850, NDBCF.

Epilogue

1. " 'Most Wanted' for Child Support," *New York Times*; "Child Support Crackdown Shows Success and Limits," *New York Times*; "Poster Parents: On the Lam," *USA Today*.

2. Coll, *Safety Net*, 105.

3. Ibid., 115.

4. The bills proposed in the U.S. Senate in 1941, 1943, and 1945 were not passed. The Uniform Support of Dependents Law allowed a complaint filed in one state to be heard in another state, avoiding the necessity of extraditing the deserter. It was subsequently passed by ten other states. After 1950, most states adopted a similar law, the Uniform Reciprocal Enforcement of Support Act. S. N. Katz, "Historical Perspective on Child-Support Laws," 17–18.

5. Coll, *Safety Net*, 164.

6. Ibid., 222.

7. Some states have also adopted the practice of publicizing the names and pictures of nonsupporting men, using the tactic that the NDB hoped would discourage desertion and shame men into paying. The Alaska program adopted the acronym SCROOGE, which stands for "Support Children, Remember Obligations, or Get Embarrassed." *Marketplace*, National Public Radio, 10 October 1991.

8. S. N. Katz, "Historical Perspective on Child-Support Laws," 24. Three years after NOLEO was implemented, the support collection rate from divorced, separated, or deserting fathers was only 18.3 percent. Coll, *Safety Net*, 185. Subsequent legislation hardly improved on that figure. In the mid-1990s, Texas, which revokes the driver's and professional licenses of nonsupporters, had—at 18.5 percent—one of the best collection rates. Advocates for tougher enforcement legislation in the 1970s and 1980s predicted that it would result in greater paternal responsibility by punishing nonsupporters, and that it would thus decrease the number of women on welfare and the financial burden carried by the state. But research conducted by Deborah Harris reveals that it in fact achieved none of these goals. Harris, "Child Support for Welfare Families."

9. "Too Many Offenses Are Made U.S. Crimes, Rehnquist Says," *New York Times*.

10. ADC became Aid to Families with Dependent Children (AFDC) in 1962. TANF stands for Temporary Assistance for Needy Families. Some policymakers predict that as TANF recipients reach their time limits, support enforcement measures will increasingly replace welfare grants. See "Child-Support Collection Net Usually Fails," *New York Times*.

11. M. B. Katz, *Price of Citizenship*, chap. 3.

12. "Welfare Chief Is Hoping to Promote Marriage," *New York Times*. Boo, "Marriage Cure," 107–8. President Bill Clinton advocated increased child-support collection and encouraging marriage in a number of speeches, including his first State of the Union address in January 1993. Vice President Dan Quayle's comment was made in an address to the Commonwealth Club in San Francisco on 19 May 1992. For "marriage bonuses," see Koontz, *Marriage, a History*, 287; Hays, *Flat Broke with Children*, 238. A useful discussion of the politics of child-support enforcement can be found in Mink, *Wages of Motherhood*, 187–89.

13. J. Levine, "Jewish Family Desertion," xvii.

bibliography

Manuscript Collections

Cincinnati, Ohio
- American Jewish Archives
  - Morris David Waldman Papers

New York, N.Y.
- Columbia University
  - Community Service Society Collection
  - Rare Book and Manuscript Library
- Tamiment Institute Library
  - Jacob Panken Collection
- YIVO Institute for Jewish Social Research
  - National Desertion Bureau Case Files
  - Charles Zunser Papers

Sleepy Hollow, N.Y.
- Rockefeller Archive Center
  - Bureau of Social Hygiene Records
  - Lawrence B. Dunham Papers

Waltham, Mass.
- American Jewish Historical Society
  - Lee Kaufer Frankel Papers
  - Incorporation Papers
  - National Association of Jewish Social Workers Papers

Cases, Statutes, and Legislative Documents

Goetting v. Normoyle 191 New York 369 (1908)

People v. De Wolf 133 New York App. Div. 879 (1909)

People v. Smith 139 New York App. Div. 361 (1910)

People ex. rel. Heinle v. Heinle 115 New York Misc. 469 (1921)

People ex rel. Case v. Case 138 New York Misc. 131 (1930)

People v. Gross 161 New York Misc. 514 (1936)

People v. McAdam 164 New York Misc. 800 (1937)

Germer v. Germer 167 New York Misc. 882 (1938)

People v. Goodwin 167 New York Misc. 627 (1938)

Laws of New York, 1910, chap. 659, sec. 74

Laws of New York, 1924, chap. 458

Penal Code of New York, 1905, chap. 168, sec. 480
New York Assembly Document 54 (1910)
New York Legislative Document 88 (1924)
New York Senate Document 30 (1909)
New York Senate Document 57 (1914)
Congressional Record, 21 December 1896
U.S. House of Representatives, *Report No. 781*, 55th Congress, 2d Session (1897–98)
Statutes at Large of the United States of America, vol. 30 (1899)
Statutes at Large of the United States of America, vol. 32, pt. 1 (1903)
Personal Responsibility and Work Opportunity Reconciliation Act of 1996, Pub. L. No. 104–193, 42 U.S.C. 601 (1996)

Primary Sources

Abbott, Edith. "Abolish the Pauper Laws." *Social Service Review* 8 (March 1934): 1–16.
——. *Public Assistance*. Vol. 1. Chicago: University of Chicago Press, 1940.
Abbott, Grace. "Recent Trends in Mothers' Aid." *Social Service Review* 8 (June 1934): 191–210.
Affachiner, Rebecca G. "The Deserted Woman." *Jewish Charity* 5 (October 1905): 23–24.
Annual Report of the Board of City Magistrates of the City of New York for the Year Ending December 31, 1920.
Annual Report of the Charity Organization Society of the City of New York. 1884–1903.
Annual Report of the Domestic Relations Court of the City of New York. 1933–39.
Annual Report of the Municipal Court of Philadelphia. 1914.
Annual Report of the New York City Magistrates' Court. 1909–32.
Aumann, F. R. "Domestic Relations Courts in Ohio." *Journal of the American Judicature Society* 15 (October 1931): 89–93.
Baldwin, William H. "The Canadian Extradition Treaty and Family Deserters." *Journal of Criminal Law and Criminology* 12 (1921–22): 199–212.
——. *Family Desertion and Non-support Laws*. Washington, D.C.: Associated Charities, 1904.
——. "Making the Deserter Pay the Piper: The District of Columbia Plan of Paying Prisoners' Wages to Their Deserted Wives." *Survey* 23 (20 November 1909): 249–52.
——. "The Most Effective Methods of Dealing with Cases of Desertion and Non-support." *Journal of the American Institute of Criminal Law* 8 (1917–18): 564–75.
——. "The Movement to Prevent Family Desertion." *City Club Bulletin* (Philadelphia) 6 (12 February 1913): 250–53.
Bartelme, Mary M. "The Opportunity for Women in Court Administration." *Annals of the American Academy of Political and Social Science* 52 (March 1914): 188–90.

Bielefeld, Rachel. "With the Pension Agent." *Jewish Charity* 5 (October 1905): 18–19.

Bijur, Nathan. "Report of Committee on Desertions." In *First National Conference of Jewish Charities in the United States: Proceedings*, 52–69. Chicago, 1900.

Bonniwell, Eugene C. "Proposed Legislation in Pennsylvania." *City Club Bulletin* (Philadelphia) 6 (February 1913): 253–56.

Borah, William E. "The Lawyer and the Public." *American Bar Association Journal* 2 (October 1916): 776–88.

"B. Rabbino Is Dead; Welfare Worker." *New York Times*, 25 November 1933.

Bradway, John S. *Law and Social Work: An Introduction to the Study of the Legal-Social Field for Social Workers*. Chicago: University of Chicago Press, 1929.

Brandt, Lilian. *Five Hundred and Seventy-four Deserters and Their Families: A Descriptive Study of Their Characteristics and Circumstances*. New York City: Charity Organization Society, 1905.

Breckinridge, Sophonisba P. *The Family and the State: Selected Documents*. 1934. Reprint, New York: Arno Press and New York Times, 1972.

——. "Neglected Widowhood in the Juvenile Court." *American Journal of Sociology* 16 (July 1910): 53–87.

Breed, Mary. "The Difference in the Treatment of the Problem of Widows, and That of Deserted Wives." In *Eleventh New York State Conference of Charities and Correction: Proceedings*, 76–90. Rochester, N.Y.: 15–17 November 1910.

——. "Report of the Committee on the Relief of the Poor in their Homes." In *Second Capital District Conference of Charities and Correction: Proceedings*, 1069–91. Albany, N.Y., 1914.

Brockelbank, W. J. "The Family Desertion Problem across State Lines." *Annals of the American Academy of Political and Social Science* 383 (May 1969): 23–33.

"Broken Affections as Repaired in Cleveland." *Literary Digest*, 31 March 1923, 56, 58–60.

Brown, Robert C. "The Duty of the Husband to Support the Wife." *Virginia Law Review* 18 (June 1932): 823–49.

Buttenweiser, Helen. "Law and the Social Worker." *Jewish Social Service Quarterly* 25 (September 1948): 143–47.

"A Bureau for Husband Finding." *Survey* 28 (11 May 1912): 265–66.

Bureau of Municipal Research, Philadelphia. *Domestic Relations Division of the Municipal Court of Philadelphia*. Philadelphia, 1930.

——. *Filing of Social Case Records in the Municipal Court of Philadelphia*. Philadelphia, 1930.

——. *History and Functions of the Municipal Court of Philadelphia*. Philadelphia, 1930.

Caccavajo, Joseph, comp. *Guide to the Municipal Government, City of New York*. Brooklyn, N.Y.: Brooklyn Daily Eagle, 1924.

Cahan, Abraham. *Bleter fun mayn leben*. Vol. 4. New York: *Forward* Association, 1928.

——. *The Education of Abraham Cahan*. Translated by Leon Stein et al. Philadelphia: Jewish Publication Society of America, 1969.

Calhoun, John W. "The Courts of Domestic Relations." *St. Louis Law Review* 7 (1922): 152–58.

Carstens, C. C. "How to Aid Deserted Wives." *Jewish Charity* 4 (February 1905): 139–43.

——. "Bringing the Wife Deserter to Terms." *New Boston*, March 1911, 482–84.

"The Case of the Widowed Mothers." *Survey* 22 (12 June 1909): 400–401.

"Charles Zunser, 94, a Family Lawyer." *New York Times*, 19 May 1976.

"Child-Support Collection Net Usually Fails." *New York Times*, 17 July 1997.

"Child Support Crackdown Shows Success and Limits." *New York Times*, 14 April 1995.

Claghorn, Kate Holladay. *The Immigrant's Day in Court*. 1923. Reprint, New York: Arno Press and New York Times, 1969.

Colcord, Joanna C. *Broken Homes: A Study of Family Desertion and Its Social Treatment*. New York: Russell Sage Foundation, 1919.

——. "Desertion and Non-support in Family Case Work." *Annals of the American Academy of Political and Social Science* 77 (May 1918): 91–102.

Collins, Hon. Cornelius F. "The Proposed Constitutional Amendment—Effect upon the Children's Court and Court of Domestic Relation." *Legal Aid Review* 17 (January 1919): 8–15.

"Compelling Deserters to Support Their Children." *Survey* 30 (28 June 1913): 431–32.

"Conserving the Family." *Outlook*, 16 July 1910, 550.

Conyngton, Mary. *How to Help: A Manual of Practical Charity*. New York: Macmillan, 1909.

Cummings, John. *Poor Laws of Massachusetts and New York*. New York: Macmillan, 1895.

DeLacy, William H. "Making Wife Desertion Unpopular: The Working of the Non-support Law of the District of Columbia." *New Boston*, March 1911, 484–85.

"The Deserted." *Survey* 33 (19 December 1914): 322–23.

"Desertion and Unemployment: An Exchange of Letters between Dr. Billikopf and Mr. Zunser." *Jewish Social Service Quarterly* 7 (March 1931): 10–12.

"Desertion Bureau Aide Quits." *New York Times*, 11 June 1948.

"A Domestic Court." *New York Times*, 30 January 1909.

"The Domestic Relations Court." *Bulletin of the New York Academy of Medicine* 12 (1936): 59–85.

"The Domestic Relations Court." *New York Times*, 2 September 1910.

Doyle, Michael Francis. "Causes of Family Desertion." *City Club Bulletin* (Philadelphia) 6 (February 1913): 246–48.

Dyson, Verne. "She Brings Husband to Time." *American Magazine*, April 1916, 53–54.

Educational Alliance. *Sholom Aleykhem tsu Immigranten*. New York: Educational Alliance, 1903.

Edwards, Richard Henry. *Popular Amusements*. New York: Association Press, 1915.

Einstein, Hannah B. "Pensions." *Jewish Charity* 3 (March 1904): 131–33.

Einstein, Mrs. William. "Pensions for Widowed Mothers as a Means of Securing for Dependent Children the Benefits of Home Training and Influence." In *Eleventh New York State Conference of Charities and Correction: Proceedings*, 224–46. Rochester, N.Y.: 1910.

Eliot, Ada. "Deserted Wives." *Charities Review*, October 1900, 346–48.

Eubank, Earle Edward. *A Study of Family Desertion*. Chicago: University of Chicago Press, 1916.

"Family Deserter Brought to Book." *Survey* 30 (12 April 1913): 57–58.

"Family Desertion in Manitoba." *Survey* 27 (22 June 1912): 456–67.

Frankel, Lee K. "Report of Committee on Desertions." In *Fourth Biennial Session of the National Conference of Jewish Charities in the United States: Proceedings*, 46–63. Philadelphia, 1906.

Gascoyne, John J. "Judicial and Probationary Treatment of Cases of Non-Support of Family." In *39th National Conference of Charities and Correction: Proceedings*, 462–64. Cleveland, 1912.

Gemmill, William N. "Chicago Court of Domestic Relations." *Annals of the American Academy of Political and Social Science* 52 (March 1914): 115–23.

——. "Employment and Compensation of Prisoners." *American Bar Association Journal* 2 (January 1916): 103–15.

Goldstein, Jonah J. *The Family in Court*. New York: Clark Boardman, 1934.

Goldstein, Monroe M. "Desertion." In *Seventh Biennial Session of the National Conference of Jewish Charities: Proceedings*, 57–123. Cleveland, 1912.

Governors' Conference of the States of the Union: Proceedings. 1911, 1912, 1914, 1926.

"A Half Million Dollars in Widows' Pensions." *Survey* 33 (26 December 1914): 336.

Hall, Fred S., and Elisabeth W. Brooke. *American Marriage Laws in Their Social Aspects*. New York: Russell Sage Foundation, 1919.

Harry, T. Everett. "A Repairer of Homes." *Harper's Weekly*, 8 August 1908, 14.

Hebberd, Robert W. Address to the National Conference on the Education of Backward, Truant, Delinquent, and Dependent Children, Held at Buffalo, N.Y., 28 August 1913. Reprinted in *Annual Report of the State Board of Charities for the Year 1913, Senate Document* 57 (1914).

——. "Supervision of Charities in New York." *Annals of the American Academy of Political and Social Science*. Reprint no. 423, May 1904.

Herzberg, Max. "How the Jewish Charities Are Dealing with the Problem." *City Club Bulletin* (Philadelphia) 6 (February 1913): 248–50.

Hexter, Maurice. "The Business Cycle, Relief Work, and Desertion." *Jewish Social Service Quarterly* 1 (February, May 1924): 3–33, 27–56.

Hoffman, Charles W. "Domestic Relations Courts and Divorce." *Delinquent* 7 (February 1917): 1–5.

Hunter, Joel DuBois. "Desertion and Non-support by Fathers in Mothers' Aid Cases." In *National Conference of Social Work: Proceedings*, 308–9. Atlantic City, N.J., 1919.

Johnson, Eleanor Hope. "The Deserted Children." *Survey* 26 (24 June 1911): 466.

"Judge Anita." *Literary Digest*, 8 May 1915, 112–15.

"Justices Reverse a 14-Year Policy." *New York Times*, 17 June 1948.

Kirchway, George W. "Social Work and the Law: Forms of Cooperation between Law and Social Work." In *National Conference of Social Work: Proceedings*, 181–89. Cleveland, 1926.

"Levy to Don Court Robe." *New York Times*, 18 June 1948.

Liebman, Walter H. "Some General Aspects of Family Desertion." *Journal of Social Hygiene* 1, no. 2 (April 1920): 197–212.

Lowenstein, Solomon. "Jewish Desertions." *Jewish Charity* 4 (February 1905): 143–45.

Lundberg, Emma Octavia. "The New York Temporary Emergency Relief Administration." *Social Service Review* 6 (December 1932): 545–66.

——. "Who Are the New York Emergency Relief Families?" *Social Service Review* 8 (December 1934): 616–27.

McCord, Clinton P. "The Psychopathic Laboratory in the Administration of Justice." *Delinquent* 7 (November 1917): 7–13.

McLean, Francis H. "New Views on Desertion." *Survey* 26 (11 July 1911): 476.

Madeira, Mrs. Louis C. "What Family Desertion Costs the Community in Dependent Children, Family Poverty, and Dollars." *City Club Bulletin* (Philadelphia) 6 (February 1913): 244–46.

Maguire, John MacArthur. *The Lance of Justice: A Semi-centennial History of the Legal Aid Society, 1876–1926*. Cambridge, Mass.: Harvard University Press, 1928.

Manual of Policies Relating to Eligibility for Relief. New York: City of New York Emergency Relief Bureau, 1936.

"Minnesota's Child Welfare Report." *Delinquent* 7 (June 1917): 12–13.

Moley, Raymond. *Tribunes of the People: The Past and Future of the New York Magistrates' Courts*. New Haven, Conn.: Yale University Press, 1932.

"Monroe Goldstein, Theatrical Lawyer." *New York Times*, 3 January 1960.

"Morris Waldman, a Jewish Leader." *New York Times*, 8 September 1963.

"'Most Wanted' for Child Support." *New York Times*, 11 July 1993.

"Mrs. Miriam Zunser, Author, Playwright." *New York Times*, 12 October 1951.

National Conference of Charities and Correction: Proceedings. Cleveland, 1912; Memphis, Tenn., 1914.

National Conference of Jewish Charities: Proceedings. Chicago, 1900; Philadelphia, 1906; St. Louis, 1910; Cleveland, 1912.

New York State Conference of Charities and Correction: Proceedings. St. Louis, 1910.
Olson, Harry. "Address by Hon. Harry Olson." *City Club Bulletin* (Philadelphia) 6 (January 1913): 135–36.
O'Neill, Frances E., and Rev. Ralph J. Glover. "Report on a Study of One Hundred Cases of Desertion." *Family* 9 (January 1929): 287–91.
Oppenheimer, Reuben. "Domestic Relations Courts—a Study in Americana." *Social Service Review* 4 (1930): 17–22.
Palzer, Nathaniel J. *Handbook of Information on Non-support, Desertion and Illegitimacy.* New York: Charity Organization Society of the City of New York, 1916.
"Pensioning Widows." *Jewish Charity* 4 (January 1905): 113–14.
Perkins, Willis B. "Family Courts." *Michigan Law Review* 17 (1919): 378–81.
"Port of Missing Husbands Reunites Parted Families." *New York Times,* 23 November 1924.
"Poster Parents: On the Lam." *USA Today,* 14 May 1991.
Pound, Roscoe. "Individual Interests in the Domestic Relations." *Michigan Law Review* 14 (January 1916): 176–96.
——. "The Administration of Justice in the Modern City." *Harvard Law Review* 27 (1912–13): 302–28.
"Probation for All Emigrant Husbands." *Survey* 30 (21 June 1913): 385–86.
Rabbino, Bernhard. *Back to the Home.* New York: n.p., 1933.
——. "Desertion from a Legal Standpoint." *Jewish Charity* 5 (December 1905–January 1906): 55–57.
——. "Domestic Relations Court." Paper read before a Joint Committee of the Board of City Magistrates of the First and Second Division on Charter Revision at the Seventh District Court, Manhattan, 30 June 1908.
——. *Domestic Relations Court: Arguments in Favor of Its Establishment; a Plea for the Preservation of the Home.* New York: Hebrew Standard Press, 1909.
Report of the New York State Commission on Relief for Widowed Mothers. Albany, N.Y.: J. B. Lyon, 1914.
Richmond, Mary E. "Married Vagabonds." *Lend a Hand* 16 (January–June 1896): 103–10.
——. *Social Diagnosis.* New York: Russell Sage Foundation, 1917.
Rippin, Jane Deeter. "The Family Court." *Journal of the American Institute of Criminal Law and Criminology* 9 (May 1918–February 1919): 187–92.
Rosenbaum, Bernard. "Marital Counseling as the Mutual Concern of Court and Family Agency." *Jewish Social Service Quarterly* 25 (December 1948): 243–53.
Rothenberg, Charles. *New York Law of Alimony.* New York: Prentice-Hall, 1932.
Rousseau, Victor. "The Court of Sorrows." *Harper's Weekly,* 30 May 1908, 14–16.
"Says Bachelor Is Unbiased." *New York Times,* 15 January 1911.
Second Capital District Conference of Charities and Correction: Proceedings. Albany, N.Y., 1914.

Sherman, Corrine. "Racial Factors in Desertion." *Family*, October 1922, 143–47; November 1922, 165–70; December 1922, 197–201; January 1923, 221–25.

Sixth Triennial Convention of the Council of Jewish Women: Proceedings. Philadelphia, 11–19 December 1911.

Smith, Reginald Heber. *Justice and the Poor*. 1919. Reprint, New York: Arno Press and New York Times, 1971.

Sokol, Philip. "Financial Resources as a Matter of Legal Right." *Jewish Social Service Quarterly* 25 (September 1948): 148–54.

Solenberger, Alice Willard. *One Thousand Homeless Men*. New York: Russell Sage Foundation, 1911.

Spadoni, Adriana. "In the Domestic Relations Court: An Experiment with a Special Court for Dealing with Family Affairs." *Collier's*, 26 August 1911, 15, 27.

"Statistics on Marital Happiness." *American Hebrew*, 7 April 1916, 636.

Stewart, S. V. "Extradition." In *Governors' Conference of the States of the Union: Proceedings*, 182–201. Madison, Wis., 1914.

The Talmud: The Steinsaltz Edition. Vol. 10: *Tractate Ketubot, Part IV*. New York: Random House, 1994.

Taussig, Frances. *Fifty Years of Social Service: The History of the United Hebrew Charities of the City of New York*. New York: Jewish Social Service Association, 1926.

"Too Many Offenses Are Made U.S. Crimes, Rehnquist Says." *New York Times*, 1 January 1999.

United States Department of Labor, Children's Bureau. *Mothers' Aid, 1931*. Publication no. 220. Washington, D.C.: Government Printing Office, 1933.

Waite, Edward F. "Courts of Domestic Relations." *Minnesota Law Review* 5 (February 1921): 161–71.

Waldman, Morris D. "Family Desertion." *Jewish Charity* 5 (December 1905–January 1906): 51–54.

——. "Family Desertion" and "Discussion." In *Sixth Biennial Session of the National Conference of Jewish Charities in the United States: Proceedings*, 54–111. St. Louis, 17–19 May 1910.

——. "Family Desertion." In *Seventh Biennial Session of the National Conference of Jewish Charities: Proceedings*, 51–123. Cleveland, 1912.

Wallstein, Leonard. "Deserted and Abandoned Children: A Test of the Value of Enforcing the City's Rights against Child Deserters." Report submitted to Mayor John Purroy Mitchel, New York City, 1916.

"Want Special Court for Domestic Woes." *New York Times*, 29 January 1909.

"Wants Marital Courts." *New York Times*, 24 January 1909.

"Welfare Chief Is Hoping to Promote Marriage." *New York Times*, 19 February 2002.

Yezierska, Anzia. *Bread Givers: A Novel*. New York: Doubleday, Page, 1925.

Zukerman, Jacob T. "How to Locate Deserting Relatives." *Legal Aid Briefcase*, October 1952, 10–15.

——. "The Family Court—Evolving Concepts." *Annals of the American Academy of Political and Social Science* 383 (May 1969): 119–28.

——. "Law and Social Welfare—Introductory Remarks." *Jewish Social Service Quarterly* 25 (September 1948): 142.

——. "The Role of the Public Agency with the Deserted Family." *Public Welfare* 15 (July 1957).

Zunser, Charles. "Court Reform Urged." *New York Times*, 25 March 1930.

——. "The Domestic Relations Courts." *Annals of the American Academy of Political and Social Science* 124. Reprint no. 1953, March 1926.

——. "The Family Court Bill." *New York Times*, 10 March 1932.

——. "Family Desertion (Report on a Study of 423 Cases)." *Annals of the American Academy of Political and Social Science* 145 (September 1929): 98–104.

——. "Family Desertion: Some International Aspects of the Problem." *Social Service Review* 6 (June 1932): 235–55.

——. "Impressions of a Worker in a New Field." *Jewish Charity* 5 (December 1905–January 1906): 59–60.

——. "The Late Walter H. Liebman." *New York Times*, 16 January 1931.

——. *The National Desertion Bureau, Its Functions, New Problems, and Relations with Local Agencies.* New York: National Desertion Bureau, 1924.

——. "The New Domestic Relations Court of New York: How Does It Work?" *Jewish Social Service Quarterly* 14 (June 1938): 372–79.

Secondary Sources

Abramovitz, Mimi. *Regulating the Lives of Women: Social Welfare Policy from Colonial Times to the Present.* Boston: South End Press, 1988.

Adler, Ruth. *Women of the Shtetl—through the Eyes of Y. L. Peretz.* Cranbury, N.J.: Associated University Presses, 1980.

Auerbach, Jerold S. "From Rags to Robes: The Legal Profession, Social Mobility and the American Jewish Experience." *American Jewish Historical Quarterly* 66 (December 1976): 249–84.

Ayers, Pat, and Jan Lambertz. "Marriage Relations, Money, and Domestic Violence in Working-Class Liverpool, 1919–1939." In *Labour and Love: Women's Experience of Home and Family, 1850–1940*, edited by Jane Lewis, 194–219. New York: Basil Blackwell, 1986.

Baker, Mark. "The Voice of the Deserted Jewish Woman, 1867–1870." *Jewish Social Studies* 2 (Fall 1995): 98–123.

Barkai, Avraham. *Branching Out: German-Jewish Immigration to the United States, 1820–1914.* New York: Holmes and Meier, 1994.

Basch, Norma. *Framing American Divorce: From the Revolutionary Generation to the Victorians.* Berkeley: University of California Press, 1999.

——. *In the Eyes of the Law.* Ithaca, N.Y.: Cornell University Press, 1982.

——. "Relief in the Premises: Divorce as a Woman's Remedy in New York and Indiana, 1815–1870." *Law and History Review* 8 (Spring 1990): 1–24.

Baum, Charlotte, Paula Hyman, and Sonya Michel. *The Jewish Woman in America.* New York: New American Library, 1975.

Bederman, Gail. *Manliness and Civilization: A Cultural History of Gender and Race in the United States, 1880–1917.* Chicago: University of Chicago Press, 1995.

Benson, Susan Porter. "Living on the Margin." In *The Sex of Things: Gender and Consumption in Historical Perspective,* edited by Victoria de Grazia, with Ellen Furlough, 212–43. Berkeley: University of California Press, 1996.

Berkowitz, Edward, and Kim McQuaid. *Creating the Welfare State: The Political Economy of Twentieth-Century Reform.* New York: Praeger, 1980.

Biale, David. "Childhood, Marriage, and the Family in the Eastern European Jewish Enlightenment." In *The Jewish Family: Myths and Reality,* edited by Steven M. Cohen and Paula E. Hyman, 45–61. New York: Holmes and Meier, 1986.

——. *Eros and the Jews: From Biblical Israel to Contemporary America.* New York: BasicBooks, 1992.

——. "Love, Marriage, and the Modernization of the Jews." In *Approaches to Modern Judaism,* edited by Marc Lee Raphael, 1–17. Chico, Calif.: Scholars' Press, 1983.

Biale, Rachel. *Women and Jewish Law: An Exploration of Women's Issues in Halakhic Sources.* New York: Schocken, 1984.

Blau, Joel. "Theories of the Welfare State." *Social Service Review* 63 (March 1989): 27–38.

Blicksilver, Edith. "The *Bintl Briv* Woman Writer: Torn between European Traditions and the American Lifestyle." *Studies in American Jewish Literature* 3 (Winter 1977–78): 36–49.

Block, Debra Susan. "Virtue out of Necessity: A Study of Jewish Philanthropy in the United States: 1890–1918." Ph.D. diss., University of Pennsylvania, 1997.

Bodek, Evelyn. "'Making Do': Jewish Women and Philanthropy." In *Jewish Life in Philadelphia, 1830–1940,* edited by Murray Friedman, 143–62. Philadelphia: Ishi Publications, 1983.

Boo, Katherine. "The Marriage Cure." *New Yorker,* 18 August 2003, 105–20.

Boris, Eileen, and Peter Bardaglio. "The Transformation of Patriarchy: The Historic Role of the State." In *Families, Politics, and Public Policy,* edited by Irene Diamond, 70–93. New York: Longman, 1983.

Boushy, Theodore Fadlo. "The Historical Development of the Domestic Relations Court." Ph.D. diss., University of Oklahoma, 1950.

Brannen, Julia, and Gail Wilson, eds. *Give and Take in Families: Studies in Resource Distribution.* Boston: Allen and Unwin, 1987.

Branscombe, Martha. *The Courts and the Poor Laws in New York State, 1784–1929.* Chicago: University of Chicago Press, 1943.

Breazale, Kenon. "In Spite of Women: *Esquire* Magazine and the Construction of the Male Consumer." *Signs* 20 (Autumn 1994): 1–22.

Bremner, Robert H. *From the Depths: The Discovery of Poverty in America.* New York: New York University Press, 1956.

Bristow, Edward J. *Prostitution and Prejudice: The Jewish Fight against White Slavery, 1870–1939.* New York: Schocken Books, 1983.

Broder, Sherri. "Informing the 'Cruelty': The Monitoring of Respectability in Philadelphia's Working-Class Neighborhoods in the Late Nineteenth Century." *Radical America* 21 (July–August 1987): 34–47.

——. *Tramps, Unfit Mothers, and Neglected Children: Negotiating the Family in Late Nineteenth-Century Philadelphia.* Philadelphia: University of Pennsylvania Press, 2002.

Brophy, Julia. "Parental Rights and Children's Welfare: Some Problems of Feminists' Strategy in the 1920s." *International Journal of the Sociology of the Law* 10 (1982): 149–68.

Brophy, Julia, and Carol Smart. "From Disregard to Disrepute: The Position of Women in Family Law." *Feminist Review* 9 (October 1981): 3–16.

Brown, Carol. "Mothers, Fathers, and Children: From Private to Public Patriarchy." In *Women and Revolution*, edited by Lydia Sargent, 239–67. Boston: South End Press, 1981.

Buchler, Samuel. *"Cohen Comes First" and Other Cases.* New York: Vanguard Press, 1933.

Chauncey, George. *Gay New York: Gender, Urban Culture, and the Making of the Gay Male World, 1890–1940.* New York: Basic Books, 1994.

Chester, Alden. *Courts and Lawyers of New York: A History, 1609–1925.* New York: American Historical Society, 1925.

Chunn, Dorothy E. "Doing Good in the Twentieth Century: The Origins of Family Courts in the United States." *Canadian Criminology Forum* 5 (Fall 1982): 25–39.

——. "Rehabilitating Deviant Families through Family Courts: The Birth of 'Socialized' Justice in Ontario, 1920–1940." *International Journal of the Sociology of the Law* 16 (May 1988): 137–58.

Cohen, Naomi. *Encounter with Emancipation: The German Jews in the United States, 1830–1914.* Philadelphia: Jewish Publication Society, 1984.

Coll, Blanche D. *Safety Net: Welfare and Social Security, 1929–1979.* New Brunswick, N.J.: Rutgers University Press, 1995.

Coontz, Stephanie. *Marriage, a History: From Obedience to Intimacy or How Love Conquered Marriage.* New York: Viking, 2005.

——. *The Way We Never Were: American Families and the Nostalgia Trap.* New York: Basic Books, 1992.

Cott, Nancy F. *Public Vows: A History of Marriage and the Nation.* Cambridge, Mass.: Harvard University Press, 2000.

Cross, Gary. *An All-Consuming Century: Why Commercialism Won in Modern America.* New York: Columbia University Press, 2000.

Dahl, Tove Stang, and Annika Snare. "The Coercion of Privacy: A Feminist Perspective." In *Women, Sexuality, and Social Control,* edited by Carol Smart and Barry Smart, 8–26. London: Routledge and Kegan Paul, 1978.

Degler, Carl N. *At Odds: Women and the Family in America from the Revolution to the Present.* New York: Oxford University Press, 1980.

Diner, Hasia R. *A Time for Gathering: The Second Migration, 1820–1880.* Baltimore: Johns Hopkins University Press, 1992.

Dobkowski, Michael N., ed. *Jewish American Voluntary Organizations.* Westport, Conn.: Greenwood Press, 1986.

Donzelot, Jacques. *The Policing of Families.* New York: Pantheon, 1979.

Drachman, Virginia G. *Sisters in Law: Women Lawyers in Modern American History.* Cambridge, Mass.: Harvard University Press, 1998.

Edsforth, Ronald. *Class Conflict and Cultural Consensus.* New Brunswick, N.J.: Rutgers University Press, 1987.

Ehrenreich, Barbara. *The Hearts of Men: American Dreams and the Flight from Commitment.* New York: Anchor Press / Doubleday, 1983.

Ehrenreich, John H. *The Altruistic Imagination: A History of Social Work and Social Policy in the United States.* Ithaca, N.Y.: Cornell University Press, 1985.

Eisenstein, Sarah. *Give Us Bread but Give Us Roses: Working Women's Consciousness in the United States, 1890 to the First World War.* Boston: Routledge and Kegan Paul, 1983.

Ellis, David M. et al. *A Short History of New York State.* Ithaca, N.Y.: Cornell University Press, 1957.

Ephraim, Miriam R. "Introduction: The Meaning of the Conference for the American Jewish Community." In *Trends and Issues in Jewish Social Welfare in the United States, 1899–1952,* edited by Robert Morris and Michael Freund, xxiii–xxix. Philadelphia: JPS, 1966.

Ewen, Elizabeth. *Immigrant Women in the Land of Dollars: Life and Culture on the Lower East Side, 1890–1925.* New York: Monthly Review Press, 1985.

Feldman, Egal. "Prostitution, the Alien Woman, and the Progressive Imagination, 1910–1915." *American Quarterly* 19 (1967): 192–206.

Fox, Richard Wightman, and T. J. Jackson Lears, eds. *The Culture of Consumption: Critical Essays in American History, 1880–1980.* New York: Pantheon, 1983.

Freeze, ChaeRan Y. *Jewish Marriage and Divorce in Imperial Russia.* Hanover, N.H.: University Press of New England [for] Brandeis University Press, 2002.

Fridkis, Ari Lloyd. "Desertion in the American Jewish Immigrant Family: The Work of the National Desertion Bureau in Cooperation with the Industrial Removal Office." *American Jewish History* 71 (December 1981): 285–99.

Friedman, Marilyn A. "Women in Poverty and Welfare Equity." In *Poverty, Justice, and the Law: New Essays on Needs, Rights, and Obligations*, edited by George R. Lucas Jr., 91–104. Lanham, Md.: University Press of America, 1986.

Friedman, Reena Sigman. " 'Send Me My Husband Who Is In New York City': Husband Desertion in the American Jewish Immigrant Community, 1900–1926." *Jewish Social Studies* 44 (Winter 1982): 1–18.

Gilfoyle, Timothy J. *City of Eros: New York City, Prostitution, and the Commercialization of Sex, 1790–1920*. New York: W. W. Norton, 1992.

Gillis, John R. *A World of Their Own Making: Myth, Ritual, and the Quest for Family Values*. Cambridge, Mass.: Harvard University Press, 1996.

Gjerde, Jon. "New Growth on Old Vines—the State of the Field: The Social History of Immigration to and Ethnicity in the United States." *Journal of American Ethnic History* 18 (Summer 1999): 40–65.

Glanz, Rudolf. *The Jewish Woman in America: Two Female Immigrant Generations, 1820–1929*.Vol. 1: *The Eastern European Jewish Woman*. New York: Ktav Publishing House and National Council of Jewish Women, 1976.

Glenn, Susan A. *Daughters of the Shtetl: Life and Labor in the Immigrant Generation*. Ithaca, N.Y.: Cornell University Press, 1990.

Glickman, Lawrence. "Inventing the 'American Standard of Living': Gender, Race, and Working Class Identity, 1880–1925." *Labor History* 34 (Spring–Summer 1993): 221–35.

Goldberg, Idana. "Gender, Religion and the Jewish Public Sphere in Mid-Nineteenth Century America." Ph.D. diss., University of Pennsylvania, 2004.

Goodwin, Joanne Lorraine. "The Differential Treatment of Motherhood: Mothers' Pensions, Chicago, 1900–1930." Paper presented at the Conference on Gender and Social Policy in conjunction with the annual meeting of the Social Science History Association, Minneapolis, 18 October 1990.

——. *Gender and the Politics of Welfare Reform: Mothers' Pensions in Chicago, 1911–1929*. Chicago: University of Chicago Press, 1997.

——. "Gender, Politics, and Welfare Reform: Mothers' Pensions in Chicago, 1900–1930," Ph.D. diss., University of Michigan, 1991.

Gordon, Linda. "Family Violence, Feminism, and Social Control." *Feminist Studies* 12 (Fall 1986): 453–78.

——. *Heroes of Their Own Lives: The Politics and History of Family Violence, Boston, 1880–1960*. New York: Viking, 1988.

——. "The New Feminist Scholarship on the Welfare State." In *Women, the State, and Welfare*, edited by Linda Gordon, 9–35. Madison: University of Wisconsin Press, 1990.

——. *Pitied but Not Entitled: Single Mothers and the History of Welfare.* New York: Free Press, 1994.

Greenberg, Louis. *The Jews in Russia: The Struggle for Emancipation.* New Haven, Conn.: Yale University Press, 1965.

Griswold, Robert L. *Family and Divorce in California, 1850–1890: Victorian Illusions and Everyday Realities.* Albany: State University of New York Press, 1982.

——. "Law, Sex, Cruelty, and Divorce in Victorian America, 1840–1900." *American Quarterly* 38 (Winter 1986): 721–45.

Grossberg, Michael. *Governing the Hearth: Law and Family in Nineteenth-Century America.* Chapel Hill: University of North Carolina Press, 1985.

Gurock, Jeffrey. *When Harlem was Jewish, 1870–1930.* New York: Columbia University Press, 1979.

Halem, Lynne Carol. *Divorce Reform: Changing Legal and Social Perspectives.* New York: Free Press, 1980.

Hareven, Tamara K. "The History of the Family and the Complexity of Social Change." *American Historical Review* 96 (February 1991): 95–124.

Harris, Deborah. "Child Support for Welfare Families: Family Policy Trapped in Its Own Rhetoric." Unpublished paper, PARSS seminar on work and welfare, University of Pennsylvania, 21 November 1988.

Hays, Sharon. *Flat Broke with Children: Women in the Age of Welfare Reform.* New York: Oxford University Press, 2003.

Heinze, Andrew. *Adapting to Abundance: Jewish Immigrants, Mass Consumption, and the Search for an American Identity.* New York: Columbia University Press, 1990.

Holcombe, Lee. *Wives and Property: Reform of the Married Women's Property Law in Nineteenth-Century England.* Toronto: University of Toronto Press, 1983.

Howard, Christopher. "Sowing the Seeds of 'Welfare': The Transformation of Mothers' Pensions, 1900–1940." *Journal of Policy History* 4 (1992): 188–227.

Howard, Ronald L. *A Social History of American Family Sociology, 1865–1940.* Westport, Conn.: Greenwood Press, 1981.

Hyman, Paula E. *Gender and Assimilation in Modern Jewish History: The Roles and Representation of Jewish Women.* Seattle: University of Washington Press, 1995.

Jacobson, Matthew Frye. *Barbarian Virtues: The United States Encounters Foreign Peoples at Home and Abroad, 1876–1917.* New York: Hill and Wang, 2000.

——. *Whiteness of a Different Color: European Immigrants and the Alchemy of Race.* Cambridge, Mass.: Harvard University Press, 1998.

Jones, Mary Somerville. *An Historical Geography of the Changing Divorce Law in the United States.* New York: Garland, 1987.

Joseph, Judith Lee Vaupen. "The Nafkeh and the Lady: Jews, Prostitutes, and Progressives in New York City, 1900–1930." Ph.D. diss., State University of New York at Stony Brook, 1986.

Katz, Michael B. *In the Shadow of the Poorhouse: A Social History of Welfare in America.* New York: Basic Books, 1986.

——. *Poverty and Policy in American History.* New York: Academic Press, 1983.

——. *The Price of Citizenship: Redefining the American Welfare State.* New York: Henry Holt, 2001.

Katz, Sanford N. "A Historical Perspective on Child-Support Laws in the United States." In *The Parental Child-Support Obligation: Research, Practice, and Social Policy*, edited by Judith Cassetty, 17–28. Lexington, Mass.: D. C. Heath, 1983.

Kerber, Linda K. *No Constitutional Right to Be Ladies: Women and the Obligations of Citizenship.* New York: Hill and Wang, 1998.

——. "Separate Spheres, Female Worlds, Woman's Place: The Rhetoric of Women's History." *Journal of American History* 75 (June 1988): 9–39.

Kessler-Harris, Alice. "Gender and the Construction of Culture." Paper presented at the Conference on Ideology and Resistance, Haifa, Israel, 8 January 1990.

——. "Gendered Interventions: Exploring the Historical Roots of U.S. Social Policy." *Japanese Journal of American Studies* 5 (1993–94): 3–22.

——. *In Pursuit of Equity: Women, Men, and the Quest for Economic Citizenship in Twentieth-Century America.* New York: Oxford University Press, 2001.

——. *Out to Work: A History of Wage-Earning Women in the United States.* New York: Oxford University Press, 1982.

——. *A Woman's Wage: Historical Meanings and Social Consequences.* Lexington: University Press of Kentucky, 1990.

Kovarsky, Marcel. "Current Purposes and Goals of Jewish Family Agencies." In *Trends and Issues in Jewish Social Welfare in the United States, 1899–1952*, edited by Robert Morris and Michael Freund, 469–75. Philadelphia: JPS, 1966.

Koven, Seth, and Sonya Michel."Womanly Duties: Maternalist Politics and the Origins of Welfare States in France, Germany, Great Britain, and the United States, 1880–1920." *American Historical Review* 95 (October 1990): 1076–1108.

Kutzik, Alfred Jacob. "The Social Basis of American Jewish Philanthropy." Ph.D. diss., Brandeis University, 1967.

Kuznets, Simon. "Immigration of Russian Jews to the United States: Background and Structure." *Perspectives in American History* 9 (1975): 35–124.

Ladd-Taylor, Molly. *Mother-Work: Women, Child Welfare, and the State, 1890–1930.* Urbana: University of Illinois Press, 1994.

Leff, Mark H. "Consensus for Reform: The Mothers'-Pension Movement in the Progressive Era." *Social Service Review* 47 (September 1973): 397–417.

Leiby, James. *A History of Social Welfare and Social Work in the United States.* New York: Columbia University Press, 1978.

Leider, Emily Wortis. "Postscript." In Miriam Shomer Zunser, *Yesterday: A Memoir of a Russian Jewish Family*, edited by Emily Wortis Leider, 253–69. New York: Harper and Row, 1978.

Levine, Daniel. *Poverty and Society: The Growth of the American Welfare State in International Comparison*. New Brunswick, N.J.: Rutgers University Press, 1988.

Levine, Jeanne. "Jewish Family Desertion in Cases Carried Cooperatively by the National Desertion Bureau and Other Social Agencies in New York City, 1934." M.A. thesis, Graduate School for Jewish Social Work, 1939.

Lewis, Thomas P., and Robert J. Levy. "Family Law and Welfare Policies: The Case for 'Dual Systems.'" In *The Law of the Poor*, edited by Jacobus tenBroek, 424–56. San Francisco, Calif.: Chandler Publishing, 1966.

Lubove, Roy. *The Professional Altruist: The Emergence of Social Work as a Career, 1880–1930*. Cambridge, Mass.: Harvard University Press, 1965.

——. *The Struggle for Social Security, 1900–1935*. Cambridge, Mass.: Harvard University Press, 1968.

Mandelker, Daniel R. "Family Responsibility under the American Poor Laws." *Michigan Law Review* 54 (1956): 497–532, 607–32.

Marcus, Jacob Rader. *The American Jewish Woman, 1654–1980*. New York: Ktav Publishing House, 1981.

May, Elaine Tyler. *Great Expectations: Marriage and Divorce in Post-Victorian America*. Chicago: University of Chicago Press, 1980.

May, Martha. "Bread before Roses: American Workingmen, Labor Unions, and the Family Wage." In *Women, Work, and Protest: A Century of U.S. Women's Labor History*, edited by Ruth Milkman, 1–21. Boston: Routledge and Kegan Paul, 1985.

——. "The 'Good Managers': Married Working Class Women and Family Budget Studies, 1895–1915." *Labor History* 25 (Summer 1984): 351–72.

——. "The 'Problem of Duty': Family Desertion in the Progressive Era." *Social Service Review* 62 (March 1988): 40–60.

McClintock, Megan. "Binding Up the Nation's Wounds: Nationalism, Civil War Pensions, and American Families, 1861–1890." Ph.D. diss., Rutgers University, 1994.

McCormick, Richard L. *The Party Period and Public Policy: American Politics from the Age of Jackson to the Progressive Era*. New York: Oxford University Press, 1986.

McIntosh, Mary. "The Welfare State and the Needs of the Dependent Family." In *Fit Work for Women*, edited by Sandra Burman, 153–72. New York: St. Martin's Press, 1979.

Mensch, Jean Ulitz. "Social Pathology in Urban America: Desertion, Prostitution, Gambling, Drugs and Crime among Eastern European Jews in New York City." Ph.D. diss., Columbia University, 1983.

Metzker, Isaac, ed. *A Bintel Brief: Sixty Years of Letters from the Lower East Side to the Jewish Daily Forward*. New York: Schocken, 1971.

Meyerowitz, Joanne J. *Women Adrift: Independent Wage Earners in Chicago, 1880–1930*. Chicago: University of Chicago Press, 1988.

Michel, Sonya. "The Limits of Maternalism: Policies toward American Wage-Earning Mothers during the Progressive Era." In *Mothers of a New World: Maternalist Politics and the Origins of Welfare States*, edited by Seth Koven and Sonya Michel, 277–320. New York: Routledge, 1993.

Mink, Gwendolyn. *The Wages of Motherhood: Inequality in the Welfare State, 1917–1942*. Ithaca, N.Y.: Cornell University Press, 1995.

Minow, Martha. " 'Forming Underneath Everything That Grows': Toward a History of Family Law." *Wisconsin Law Review* (1985): 819–98.

Moloney, Deirdre M. *American Catholic Lay Groups and Transatlantic Social Reform in the Progressive Era*. Chapel Hill: University of North Carolina Press, 2002.

Morris, Robert, and Michael Freund, eds. *Trends and Issues in Jewish Social Welfare in the United States, 1899–1952*. Philadelphia: JPS, 1966.

Neckerman, Kathryn M. "The Emergence of 'Underclass' Family Patterns, 1900–1940." In *The Underclass Debate: Views from History*, edited by Michael B. Katz, 194–219. Princeton, N.J.: Princeton University Press, 1993.

Olsen, Frances E. "The Family and the Market: A Study of Ideology and Legal Reform." *Harvard Law Review* 96 (May 1983): 1497–1578.

O'Neill, William L. *Divorce in the Progressive Era*. New Haven, Conn.: Yale University Press, 1967.

Oren, Laura. "The Welfare of Women in Laboring Families: England, 1860–1950." In *Clio's Consciousness Raised*, edited by Mary S. Hartman and Lois Banner, 226–44. New York: Harper and Row, 1974.

Orloff, Ann Shola, and Theda Skocpol. "Why Not Equal Protection? Explaining the Politics of Public Social Spending in Britain, 1900–1911, and the United States, 1880s–1920." *American Sociological Review* 49 (December 1984): 726–50.

Parush, Iris. *Reading Jewish Women: Marginality and Modernization in Nineteenth-Century Eastern European Jewish Society*. Waltham, Mass.: Brandeis University Press, 2004.

Pascoe, Peggy. *Relations of Rescue: The Search for Female Moral Authority in the American West, 1874–1939*. New York: Oxford University Press, 1990.

Patterson, James T. *America's Struggle against Poverty, 1900–1980*. Cambridge, Mass.: Harvard University Press, 1981.

Piven, Frances Fox, and Richard Cloward. *Regulating the Poor: The Functions of Public Welfare*. New York: Random House, 1971.

Platt, Anthony M. *The Child Savers*. Chicago: University of Chicago Press, 1969.

Prell, Riv-Ellen. *Fighting to Become Americans: Jews, Gender, and the Anxiety of Assimilation*. Boston: Beacon Press, 1999.

Pumphrey, Muriel W., and Ralph E. Pumphrey. "The Widows' Pension Movement, 1900–1930: Preventive Child-Saving or Social Control?" In *Social Welfare or Social Control?: Some Historical Reflections on Regulating the Poor*, edited by Walter I. Trattner, 51–66. Knoxville: University of Tennessee Press, 1983.

Ringenbach, Paul T. *Tramps and Reformers, 1873–1916: The Discovery of Unemployment in New York*. Westport, Conn.: Greenwood Press, 1973.

Robles, Arodys, and Susan Cotts Watkins. "Immigration and Family Separation in the U.S. at the Turn of the Twentieth Century." *Journal of Family History* 18 (1993): 191–211.

Rodgers, Daniel T. *Atlantic Crossings: Social Politics in a Progressive Age*. Cambridge, Mass.: Harvard University Press, 1998.

Rogow, Faith. *Gone to Another Meeting: The National Council of Jewish Women, 1893–1993*. Tuscaloosa: University of Alabama Press, 1993.

Romanofsky, Peter, and Gary E. Rubin, "Jewish Family Service (JFS)." In *Jewish American Voluntary Organizations*, edited by Michael N. Dobkowski, 245–55. Westport, Conn.: Greenwood Press, 1986.

Rosenberg, Emily S. "Rescuing Women and Children." *Journal of American History* 89 (September 2002): 456–65.

Roskies, David G. "Yiddish Popular Literature and the Female Reader." *Journal of Popular Culture* 10 (Spring 1977): 852–58.

Ross, Ellen. " 'Fierce Questions and Taunts': Married Life in Working-Class London, 1870–1914." *Feminist Studies* 8 (Fall 1982): 577–602.

Rothbart, Ron. " 'Homes Are What Any Strike Is About': Immigrant Labor and the Family Wage." *Journal of Social History* 23 (1989): 267–84.

Rothman, David J. "The State as Parent: Social Policy in the Progressive Era." In *Doing Good: The Limits of Benevolence*, edited by William Gaylin et al., 67–95. New York: Pantheon, 1978.

Rubin, Gary E. "Conference of Jewish Communal Service (CJCS)." In *Jewish American Voluntary Organizations*, edited by Michael N. Dobkowski, 125–30. Westport, Conn.: Greenwood Press, 1986.

Schneider, David M., and Albert Deutsch. *The History of Public Welfare in New York State, 1867–1940*. Chicago: University of Chicago Press, 1941.

Skocpol, Theda. *Protecting Soldiers and Mothers: The Politics of Social Provision in the United States, 1870s–1920s*. Cambridge, Mass.: Harvard University Press, 1992.

Smith, Judith E. "Our Own Kind: Family and Community Networks in Providence." In *A Heritage of Our Own*, edited by Nancy Cott and Elizabeth H. Pleck, 393–411. New York: Simon and Schuster, 1979.

Smith, Merril D. *Breaking the Bonds: Marital Discord in Pennsylvania, 1730–1830*. New York: New York University Press, 1991.

Soyer, Daniel. *Jewish Immigrant Associations and American Identity in New York, 1880–1939*. Cambridge, Mass.: Harvard University Press, 1997.

Stadum, Beverly. *Poor Women and Their Families: Hard Working Charity Cases, 1900–1930*. Albany: State University of New York Press, 1992.

Stansell, Christine. *City of Women: Sex and Class in New York, 1789–1860*. New York: Alfred A. Knopf, 1986.

Stein, Sarah Abreyva. *Making Jews Modern: The Yiddish and Ladino Press in the Russian and Ottoman Empires.* Bloomington: Indiana University Press, 2004.

Stone, Lawrence. *The Family, Sex and Marriage in England, 1500–1800.* New York: Harper and Row, 1979.

Summers, Robert S. "Pragmatic Instrumentalism in Twentieth Century American Legal Thought—a Synthesis and Critique of Our Dominant General Theory about Law and Its Use." *Cornell Law Review* 66 (June 1981): 861–948.

Szajkowski, Zosa. "The *Yahudi* and the Immigrant: A Reappraisal." *American Jewish Historical Quarterly* 63 (September 1973): 13–44.

TenBroek, Jacobus. "California's Dual System of Family Law: Its Origin, Development, and Present Status." *Stanford Law Review* 16–17 (1964–65): 257–317, 900–981, 614–82.

——, ed. *The Law of The Poor.* San Francisco, Calif.: Chandler Publishing, 1966.

Thane, Pat. "Women and the Poor Law in Victorian and Edwardian England." *History Workshop* 6 (Autumn 1978): 29–51.

Tiffin, Susan. *In Whose Best Interest? Child Welfare Reform in the Progressive Era.* Westport, Conn.: Greenwood Press, 1982.

Traverso, Susan. *Welfare Politics in Boston, 1910–1940.* Amherst: University of Massachusetts Press, 2003.

Tweed, Harrison. *The Legal Aid Society, New York City, 1876–1951.* New York: Legal Aid Society, 1954.

Walkowitz, Daniel J. "The Making of a Feminine Professional Identity: Social Workers in the 1920s." *American Historical Review* 95 (October 1990): 1051–75.

Wenger, Beth S. *New York Jews and the Great Depression: Uncertain Promise.* New Haven, Conn.: Yale University Press, 1996.

Weyrauch, Walter O. "Dual Systems of Family Law: A Comment." In *The Law of The Poor*, edited by Jacobus tenBroek, 457–67. San Francisco, Calif.: Chandler Publishing, 1966.

White, G. Edward. *Patterns of American Legal Thought.* Indianapolis: Bobbs-Merrill, 1978.

White, Morton. *Social Thought in America: The Revolt against Formalism.* Boston: Beacon Press, 1947.

Wiebe, Robert H. *The Search for Order, 1877–1920.* New York: Hill and Wang, 1967.

Willrich, Michael. *City of Courts: Socializing Justice in Progressive Era Chicago.* New York: Cambridge University Press, 2003.

Wilson, Elizabeth. *Women and the Welfare State.* London: Tavistock Publications, 1977.

Wittig, Monique. *The Straight Mind.* Boston: Beacon Press, 1992.

Zelizer, Viviana A. *The Social Meaning of Money.* New York: Basic Books, 1994.

——. "The Social Meaning of Money: 'Special Monies.'" *American Journal of Sociology* 95 (September 1989): 342–77.